The Dust Poet has tertiary qualifications in the study of religions and ideologies. Her post graduate work involved in-depth academic study and research across four continents. She has taught at University level and written on religious movements. Recently, she returned to writing poetry and prose. The Dust Poet lives in Brisbane with her husband and two dogs.

HANNAH'S SONG

A story of love and betrayal
of a woman psychically stalked
and called to walk
the ultimate Camino,
the Eiger of the Soul

The Dust Poet

American spelling has been used throughout this book.

Published by The Dust Poet

First published 2014, reprinted 2015
This edition published 2021

© 2013 The Dust Poet

The moral right of the author has been asserted.

All rights reserved. Without limiting the rights under copyright restricted above, no part of this publication may be reproduced, stored in or introduced into a retrieval system, or transmitted, in any form or by any means (electronic, mechanical, photocopying, recording or otherwise), without the prior written permission of the copyright owner.

 A catalogue record for this book is available from the National Library of Australia

ISBN: 978 0 9944026 2 2

Cover designed by Carolyn Nowicki
Typeset by Palmer Higgs
Printed and distributed by Publicious Publishing

The central character of this story wishes to remain anonymous. Names and details in relation to her in many instances, and specifically visionary experiences, have been obfuscated, dovetailed or changed so that no reference to any living person or institution is intended at these points. Otherwise events reflect reality. The visionary experiences themselves are, as much as possible, in italics.

This book is for discernment by all who read it. Conclusions drawn flow from the experiences and are not intended in any way to be construed as strictly judgmental, but rather as points to ponder.

A percentage of the profits from the sale of this book will go to charity.

Concepts of time and space starting to rupture badly …

The wizards of the mindspace have lost control … we are spinning between Eden and Armageddon.

2013 (our time) … But where are we really?

And what are we? Who are we? Concepts in anthropology, psychology and sociology start to warp. What is left of scientific theory if this reflects truth? More to the point:

who controls the mindspace of mankind? Who or what controls the way we think and perceive 'reality'?

Who is telling you what to do?

Persevere. You are going to climb a mountain –

you are invited to break out of a tomb.

Dedication

This book is written and dedicated to wisdom on behalf of myself, my husband, our families and those we love. And most especially to the people you will read of – the 'keepers of the flame'.

It is also dedicated to the chosen, and those of us who strive to be among the chosen. To the fallen of many lands. To the British people and the people who have given us a home, the Australians. Finally to the abused and the falsely accused, not just of the land of my fathers, the Irish; but the abused of all nations, creeds and religions.

Shalom.

"For wisdom is better than rubies:
And all the things that may be desired
Are not to be compared to it."

Proverbs 8:11; kjv

Beverages, Refreshments and Soundscape for the Climb

Mountain climbing is not to be undertaken without some form of physical sustenance. So suggestions are:

Opening chapters

Ceylon tea or fair-trade hot chocolate. Shortbread to nibble.

Musical suggestion: something from The Beatles?

Christmas 1971

A pot of coffee, cheese biscuits.

Soundscape for South Africa: Juluka; preferably *Scatterlings of Africa* or *African Sky Blue*.

If feeling rebellious, Pink Floyd's *The Wall*.

Night

This is where Chanel slowly morphs into hell so, hit the Mumm Cordon Bleu (if you can run to it: one flute max; you need your wits about you). If you don't like champagne, a good fizz or sparkling mineral water with lime might be in order, to engage the feel of London in the eighties with Linda Evangelista and Lady Di.

Accompaniment: very dark chocolate. With bite.

Music: it's got to be Kim Carne's *Bette Davis Eyes* and Bryan Ferry's *These Foolish Things*. (*Bette Davis Eyes* is for Laura; you'll see what I mean when you get there.)

The Winter Is Past

Hit the double Scotch (a demi-shot) and sip very slowly: as if it's medicine.

As things lighten up you might like to play *Jerusalem*.

You Are Once Again Entering The Night

For this part of the climb it's definitely a double espresso; even if you don't like coffee. To eat: slices of spicy Spanish omelet.

For the mindscape, Bob Dylan. (I can't give the real tune that recurred I'm afraid. The subject won't reveal it.)

And As You Turn The Last Page Of The Climb

Bravo! You have reached the summit to look out across the landscape, reflect, see into the abyss across the clouded valleys, shadowed fields, streams and rivers. Pause.

Again, maybe one flute of champagne. Grapes, figs and good cheese; with the option of organic tofu with dukka for vegans.

For such a moment you can't beat Vidor's *Toccata*. And for a grand finale: William Blake's

Jerusalem.

And decide:

that is freedom!

I slept but my heart was awake.
Listen! My lover is knocking;
Open to me, my sister, my darling,
My dove, my flawless one.

My head is drenched with dew,
My hair with the dampness of the night.

The Song of Songs

And it was night.
The Gospel of John

Humanity's Dark Night of the Soul.

The betrayal of Christ

Israel: 1996

Beneath a converted convent on the Via Dolorosa

An ancient cavern where Jesus is believed to have been scourged.

We sit in a semi-circle as an account of events leading up to the crucifixion is read.

A young woman doctor from Holland is among those of us who weep.

1996

The Sea of Galilee

Christ Walks the Lightning

I slept but my heart was awake.
The Song of Songs

BEGINNINGS: MEMORIES, VISIONS … DREAMS.
(And as for psychoanalysis; well – "Huh!")

I was born in a poor suburb of a city in Wales. There were mice in the fireplace.

It was night.

There was a fierce electrical storm. The electricity cables were down.

My father had to go out and fetch the midwife.

Years later my mother, who in a way saw visions (I know you don't talk about these things nowadays. But she did tell me). She said she saw me; she saw me before I was born. Waiting. Waiting to be born.

She also said that she prayed for me while I was in the womb. That my eyes would be beautiful. That my lips would be beautiful. And so on. She had great generosity of spirit at times. At other times she could be terrible.

But aren't most of us like that?

My mother came from a Protestant family. Most of her family were unbaptized. There was May, her older sister. She was married to Henry, and by the time I was old enough to know them they had a shop selling musical instruments. I have fond memories of going there. May and Henry used to give us presents of small amounts of money. May was very athletic and had two daughters, Rita and Karen. My mother's older brother was Phil. He got married and had a daughter called Cathy who was mentally retarded. Someone – I don't know who – said it was a result of syphilis. My father's family lived nearby and Dad told us people would call her "Crazy Cathy" because she used to smear lipstick on her face. I thought that was funny when I first heard. Huh! Now, of course, I think it's just sickening; there but for the grace of God go you or I. Phil's marriage broke up and Cathy was sent out to Australia in her teenage years. I think she went to Adelaide. My mother's other older sister was Elizabeth. Elizabeth was very beautiful, and I think my mother was a little envious. I only recall one photograph of Elizabeth, taken when she was around eighteen or nineteen. Yet even in that faded black and white still, she was tall and slim and elegant. She evoked the grace of a dancer. So incandescent was her loveliness, I can still remember her image to this day. She was as beautiful as light.

Light.

Elizabeth had a suitor who migrated to Australia. He wrote, and sent an amount to cover her passage so that she could join him. But my mother opened Elizabeth's post, read the letter, and sent the money back together with a note saying Elizabeth would only spend the cash on a coat or something. Elizabeth later married into a wealthy local family, the Hileses. Her husband, Fred Hiles, was ebullient and popular (particularly with my father) and the couple bought a stately house in the Usk Valley where Elizabeth wore film-star clothes. She gave one evening dress to my mother, a siren-like black sheath dress with an ornate jacket embroidered with gold filigree work. My mother bequeathed the dress to me. But by the time I got it, someone had put a razor though the jacket.

My father and mother described Elizabeth as really good fun but a bit scatty. All over the place. A bit like my sister Alice in character. Elizabeth and Fred fell on hard times. I really cannot remember ever seeing her in person. Over the years Elizabeth would say she was coming to visit and then wouldn't show. It upset my mother a bit, when she had cooked and Elizabeth didn't turn up.

My mother's other sibling was Ted. Mum would tell how, on the day Ted died, her Aunt Mildred came to the door. My mother said she didn't want to open the door; she just "knew" it was bad news. Mildred was psychic and had received a premonition. When my mother opened the door, Mildred announced Ted was going to die. Ted died later that day in a motorcycle accident. My mother was bereft.

I remember my maternal grandmother as a tall, striking woman. My father told me he always remembered Grandma's hands. Apparently they were very large hands, the most beautiful hands he had ever seen. I remember asking Dad if my hands were like Grandma's. Dad looked at my hands and answered, "No". I felt rather miffed about that. Although Mum's parents lived nearby, I can't say much about them because they both died when I was very young. But I do recall my mother telling me Grandfather painted, and I have vague recollections of some of his pictures, including one of fishing boats on a seashore which I wrote a poem about later on. Grandpa and Grandma had a lovely little house near us which I visited. It had a big Grandfather clock and pretty, but frayed, chintzy furniture. Grandfather died of a heart attack in his nineties, on his way to place a bet while walking up a hill pushing his bike. Grandma developed Alzheimer's after that. The poor woman would go wandering. She had an obsession with Elizabeth and would keep going round to see her. (Shades of things to come.) It was so difficult someone decided to put Gran in a home. Still, she escaped and ended up at our place, and Mum and Dad had to take her back to the home. My father expressed the view that Gran was not as far gone as some members of the family made out, but I don't think my parents were that intimately involved with Grandma's care. The home Gran went to was closed some years later because of reports of abuse.

The story my father told was that he was out one day with some friends when he first saw my mother. Dad told his friends, "This is the girl I am going to marry". It was strange, but he was immediately very much in love with Mum. Looking back, I often think of that, that telling of his love. A kind of mad Celtic thing. Wildness – Irish or Welsh - I don't know. I think a little bit of that is in me. It has driven me, that madness; driven me in my search for truth. So in different ways it drove us both, Dad and me, almost to destruction.

Anyway, my mother used to say that during the early years she and Dad were very happy. Dad was handsome, with vibrant and deep blue eyes, dark hair and an incredible bone structure. He wrote letters to my mother during the early years of their relationship, and while I don't have the letters something of my father's religious devotion comes across even in the memory of them. A photograph I have of him in army uniform also reflects a sense of spiritual, almost mystical, purity. I remember him telling me he wanted to be a priest, but couldn't handle not having a family. When I look now at that picture I often ponder how life would have been had he been able to fulfill his vocation. Because that mystical aura tarnished as the years wore on, only to return in his last days when that handsome beauty was shattered by suffering. And only then, once more, could you discern that glowing, opalescent quality again, in his eyes – in his gaze. And recall the glorious pearl glow of his soul as it returned to its pristine, virginal state: beyond the ruined vessel that had become his body.

Dad's parents were of Irish and Welsh descent. His family, the Ryans, were very poor but devout Catholics from around the Cork area. Dad's father ran a pub in the docks for a while and then, when the grog started to become a problem for Granddad, the family pulled out. Granddad Ryan then took up a coal haulage business. There were loads of kids of course; I think ten. The ones I remember most were Pam and Mary who became nuns, and Edgar who became a schoolteacher. Dad's mum was an incredibly devout woman, and I sometimes think we owe a lot to her daily recitation of the rosary; with all those kids as well! It was inculcated in me that the Virgin Mary was a good one to call on with anything to do with marriage and purity.

When war broke out there was some problem in my mother's family, and so my mother went to live with the Ryans. Mum told me about her experience of 'finding the faith'. Apparently she was doubtful about Catholicism until she read the beginning of the Gospel of John. That was it! For her wedding Mum bought a blue dress. It really was 'Dior New Look' before 'Dior New Look', made of satin with huge white flowers scattered across the shiny material. She must have looked wonderful, but I don't have any pictures of the wedding. My mother bequeathed my sister Alice her wedding dress, which is nice because it matches the color of Alice's eyes. At the time of her wedding, Mum was working as a bookkeeper and secretary. She didn't seem to like my father's family and frequently complained Gran Ryan had asked too much money for her keep. I also recall her saying, with disdain, how the Ryans had fish and chips one night when she was with them and that someone had used their hands to portion out the chips. Still, as the Ryans had taken her in, I couldn't quite understand her dislike.

While she was living with the Ryans, Mum gave birth to Patrick. I was born ten years later when my parents had moved to rented rooms. Patrick gave me a little teddy bear when I was very young which I kept for years but then lost. Michael (my husband) didn't like the teddy at all because it looked dirty, and I think he might have ditched the bear somewhere; something he denies emphatically. Anyway, I was an incredibly healthy child with very blonde hair and wonderful skin. This my mother put down to heredity and – for some curiously intuitive reason – breastfeeding and rose-hip syrup. I was big; what might be called a bit of a bruiser, because it was fashionable then to feed your babies up. One of my first memories was being with some rellies and looking up at the sun in my pram. I recall feeling like,

"Hello world. I've arrived!" The glorious, mesmeric sunlight.

Light.

I remember my early years as being content, but later learnt, piecing together things my brother and his wife Genevieve said, that my mother and father would row a lot about money. It affected my brother deeply as he overheard, and it made him really careful about finances. Patrick was always diligent in saving and bought his first house as soon as he and Genevieve married. When Michael and I used to visit after we left Newport, Patrick would give us advice about shares and things; stuff like that that we never paid enough attention to. Patrick never had children – I think he might have been afraid of being poor. He was burnt from those rows.

My parents moved again to a house in Llanarth in Newport. A property rented from the council on one of the big, new, post-war estates. There my brother was given a dog called Boxer. For ages my mother told me Boxer had died in a car accident. Then one day I heard the truth, when she informed me that she had seen me playing near Boxer's kennel, crawling round. Mum thought Boxer might bite me, she explained, not without her face and voice betraying a trace of guilt as she added by way of explanation:

"I thought he would scar your face."

Mum made my father take Boxer and have him put down. My father told me he went straight to the pub after and got drunk. I found it difficult to believe Mum could be so callous; I mean, she could have found Boxer a new home or something.

We would go and visit the Ryan family in those early years for special occasions such as birthdays. I remember they all seemed to have nice old houses, probably built in the 30s. Rambling places that were interesting to be in and beguiling to explore, with lots of cupboards to examine and rooms and staircases. They also had lovely china. I always liked china, as I found the shapes of the cups and the feel of the material and ambience of the colors fascinating. The Ryans were better off than we were and, even when I was young, I did feel a bit inferior – rather the poor relative. Still, I really liked my cousins. Two of whom, Eva and Maria, I remember especially well were about the same age as me. Later on I was at school with them and was envious of how brilliantly they excelled in exams. Their father was highly educated, a teacher and then headmaster, and very erudite. Many years later I was proud when I heard him on the radio discussing issues in education. Other relatives I can't remember so well, but I know one of my uncles was a butcher who wound up emigrating to New Zealand. I often wonder how that branch of the family are doing.

All in all I was a mixed bag as a kid. I remember I was accused of holding on to a lamp-post claiming it to be my own, much to the disgust of my better behaved friend, Brenda Neilson. At least that was what Mrs Neilson told my mother. It was "shocking behavior!" Mrs. Neilson declared when she came round to our house complaining about the occurrence. The lamp-post was public property and delicate Brenda was upset. My mother wouldn't believe Mrs Neilson – or Brenda for that matter – even though I didn't defend myself. Mum's attitude was: "None of my children would do a thing like that". To my shame of course, I did. I didn't admit it though. I also had incredible strength, being very athletic, and could outrun anybody my own age. Out in the streets the local kids and I would play a game called 'British Bulldogs' in which we would form two sides and run at each other, trying to rugby-tackle our opponents to the ground. I was so strong I could easily take two or three older boys down at once. The girls steered clear of me, and I don't blame them, looking back. I became so good eventually even the boys took fright and wouldn't play anymore. I was really upset. I liked playing Bulldogs and no-one would play with me. It didn't make me very popular.

My first school was Church of England. I can remember being happy there. The atmosphere was nice. After that I went to the local Catholic school. I felt the atmosphere change: it didn't seem as friendly. The school had a high fence around the playground and I used to peer out through the wire. I felt I had gone to prison. By that time my twin sisters, Laura and Alice, were on the way. As it was twins, Mum had to go to hospital for the birth. Dad was left to cook and he was always working, so it was a problem. He was also a terrible cook and couldn't cook anything; except eggs. So we ate eggs for almost a week; morning, noon and night. Always hard boiled. As a result I came out in a massive allergic reaction, red and itchy all over.

My mother went a bit crazy when she was pregnant. Mum was always on about my father not being ambitious and something about being pregnant again seemed to fire her up about this. When the twins were born things became really difficult. With hindsight, I think she might have been suffering post-natal depression. Mum was breastfeeding the twins and studying for exams at the same time. She wanted to teach, and was acquiring more and more qualifications. In fact she worked so hard she never seemed to sleep. It was the ambition thing, and I think she was probably also concerned about money. Although I always remembered us having enough. Anyway, life became turbulent and Mum was very difficult to deal with. By then Dad was flat out running the coal business he had taken over from Granddad Ryan. Dad used to come home late and covered in coal dust and would head for his bath while Mum would prepare dinner and complain to us and bicker with him afterwards. It was unpleasant for everyone.

Apart from that, I remember my mother very much as a free thinker. She was very careful when it came to minimizing exposure to chemicals, always wearing a covering over her face and mouth when she used them. In fact, Mum seemed to have an inbuilt sense of self-preservation, and would keep away from anyone with an illness as much as possible, even people with cancer, because in that case she believed nobody knew if you could catch it. She was very careful about food early on and would always try to cook nice, fresh produce and buy the best we could afford. Mum would never buy veal, though, as she knew how the animals were kept. She also always made the butcher mince the finest steak in front of her as she wanted to be sure of what we would be eating. Really, she never quite trusted butchers, or anyone outside the family for that matter. My father would often get paid by way of a sort of barter system when people couldn't pay cash, so Dad would bring home a chicken or rabbit for dinner. Fruit and nuts and turkeys at Christmas also came in very useful. Memories of plucking the Christmas bird, however, would haunt me because even though preparing the bird was thought of as something joyous to do before the feast, as I tugged each little feather out of that damp and white skin, once so full of life, something deep inside me rebelled, an inchoate anguish that I couldn't totally suppress; this was wrong. That bird I was pulling at – hanging limp on a nail – was a lost existence. It was the same with pulling the innards out of a chicken or rabbit, experiencing the disgusting slimy, red and dead flesh chill against my fingers. Deep down within me raged empathy for the anguish and pain this creature felt losing its short life. But I buried the sensation; the awakening, buried it. That intimation of stolen freedom, lost life and joy, something terribly wrong! The feeling deep, deep, that I didn't want to do this, not really; not ever.

All in all, my mother was incredibly put together in many ways. She did all my father's books and was a very good and trustworthy manager, exceedingly meticulous with detail.

The voice of my beloved!

The Song of Solomon; kjv

Then came the vaccination. It was just routine. For polio, whooping cough and diphtheria. I believe some children died. Anyway I became very ill; in fact I was in a terrible state. Lying on a bed in the front room of our house and looking up at the sky, I recall a voice from heaven and God saying to me, *"You're not going to die"*. I can't remember if I told anybody at the time; but I did later. And I did recover, of course. But shortly after I came out in horrendous, huge skin bubbles filled with fluid all over my body. My mother told me the doctor said the injection had destroyed my immune system, and that I would have to take vitamin B6 for the rest of my life (I wasn't given any B6 then but I take a supplement now). Anyway, that was it. I didn't run fast any more and I seemed to tire more and more easily as the years passed. I started getting colds and allergies and I remember snivelling a lot; something which Patrick hated about me. I can understand this as it was so unhealthy, and it was always very embarrassing as I never seemed to have a hankie at the right moment, so I tended to use my sleeve or skirt: I felt filthy.

Mum had a strange attitude to sexuality and babies. She would always urge me never to have children because, "Babies are awful", she declared. And if we passed a baby in a pram instead of goggling at it like other mothers would, she would just turn to me and say, "Doesn't he smell!" (Or "she" of course.) Especially over dinner Mum would recall details of her breech births in descriptions as vividly evocative as her film-star looks demanded, "All my children were breech birth and you all have such beautiful, large heads to thank me for because of it. But that made it excruciating. The agony of your head!" She would emote, looking at my head, her enormous, dark eyes rounding with incredulity and accusation, "Was unbelievable! If I had had forceps they would have pulled it, and it would have been misshapen. But I didn't. I put up with the pain and wouldn't let them touch me. But look at the shape of your head; it's incredible".

And then she would turn to the twins (so they got their turn), "But you: you two ruined me – two breech babies. They tried to turn you round, Laura, but they couldn't do it. And you both got stuck. I was ruined after you! I've never been the same since". My jaw would drop. I didn't even look at my two tiny sisters; God knows what they were thinking on hearing this at all of three years of age. Mum seemed to imply it was our fault, and the fault of the medicos, and the fault of my father (because he also had a big head). I was horrified by her vivid descriptions of female anguish, but she would not cease, "And the pain! But I wouldn't take anything, because I knew it would affect you mentally. And you must never take anything; my mother told me that. And her mother told her: you never take anything when you're pregnant". She stressed this, all the while her voice rising and falling in penetrating acuity. Armed with this information, of course, I could not understand why any woman would ever want a baby. Equally, I could not quite fathom why Mum also paradoxically admitted, "My dream was always to have a family. That's why I married your father ..."

"One?" I thought. "But four of us?"

If Mum's way of looking at the world didn't make sense in this respect, I didn't think much about it then. What I did pick up, though, was her possessiveness. I should have linked the two things, but I was only a kid. Anyway, sometimes it felt emotionally like Mum was clinging on to me and would never let go.

Mum was so super-charged she sometimes had a weird way of draining energy out of you. I remember a priest who came round to the house told her to her face that she literally seemed to "drain him" – he noticed it, too. Other people said they felt like rags after being with her. I thought it was a bit eerie.

We often went to birthday parties in the house of one of my friends, Linda Screed. Her mother was a pillar of the church, a lovely lady who was very sociable and always doing things for other people. Linda's sister, Ethel, was a sweet, ethereal and willowy being who developed a terrible cancer. I remember being quite young and seeing Ethel in the church cloakroom doing her make up and thinking how sophisticated she looked. Young and lovely and primped with pretty clothes; a real picture. When Ethel died, Linda and the entire family were devastated. It hit me, in that I realized I couldn't take it in; Ethel's death, I mean. I remember asking Linda some stupid question about whether or not she missed Ethel. And Linda's face screwing up as she tried not to cry. Dear Linda. And my God, what a ridiculous, awful question!

Holidays with my family were horrendous to the point of farce. Something always went wrong. I cannot recall having holidays when I was really young, but we usually managed an annual vacation after I turned six or seven. To give an example: one year we went to stay in a caravan on a farm in the West Country. The caravan was small, box-like, and you could hardly move without bumping into someone. With the door closed it had the feel of a huge tin can. Scuffle-like arguments broke out because we were all such strong, dynamic characters. Anyway, at least the weather was okay, because inevitably it rained; (it always seems to rain when you go on holiday in Britain, of course). Near the caravan there was this cesspit with no visible demarcation as to where it began and ended within a sea of grass. I used to go walking, and kept finding it and getting stuck, and then wading my feet out trying to find an exit because I kept forgetting it was there – and I didn't even know it was a cesspit. To be honest, I didn't know what cesspits were until I got in real deep one day because I couldn't find solid ground. Eventually I pulled out my stinking legs. I remember the look of horror on Dad's face as I walked back towards the caravan slathered to the thighs in brown sludge which I thought was just mud. I mean, I thought … I was so naïve. I couldn't fathom why the owners of the caravan site had all this fetid mud all over the place.

It was very unpleasant. Dad was beside himself, of course. He said, with a look of despair on his face, "What the hell are you doing in the cesspit?"

"What's a cesspit Dad?" The voice of innocence. But by then the penny was dropping. I was never quick. Never have been, never will be. But … the smell! To cap it, there were no bathing facilities on the site. I can't even remember how my parents cleaned me up. I can remember feeling humiliated. I was a dullard who didn't even know about cesspits. I developed a vehement hatred of camp sites after that. I would rather never go on holiday ever again than go on holiday to a camp site.

Another time we went by train and stayed at a guest-house in West Wales. It started off okay. But we were all in one room. It was terribly small, only big enough for two people at most, and there were five of us (Patrick wasn't with us). The owners catered institutional-style meals of which I have dim, disdainful glimpses of recollection. Stuff like colored jelly for dessert. All sorts of unhealthy shades like bottle green and scarlet, colors desserts shouldn't be. Almost immediately we arrived, Laura came down with a terrible bout of measles. That wouldn't have been too bad, but there was a smallpox epidemic in Britain at the time and people were dying fly-like all over the place. So here we were with Laura covered in spots and in a terrible state because she was such a thin whippet-of-a-thing to start with, and the people running the guest-house wanted us out. But Laura was too sick to move, so we had to stay: we became pariahs. I remember my parents taking Alice out one afternoon and me staying with little Laura who was desperately ill, so ill I believed she was dying. Thin to begin with, she was now emaciated. I remember holding her little hand, lying on the bed with her, praying she would live. She did. But the train ride home was a debacle. People backed off, moved away, if we came anywhere near them; it was like we had the plague. Laura was vivid vermillion, so blotchy with spots there was very little white skin showing.

I remember years later recounting this and similar stories of our holidays to my best friend, Alison Hayes. She came from a private estate just down the road and was very cultured and cultivated, quite brilliant later on in English language and literature. With a deadpan face and flat voice Alison remarked, "I don't think I'd go on holidays if mine were as bad as yours". Alison was totally matter of fact. We sat there together considering, staring into the air in front of us, sitting on a wall outside her house. We got on amiably, Alison and I. Alison later became the first person I knew in real life who had a nose job. She persuaded the doctors she had a psychological problem with it. So she had it done on the National Health Service. Mum thought it was a coup, and said she would have had a nose job too if she had been younger. I knew it wasn't a good idea even then. I mean, Mum had this classical face and her Roman nose imbued her with chutzpah. It was there, it stuck out, it existed; there was nothing wrong with it! It wasn't some namby-pamby nose you got off the conveyor belt of a plastic surgeon's shrunken imagination. Now everybody's getting nose jobs so that all the women that have them can be trophy wives. Everybody in the 'in' crowd is looking more and more alike, like eggs in a carton. Thank God Mum didn't have the opportunity for that nose job; hers was a one-off, designer nose.

Very infrequently over the years Mary, my father's sister who had become a nun, came to visit. Mary was a bit strict, and scared me. She taught orphaned and disadvantaged children. I always remember a conversation Sister Mary had with Mum. Mary had lovely long hair – Ryan hair. I peaked at it once under her veil. It was thick and flaxen, falling well below her waist. I didn't know nuns had hair, for some reason I thought they were all sort of bald. Anyway, this one time Mum was 'doing a Mum' and envisioning her view of reality. So she waxed lyrically on about Man being the "microcosm in the macrocosm". I knew Mum was trying to impress, but I felt rather proud of this, to me, revolutionary idea. Mary, the pragmatist, on the other hand, looked gob-smacked, and I had the distinct impression she thought Mum was 'up herself'. Or barmy or something. For my part, I was totally mystified and intrigued, and tried to work out what the hell Mum was on about. (I like things I can't quite work out, because they stretch you intellectually and in other ways.) Of course, Mum really did seem rather 'up herself' in that instance, but she could be profound.

Anyway, we also went to visit Pamela, my father's other sister who had become a nun. Pamela had adopted her second name when she took vows and was now called Sister Molly. I remember the convent she was in as atmospherically austere. Sister Molly was brought in to see us after we arrived. I can't remember what Molly looked like now at all, but I felt immediately that this was a saintly person; she had incredible presence. Indeed, the aura of her intense sanctity had the effect of making me behave unusually well. I felt I wanted to – had to – be very, very good. I was so happy just being in the convent with her. I dimly recall entering a small, but beautiful chapel, where Mass was said and looking in through the open door, and sensing a great sanctity of space in a solemnity of darkness, and dark wood, and mood, and symbolism redolent of holiness: a sacred place.

I wanted to be holy, without quite being able to explain it.

My mother would tell a story about Sister Molly 'seeing' things. Molly taught disadvantaged children in a school attached to the convent, and apparently she walked into the girl's dormitory one night, and saw one of the little girls awake and talking to a small devil. The devil disappeared, leaving Sister Molly staring at the girl. The little girl looked at Molly and said, "You saw him, didn't you?" Shortly following our visit, Molly died. My father went to the funeral, and came home terribly distressed. Dad said all the children at the school where Molly taught were in tears, he was shaken; Molly was someone you just loved. I think even my mother liked her. It horrified Mum and Dad that Sister Mary wasn't able to go to the funeral; that was the rule in the Catholic Church at the time. Anyway, Molly had left only two items in her will, her holy water bottle and her rosary beads. She wanted me to have the holy water bottle, I don't know who got the rosary.

I must have been six or seven, and Mother demanded that she have the holy water bottle. An argument ensued. But for once my father stood his ground; Molly wanted me to have it, and I was going to get it. So I was given the holy water container. I couldn't understand why Molly had left it to me, and felt puzzled. After all, I only recalled meeting her once or twice. (The twice I'm not sure about.) So I put it by my bed, feeling vaguely privileged and knowing it was holy. Then, one day when I was feeling good, I decided to pray and clean the house for Mum, offering it all up to God. I can't remember exactly why, as I tended to be lazy, and didn't like cleaning because it was boring and hard work. There was holy water left in the holy water bottle, and I went round sprinkling it everywhere, spraying spurts and droplets over the walls, cleaning and praying at the same time. Then I took the bottle, and knelt down by my bed and prayed to Our Lady,

I remember this incredible feeling of joy, pure joy, welling up within me.

It was unlike anything I had ever experienced, or experienced since; it was unworldly, heavenly. And I felt it was Our Lady telling me that this was how to pray, to offer everything you do up to God.

I still have that holy water bottle. However, I wish trying to be good had made me more hygienic, because I cleaned the toilet using Mum's toothbrush. I remember her asking me about it over dinner, a pained expression on her face, "You didn't clean the toilet bowl with my toothbrush, did you, dear?" I really didn't know what to say. At the time it seemed a good idea for getting at the difficult bits. So I just looked down, with my fringe falling across my eyes and mumbled, "No, Mum". I don't think I actually used the negative, because I felt bad about it. It was a mark of my lack of intellectual perspicuity that it was only several years later that I looked back and thought, "Oh hell! I could have made her really, really sick". That particular night Dad, who was working evening shifts at the docks, came home with musical boxes he'd been given by a foreign seafarer, so I didn't dwell on the toilet episode. I thought it was nice of the sailor, whoever he was. As there were three boxes, we girls had one each. I played with mine. It had a little dancer that went round and round, and a picture of Mount Fuji on a glittery, glass mirror. I played with it so much the dancer fell off, and the glitter came off the mirror where I rubbed it.

Around this time I began having more dreams; strange dreams. Some of a recurring, repetitive nature. One was particularly memorable:

it was of a globe. The globe would appear in my dreams and spin round, right round the world. And then it would stop. At Indonesia, Sumatra and Borneo, before finally coming to rest at Australia.

This same curious dream recurred over and over well into my adulthood. By that time, I put the repetitive nature of the dream down to the fact that my mother had wanted to go to Australia, but my father had been against it. Mum didn't seem too perturbed when she reflected on the idea either, apparently life as a migrant wasn't too good. News had got out about migrant camps; they weren't the Ritz.

I can also remember a dream about someone standing at the end of my bed,

I might even have been awake. The woman was just looking at me. I'm pretty sure it was a nun, though my memory might be incorrect. It wasn't nasty or anything. I told my mother, and she said dreams like this happened to her when someone in the family died, and that it had happened when May (Mum's sister) died. We left it at that.

But for some reason I did not feel it was someone in my family.

Mum was the dominant one at home, and Dad adored her, although she drove him mad! My twin sisters, Laura and Alice, grew into really lovely looking children. Much smaller than me, petite, which made me feel even more a big, galumphing thing (to employ a word from an Ezra Pound poem, perhaps in the wrong way). I think my father's favorite was Laura, because he saw something of my mother in her.

My father had a beautiful singing voice, and he used to sing infrequently in the bath. I always thought it must have been the most wonderful thing, to sing. My mother related a rather diminishing story of how she and Dad were at a big family get-together with my father's family, in the Irish tradition, where everyone would play the piano or sing or tell stories or do anything they excelled at. As Dad's family all seemed to be both intellectually gifted and multi-talented, this must have been awesome. Anyway, on this particular occasion Dad was asked to sing, and my mother mused – with a curious mixture of regret and disdain – how nervous he was and how his voice was weak and had cracked. Listening to her, I felt both embarrassed and sorry for my father. I knew Dad suffered from a lack of confidence, and wondered if this stemmed from his education being curtailed; Dad having left school early to work to help pay to put his siblings through university. As being intellectually brilliant was important in the Ryan family, it must have affected him. Anyway, while I have nil vocal ability, both Laura and Alice have beautiful voices, so they must have inherited his talent.

At least I can read well on occasion; this is another Ryan thing. The trouble with me is I'm erratic as my energy wavers, so sometimes I read well and at other times it's plain awful. One aunt, Julia Bartlett, was a reader at her local church, and had a fabulous reading voice. Aunt Julia smoked like a trooper, and this really paid off as it gave her voice a husky timbre that was mesmerizing. (Not that I'm suggesting the fags for a similar effect – they probably killed her in the end.)

We went to church on Sundays and Holy Days of Obligation and ate fish on Friday, like good Catholics. But we weren't amazingly religious. In fact, I used to marvel at individuals who went to daily Mass. But spirituality was very important in a by-product sort of way. For instance, I can remember Christmases as being really happy. We all had stockings, and there was tons of food, and we played board games until they became monotonous. Church itself was wonderful, with the ritual and music and sense of community. I could pick up the Spirit, the sense of joy in the world; that wonderful intimation of a new reality breaking through. Easter was also lovely, although I wasn't too hung-up on the tragic developments of the week leading up to Easter Sunday. Unfortunately, I began to pick up the feeling of love engendered on these occasions through food, so I came to associate food with feeling happy. That's not all bad. But with Mum and Dad worked off their feet, they really didn't have enough time to dedicate to our emotional needs, so I tended to eat because it filled a void – which didn't help my girth.

We children were four very different human beings, each with our own needs. My brother was tall and good looking, but so much older than I it was difficult to feel close. Alice had my father's cornflower blue eyes and lovely skin. I always remember Alice wanting a dog, so she would walk round with this little trail of rope at the end of which was her imaginary dog. Laura was darker, more determined, with big, round eyes and long, fluttering lashes. I, however, was still referred to as 'well-built', which is not something little girls want to be called. In fact, it made me feel awful. I was the tallest in my year, and used to be singled out and positioned at the back in school photographs. Unfortunately, I wasn't particularly popular in school. I was shy, and because of my size and height, didn't have good self-esteem. I considered myself ugly, and spent a lot of time at night praying to be beautiful. People did comment on my good skin though, which helped.

Something I vividly remember was singing hymns at assembly time. One had a line that repeats about being "true to Christ till death". I used to wonder if we would. Another thing that hit me was a passage in the Bible where Christ talks about the "lilies of the field". I sort of took to that idea. I kind of looked to God to protect me. I was a lily. Sort of.

I had difficulty getting to sleep by now, so I would usually daydream my way into sleep. At around the age of nine or ten I had a really weird dream, of a type that would recur and which seems relevant to current discussions you hear on radio and TV chat shows:

I woke in the night to see a huge saucer-like object over the houses opposite. It was quite terrifying. I seemed to be able to see into this spaceship, and there were people, and something nasty going on. I thought I went back to sleep, but then awoke to find some sort of robot in the room – a kind of rectangular metal box thing. The robot, in the form of a metal box, seemed to do something to the back of my neck that felt really odd. It wasn't a nice experience at all: in fact it was malevolent.

Junior school, which stretched from when I was about seven to when I was about eleven, was wretchedly uninspiring. I did fairly well academically, but deep down still felt incarcerated. My health wasn't terribly good, and I didn't help, because I would occasionally attempt to get sick by asking other girls to breathe over me if they were ill. That way I worked out I could get to stay home, and Mum would give me attention and cook me nice things. I was in the second to top class, and got put into the top class near the time of the General Examination, but that only lasted a week. It was odd; I didn't do anything wrong. I got the impression the teacher didn't like me. Anyway, it wasn't too bad and the Headmaster was nice. You got caned if you were late, which I was from time to time. But occasionally he would go to swipe you with the cane, and then change his mind. I think it might have been that he didn't like the fear in our eyes – he had an expression on his face as if to say he couldn't stomach it.

I passed my exams at eleven only well enough to get into a secondary modern school, not a grammar school. Even so, I had done well enough to get into the top stream, which meant you could do 'O' levels, and 'O' levels meant you could get to college. But now my life changed dramatically for the worse. The head nun, Sister Agatha, was a horrid creature. Generally, nobody ever said anything negative about priests or nuns. (Though to tell the truth – in my father's family – I did overhear someone say that the priests in Ireland before they migrated could be pretty grim. So my own family used to be open about these things.) But Sister Agatha was something else. She took a dislike to me that bordered on out-and-out hatred. On one occasion I saw her coming and became so terrified I stood up without looking above me, and accidentally knocked down a pot plant balanced on a plinth. Sister was furious, and grabbed me by the arm, and punched me up and down the corridor, hard; in the ribs. I can't even remember if I was bruised, but I was horrified, terrified. The effect this woman had on me was totally demoralizing. I remember sitting in the school grounds feeling a bit down. The next assembly Sister Agatha gave a talk on 'pervy girls' who sat in the school grounds looking at the boys, staring from time to time at me as if I were a perv myself. I hadn't been looking at the boys at all, but I felt I was the object of this tirade. Sister also made weird comments about having a "little bird" on her shoulder that told her what was going on. This quite spooked me. I imagined this bird thing and her. Talking? It seemed very peculiar, kind of evil. She also seemed to have a thing about our use of toilets, and was peculiar about anyone spending too much time in the toilet. She introduced a rule, putting on monitor-prefects to time you when you went into the cubicle and when you came out. Two minutes was max. I was so concerned by the introduction of this rule, that I attempted not to go to the toilet at all in school time. It was extremely difficult.

Another bad memory from this dismal scholastic sojourn, was the experience of break time. You would be in the hall (if it rained) and they would play Beatles music; all break. I liked music, but I couldn't stand the Beatles. I particularly thought one of their most popular renditions – played on a daily basis – gross, lacking in imagination and excruciatingly repetitive. But we would be expected, forced, to get up and dance. I liked to dance, but was introverted, unwilling to perform in this manner in public. Sister Agatha, however, gave the distinct impression that if you didn't dance you were likely to be sitting round thinking unsavory thoughts. I don't know what the hell she was thinking herself, but the teachers would go round and, if you were sitting down, they would force you to dance. I detested, hated, this. But I didn't want to get into trouble, so I got up and danced; everyone did. I felt we were like robots dancing to this awful music. The peculiar thing was that, over time, I started to like the music. I even began to think the Beatles were good-looking (pretty much everyone else my age did). Slowly, I became hooked. To such an extent that when Mum purchased our first record player, I was so impatient to hear Beatles' music I picked the contraption up from town myself, carrying it home on the bus; something Mum didn't agree with. Since the record player was both extremely heavy – and an awkward shape – this was indeed a feat, and I almost wrenched my arms from their sockets.

As time went on, alone at home, I would even dance round the room to this awful music. I did determine never to go so far as to wail and scream in the sort of quasi-religious ecstasy my female peers displayed. And, while I considered the way the Beatles dressed naff, even spivvy, just being on the screen seemed to imbue them with an in-your-face allure I couldn't quite figure. I admit I went along with it all in the end, so that when one of my classmates emoted the lovesick remark, "I like George. Who do you like?" I responded, "I like Paul ... I think".

Because I didn't. I didn't really like him; in the sense of fancy him, I mean. Still, as things turned out at least our Paul wasn't such a bad bet. He and Linda have had an enormous impact in raising awareness of the need for the ethical treatment of animals. And, of course, Stella McCartney's not only vegy-friendly, she's hip-chic. But the whole thing had an impact on me later as I came to reflect on how I could have been induced to feel I liked something I abhorred: I felt I had been brainwashed.

I suppose there were times which just might have been interpreted more positively. Like the time I was involved in the Christmas play. As I was tall, and rather large, I got to play the part of Mother Hen. So I was garbed in this big balloon of fabric with a triangular yellow plume of cardboard pinned to my head, (I think the teacher must have been confused because the plume was really more fitting for a rooster) with my face painted red with yellow spots. I looked totally, absolutely, horrendous. In compensation, I threw myself into the part and clucked brilliantly and with great gusto at all the designated, relevant intervals. This did little for my ego, even though my performance received enthusiastic applause. The following Christmas dance, similarly, was something I began by looking forward to, but it turned out even worse. Mum took me out to town to pick a dress. Being sartorially naïve, I chose a yellow tulle affair with a huge skirt that made me look like Dorothy out of *The Wizard of Oz*. My mother, love her, tried to dissuade me, but I wouldn't change my mind; I liked yellow and thought it looked gay. I realized only when I was dressing in a corner of the classroom before the dance how wretched the frock was. But by then it was too late. Everyone else in my class had these sort of modish clothes which were fashionable at the time. Looking round, I knew I was going to be a frump. Being painfully shy, I would never undress in public and so, in an attempt to preserve my modesty, I wriggled into the dress while – at the same time – attempting to remove my school uniform so as not to reveal any flesh. Being rushed by the teacher, I forgot to take the skirt off and left it round my waist, with the yellow dress over the top.

The dance, only girls of course, was a tortuous event. I felt quite incomparably old fashioned, frumpy, and indeed; hideous. To make matters worse the following day one of my schoolmates commented, quite gently and sympathetically, "You have the worst case of midriff-bulge I've ever seen". She seemed terribly sorry for me. I was twelve years old at the time.

I also got into playing the violin. As I said I liked music, classical really being my style. But I turned out to be a desperately poor violin player, although towards the end I managed an impressive trill on the strings. But I loved it anyway, and ended up with the third violins in the school orchestra, where I would play ecstatically, mostly out of tune, and I started and stopped not by looking at the music sheet, but by watching what everyone else in the thirds was doing. I was transported at times by the sheer beauty of the music. For practice purposes we would sometimes go to a local Anglican school. I felt the atmosphere was warm and welcoming, and I just adored being there. The girls were friendly and there seemed to be a lot of love around.

At my own school I was feeling more and more negative about myself. After all, Sister Agatha thought I was bad, so I had to be bad. There was something wrong with me, although I couldn't quite work out what. I began to neglect my appearance and became depressed. In reality I was very well-behaved; I was too terrified of Sister to be otherwise. But I now looked so dreadful even my father was taken aback at the state I was in. I wasn't washing, and I constantly moped with my head hanging down so that my hair hid my face because I didn't want people to look at me. My mother had never encouraged us to wash – it was a family tradition which seemed to have stemmed back centuries that washing gave rise to illness. But I no longer cared about myself. Now my long hair was always stringy with dirt: I got head lice in the end. I remember walking upstairs and seeing one nit running round and round on a bookcase. (It must have dropped out of my head.) "How gross!" I thought. Mum was duly alerted and took me to a hairdresser where I was shorn into a Twiggy look-alike. It didn't suit me, and I didn't want to look like Twiggy, and the hairdo had this wretched fringe that flopped into my eyes all the time. About which the music master would make repetitive, rude comments such as ordering me to,

"Get your fringe cut, for heaven's sake!"

I despised that man. I also felt concerned about the hairdresser as well, because of being lousy with lice. Mum didn't seem to care, she was totally ruthless about it all. But I was worried the hairdresser would see them – the nits, I mean. Or catch them. Or that I might have passed the horrid little things on to some poor, unsuspecting individual come in for a nice hairdo. When we got home, Mum poured something acrid on my head and the lice all died; probably more from the stench and glug of the stuff than from poisoning. The sticky white fluid took ages to wash out, and I must have stunk of it for days. It was such a revolting experience, it made me paranoid later on in life about being spotlessly clean.

I spent long nights praying to get out of that school. It was exhausting, but eventually my prayers were answered when high achievers were given the chance to be transferred to the grammar school. My mother and father had put my name forward as a promising candidate, and subsequently were invited to a meeting with the school governors where my fate would be decided. Sister was so damning in her assessment of me that one of the school governors exclaimed that if a child was as badly behaved as I was, they ought to be transferred to an approved school; a school for delinquents. Basically, the bitch-of-a-thing radically overdid it. My father, according to my mother, came into his own and staunchly defended me. Dad always had a lot of guts when the going got tough, and he was very bright despite his lack of formal education. The school governors didn't need to be convinced after Sister's damning remarks; I had to be moved. It couldn't go on. So I was transferred to the grammar school.

I later found out that my brother had trouble at school as well. He'd been boxed in the ears so often it damaged his right eardrum, and later on Genevieve told me she suspected it resulted in his partial deafness. Random beatings by certain teachers were just to be expected, but Patrick was emotionally resilient, thank God.

Night

Catch for us the foxes, the little foxes that ruin the vineyards, our vineyards that are in bloom.

Song of Songs

After the change of school I blossomed; well, I washed. But not before I announced to my family that I would never again go to church; I definitely didn't believe any of it any longer. No-one ever seemed to stand up to Sister Agatha while I was in school, in fact they were often raving sycophants of this wretched female. So I rebelled. If this was what Christians were like, I certainly didn't want to be numbered amongst them. After all, if even individuals called to the religious life were that nasty and couldn't get it right, how could I? (I seemed to forget my saintly aunt with the holy water bottle, which doesn't show much for my reasoning powers at the time.) No! Catholics, except for my own family I felt, who – to give them their due – were free thinkers, existed in a fairyland where priests and nuns were all saints. I just couldn't handle it; it was like a spiritual fog on the landscape. Dad was furious with me, and there ensued a devil of an argument which ended up with me sitting on the local playing field for hours while he cooled down.

I labeled myself an 'atheist'. With the religious experiences I'd had, and kept having, this was somewhat untenable at a certain level, but I totally wrote off those experiences. No-one ever talked about visions and voices unless they were barking mad. Except for saintly visionaries, of course: and I certainly wasn't one of those. Still, it was difficult. So I vacillated between atheism and agnosticism, while still finding myself drawn to prayer in times of difficulty. It became a sort of subconscious Pascal's wager situation.

Dad now did a lot of the cooking. This was the era when feminism was gaining ground. Mum was part of that. She was a new woman, a sort of crypto-feminist. (She would never use the word 'feminist' though, it wasn't her style; she didn't like labels.) Mum had an incredible capacity for work, and a love of earning her own living, and was reputedly an excellent teacher. Her lectures often went on into the late evening, so someone had to feed us, and it had to be Dad. Poor bloke, he was as hopeless a cook as ever, but he did his best. His *piece de résistance* became a repetitive lamb stew. In fact, it was almost always lamb stew. Or that's all I can remember. Of course, it was better than the boiled eggs of my early childhood, although I felt the stew would have been considerably enhanced by a stock cube or two; I don't think Dad realized these existed. Dad's lamb stew had a brown, swilly appearance, gravelly texture and was generally served lukewarm. Special times we had hunks of bread, or rather that sliced, spongy stuff bakeries churned out and labeled 'bread'. Still, this addition improved the stew considerably. I really should have taken on the cooking as I was a good cook, but I was lazy and always tired. I did do weekend things and special occasion food, like cakes and biscuits. But generally the quality of the tucker deteriorated dramatically in our house. In a way we were all being neglected. Parents were now working full time, but no-one had thought of how the kids were going to be cared for. Or how dads and mums were going to get time to actually sit down and talk to each other in peace, now that they were on the go from dawn till late at night. Unless, that is, one was lucky enough to come from an extended family, or be rich enough to have a nanny or maid.

We would still see my father's relatives from time to time. I remember especially going to see Alexandria, one of my cousins. This planted a seed of the modeling bug in me. Alex was a lot older than me. (Well, twenty seems a lot older when you're barely fourteen.) She opened the door of her house in response to my knock, dressed in these wonderful clothes. Alex was sylph-like and beautiful, and I was gobsmacked at her fashionable gear and, most of all, by a pair of amazing and decidedly expensive knee-high boots she wore. Our family was often better looking than most models and film stars, that was just de rigueur, but Alex in those clothes was sixties' glamor personified. "This is elegance; this is fashion. This is style with a capital "S"!" I mused, "This is how I want to look". Alex, the model. I day-dreamed and gawped, thinking, "That's what I want to do. Then I can wear wonderful things and I'll be beautiful and everyone will love me".

Ah, the gullibility of youth! You see, I didn't for a minute recall the times my mother had taken me to a wholesaler friend to purchase outfits for special occasions. The lady wholesaler used to be scornful about my shyness when changing, always going into a little room on my own when, as the wholesaler pointed out, the models she employed used to walk round stark naked. And think nothing of it. I had no time for this at all. It was vile; tasteless. I wouldn't want to do that for anything; I mean, you have to have some sense of self-respect.

Mother was going from strength to strength and had become the main income earner. Flexing her monetary might and status as a professional, Mum began treating my father atrociously and would harangue him over dinner about his lack of ambition. Having given up his coal business because things had become difficult, Dad had taken rather low-paid jobs, including one as a night watchman and later a short stint as a special policeman. Coming under the influence of my mother, I began to look down upon my father. Simultaneously, Dad began to lose a lot of his self-respect and started to mope round submissively and neglect his appearance, just the way I had earlier at school. It wasn't at all unusual now for my mother to restrict what he ate. She did this by chiding him about the cost of food, and commenting on how much butter he was putting on his bread or how much meat he was eating, and so on. Even though I was really horrid to him myself on many occasions, it was heart-rending to watch him replace a second slice of meat on the serving dish, or scrape butter off his toast and put it back in the butter dish. It was emotional and psychological torment; my mother did a neat job in that at times. And I didn't help either.

As always, Dad remained a thoughtful man. He often used to sit at night, warming his hands in front of the fire in our living room, as though pensively reflecting on things long ago, far away. Sometimes, when Mum went on at Dad a lot, he wouldn't speak to anyone at home for weeks on end. I remember it got so bad that at one point when I was walking to school, we passed each other in the street without acknowledging one another, not speaking; not a word. It was as if I had lost my voice, my real self. The horror of it! My own Dad. How could I?

At other times Dad was kind and 'devil-may-care'. When I was sick and had to miss school he wasn't at all concerned. Dad really didn't give a hoot if we turned out brilliant or stupid. All he wanted was for us to be happy. He gave me a sense that women should be pure, somehow a bit mysterious, and would remark, employing vanity as an enticement, that nuns had "the most beautiful skin". But I did feel just a little sad that he seemed to love Laura most of all.

Something that transpired around this time sticks in my mind. My father was reading books by a popular author. They were horror stories of the occult variety. The writer was enormously popular, and I remember coming across one of these books in my parents' bedroom, and reading bits, and being influenced. I thought they were a good read, exciting and strange. As I liked music and dancing, I did this daft thing and did a dance. I thought I could dance so well I could convert the devil, or something like that. I had developed into a very sensitive adolescent, and it worried me later on when I thought about it. Things that kids take in can influence them in ways they might not understand. In fact, I would go further; everything you do has an impact on your psyche at some level or other: *what seems to happen is that you literally can open a window in your soul*. If you view your soul as a house or a castle of crystal (as St. Teresa of Avila did) *it's as if holy things open windows to heaven, while unholy things open windows to all sorts of negativity.*

Windows to other worlds and dimensions of consciousness.

Windows on heaven, windows to hell.

Around that time my brother met Genevieve. When she came to stay, Genevieve used to sleep in the bedroom I shared with my sisters. Usually Laura was turfed out. Laura was very amiable about it and would sleep downstairs on the sofa, which must have been uncomfortable. So Gen would have Laura's bed. Sleeping became even more problematic, and I began to read late into the night to try to resolve the problem, using a torch under the blankets so I wouldn't disturb anyone. I couldn't put my finger on it, but things didn't feel right anymore in the room, and I had this terrible visionary nightmare of *a black coach driven by horses, out of the 1800s. It seemed to be a hearse. I couldn't see who was inside, but there was a malevolent message: the House of the Witch.* (I am not giving details of this vision for certain reasons, or relating definitively to this time point, but this gives a sense of what transpired.)

Looking back it was as if a window had opened in my soul;

and outside it was darkness:

night.

Disturbing things were out there.

Later, Genevieve mentioned that her Aunt Christa was involved in the occult. Christa lived in an old house and, among other things, someone who worked for her had reported hearing ghostly voices of children. I don't know if this had anything to do with my deteriorating sleeping patterns, or whether it was reading those books, but something seemed to be disturbing me, spiritually and psychologically.

Anyway, apart from this, Genevieve added a novel and unique dimension to our lives. She dressed in Jean Muir with touches of art-house, and had blonde hair sprinkled with auburn that couldn't be totally natural, but still fascinated me, and which I knew my brother adored. Genevieve knew how to use cutlery, eating delicately – and only very little – while watching with undisguised horror we girls and Patrick literally descend upon our food like starving puppies, woofing it down with voracious appetite. Gen gave us presents at Christmas and birthdays concealed beneath tinsel, lace, ribbons, bows and colored tissue that were really too gorgeous to unwrap. Yet my father, privately, declared Genevieve's family to be little more than "mountain goats" from Wales. Because he knew, we knew, we were losing Patrick to this woman of the hill country. When the engagement was announced, I was called upon to cook for Patrick and Genevieve's party. So I excelled myself, and prepared masses of finger-food, canapés; that sort of thing. But I was so tired from an increasing lack of energy, that I couldn't stay to eat anything or join in once the party began. Instead, I had to go to bed. Downstairs I could hear the glasses clinking, and voices of happiness as I drifted into well-deserved sleep.

At grammar school I studied hard. I also continued to have intriguing dreams about Australia. Around the age of fourteen, I experienced an intensely creative period when I wrote mysterious poetry I couldn't fully understand. I still have it somewhere. One poem was about an existential 'pit'. Others were about real experiences I would go through much later in life. Looking back, it was as if I was writing poetry from the "Dark Night of the Soul", as if I was writing my own life; what was to be:

I remember feeling as if the poetry was coming from somewhere else – as if existence had opened up.

Of course, I wasn't religious at this time. Mum thought my poetry was good enough to be published, so she collated it and typed it out. Examining the poems years later I couldn't agree with her optimistic assessment, but I kept the little booklet because of the poems' strange, mystical intrigue.

At school we had religious education classes several times a week, with years spent studying the Gospel of Mark for examination purposes. It was dreary stuff titled something like "God's plan for Man". Bored while the teacher was teaching, I used to spend most of these lessons reading the Apocalypse, which seemed at once mysterious and intriguing. I couldn't understand the Apocalypse at all really, which was precisely what fascinated me; *the inscrutability of God.*

The religious education teacher, Mrs. Edwards, was a lovely woman. Great teachers, like bad teachers, set a stamp of remembrance: they can change your life. Mrs. Edwards was memorable far more for the way she acted than for what she taught. She was a deeply caring, spiritual person. You respected her, this salt of the earth lady with a good mind and a good heart. I even recall her face, the soft brown hair, the prettiness and femininity, the firmness and the gentleness of her. When Mrs. Edwards became pregnant she had a hard time, and I once saw her stooping, gripping her stomach on the school stairs, her face contorted by pain. I wanted to reach out to her, but something stopped me; I knew then I should care more: she was a dear woman. She lost that first child, but her second came soon after. God bless you, Mrs. Edwards.

At home we used to have heated discussions when my parents were around, delving into all manner of topics. My parents encouraged us to think – not just about religion – but also about politics and social issues. My father was for some while a trade unionist which, in a way, was a bit of an oxymoron as he was also a member of the Conservative Party. Often during these discussions, I would ask difficult questions, which drove him mad. I remember him almost tearing his hair out, asking, "Why do you always have to be asking 'why'? Why, why, why! Why can't you just accept things like other people do?" Even today, my husband Mike often has the same reaction to the way I seldom accept anything at face value. It drives him a bit crazy too.

I always seemed to push the box to its ultimate. For instance, in regard to Catholicism, I used to protest it was terribly unfair that babies went to limbo if they were born prematurely. I thought it was horrible; it upset me. I also puzzled a lot about all the Protestants and non-Christians who went to hell, or somewhere horrendous. This also seemed a bit much to swallow. I think my parents agreed, despite their non-committal reaction. Controversial issues like that really made me think. My parents were also quite unprejudiced.

You took people as they came, and issues of race and religion, though they might be talked about and even joked over, didn't really matter in the end; a decent person was a decent person.

I fell ill with whooping cough, and was off school for a year and Mrs. Edwards got someone to bring a huge basket of fruit round to the house. Following the whooping cough, I became even more depleted of energy, and suddenly found it difficult to get out of bed in the morning at all (so much for that whooping cough vaccination of years ago).

I left the grammar school to do my A levels at a college. I remember the day I left school, looking out of the door of our house, feeling free, standing at the open door of my father's house;

the intimation of a new world.

Freedom; it was the most wonderful feeling.

The trouble was, I was a handful at times. Looking back, I squirm. Spoilt, petulant and selfish in some ways, prone to outbursts of swearing, having great difficulty with the passage from childhood to womanhood, in a word, sporadically – horrible.

Leaving grammar school, and starting college, I didn't study as much as I should have. As a result, I didn't do well. In fact, I became lazy and crazy. I bought a guitar and made my sisters' lives unpleasant, constantly attempting to get them to sing along with me. I fancied being famous; which is all the rage now, of course. As I had a ghastly singing voice, my attempt to become a famous singer was somewhat improbable. But at college I at least made some memorable friends. One was a very wealthy girl, called Antoinette, who lived in a Manor House in the country. Antoinette took me there once. It was huge, and I was flabbergasted by the amazing oil paintings of her ancestors lining the staircases, and hanging on the walls of rooms of elegantly faded grandeur. As we passed the portraits, Antoinette mused about reincarnation, and how she believed that she might be one of her ancestors "come back". Antoinette talked about a man who was doing research into reincarnation and how she was thinking about going to him and being regressed into her "past lives". I thought it all sounded a bit weird, and didn't fancy it at all. I mean, most people who lived in the past seem to have had pretty wretched existences. But I did connect to how wonderful it was to be rich. The house Antoinette lived in was enormous, and the sheer sense of empty space and glorious views over the countryside from wide and elegantly shaped windows, bestowed a wonderful sense of freedom; while we, in contrast, were six highly individual people in a small two bedroom and box room place, constantly bumping into one another.

After Antoinette discovered I resided in a council house our friendship cooled, and she didn't seem to want to know me any more. I had been mute about where I lived, as there was a lot of prejudice about council property. But Antoinette had dropped in unexpectedly one day when I was at home; I don't know how she got my address. Anyway, it was terrible; Mother even gave her a cup of tea in a chipped cup. I was really cross as we had a few good cups, and Mum should have known better. I could see Antoinette looking round and sort of 'sniffing'. Antoinette, disdainful, 'sniffing' at our old furniture and the cheap patterned wallpaper on the walls; 'sniffing' at our little house that was a doll's house compared to hers, then examining the chip in the cup and looking at me, an expression of disapproval distorting her features. Antoinette didn't stay long, I don't think she wanted to.

Strangely enough, council houses at that time were really good, built very well to high standards, and with gardens. And our neighbors were decent, genuine folk. There was hardly any violence, and everyone knew one another. Later, I actually felt quite sorry for Antoinette when I recalled an incident she related about her friendship with a stable hand. Antoinette had dropped him because, as she definitively pronounced, "You can't mix classes". I couldn't believe it, and realized this was a ruddy awful way to live. After all, that stable hand could have been the love of her life, and made her forever happy. But that was the attitude among some of the middle and upper class girls I knew: you married for status and money. That was just the way it was.

Another of my friends was a Jewish boy. I learnt a bit about Judaism from him, and we and his friends used to spend hours talking about subjects such as psychology, particularly in this case, Jung and Freud. Along with the studies I was doing in politics, economics, history and law, it was all very engrossing. And I was reading masses. Lots of poetry by Yeats and others, and American literature. Maybe this influenced me, because around this time I had the crazy idea I'd like to be a writer. So I would write bits and pieces. No particular topic grabbed me though, so it was all a bit random.

I had no idea at all of what I wanted to do after leaving school. As I was interested in religion and philosophy, I considered going to university to do a Religious Studies degree, but changed my mind. (This was a bad move, thinking back.) My parents were a bit desperate to help me make a decision, and my mother came up with the idea of Domestic Science College. Apparently, domestic science teachers she worked with had easy lives at school making cakes and pasties and pies and things. So it seemed okay. The problem was, I couldn't sew, and wasn't even slightly interested in learning how to wash clothes and dry them in the best wind conditions etc., topics which formed sizable chunks of the course in the first year. The most soul-destroying part of this little escapade down a career track traditional to the family ethos came in the form of sewing classes; I have a horror of pins and needles and anything sharp and detest mechanical devices. Threading those blasted sewing machines became an exercise in futility, so much so that during my nine months at college, I only managed a drab black skirt with a (somewhat incongruously) modest slit in the front. In fact, I would usually spend the entire three-hour lesson attempting to poke thread through the funny little slots and metal holes of these intricate contraptions which morphed before my eyes into instruments of torture. I never seemed to get the bloody thing right, which meant the machine wouldn't stitch, and I repeatedly had to start from the beginning. Hours passed while others beavered away, some creating masterpieces of dressmaking that could carry the label 'couture', while I would thread and rethread. I wanted to run out screaming or cry or throw the blasted thing out of the window! Of course, I became too embarrassed to keep asking other students for help. My ability was truly, unbelievably, pathetic; indeed, it was appalling. The sewing teacher (probably and understandably because I was the worst student she had ever encountered) detested me. But her aversion didn't help. Periodically, guiltily, I would furtively glimpse round the room and catch this unpleasantly mannered, raven-haired Welsh woman glaring at me: she bloody well knew I was threading away. And I would shrivel, spiritually and mentally, if not physically, but still poking cotton through those wretched holes.

Apart from this, I spent most of the time when I was supposed to be garnering information about laundry and clothes driers, reading books on German playwrights and literature – of which there was a good supply, funnily enough, in the college library. Thankfully!

I dropped out after those nine months, the overriding reason being poor health. I had so little energy it was problematic getting up, and the college was a long and, for me, arduous journey of two bus rides from home. I had odd jobs here and there, and following a birthday gift of an enrollment in a modeling course, I was offered work as a model. One job was amazing and involved a television appearance. It could have led to further work, but I couldn't get up to go to the studios. Of course, in those days lack of energy was written off as laziness. But the truth told, I was also influenced by my father's disapproval of modeling as a career. (The course itself had been Mum's idea; she sometimes indulged me.) In retrospect, it was Dad who was wise. Returning to modeling later in life, I finally came to my senses and rediscovered that behind the scenes, beneath the glitz, it can be the pits.

At about that time I went with Alison to a medium. I went only because Alison didn't want to go alone; I wasn't really interested. I can remember entering an old house in Caerleon, and waiting in a dingy room with pots and pots of musty green plants. When I went into the room where the reading would take place, the elderly lady medium asked me for something that belonged to me. I gave her my plastic watch, and the medium looked rather vague and rubbed it and began reeling off a list of names of girls she said I "knew". She really did make a bit of a mess of it, as I didn't know any girls with the particular names she came up with. I told her this, and she informed me I would meet them "in the future". I left, disappointed at the total waste of time and money, convinced the medium was just making it up. After all, she had come up with about fifteen names, none of which applied, so it wasn't even good guesswork. I found out Alison had been told she would meet someone who was like a "ship in the night". I wonder if she ever did: I somehow doubt it.

When Patrick married Genevieve, I moved into his room at the front of the house. This was the box room, which my parents, out of their tender love for me, re-decorated, adding blue curtains and putting up lilac wallpaper; lilac being my favorite color at the time. I was moved by their care, and having acquired these very feminine touches, the room was light in ambience to the point of being exquisitely pretty. Anyway, despite this, after a while I started to feel something was very wrong: *it was as if there was all this negative energy around in my new bedroom. I could almost see balls of energy at times. It began to unnerve me. Sometimes I even thought I was being attacked by an evil spirit or spirits.*

Now, looking back, I wonder: it was as if the visit to the medium had opened another window in my soul.

And outside there were nasty things:

it was darkness;

night.

I didn't articulate anything for a while. Indeed, I had one experience in this room so puzzling I have put it down to imagination and haven't included it here. But then – and suddenly – I broached the topic of these nocturnal visitations to my parents. By that point I was fervently, constantly, praying through the long night hours and into the day for the thing or things to go away. As a result, I was feeling even more excruciatingly tired than normal. At first my parents were unconcerned, even dismissive, but then my father came across a weird, large, very dead and very black bird in our garden. The bird had either fallen dead – or been thrown – into the garden because we had no trees, just shrubs, and my father wouldn't discuss it. So I don't know, but for some reason that breached the dam-wall of my parents' lack of interest, and Dad immediately arranged for me to see a priest. Not our local priest;

I think my parents didn't want embarrassing gossip amongst our Catholic neighbors. Speedily, and at dusk, following my father's return home from work one night, I was transported in our old Ford for an interview with a priest in a parish some miles away. This turned out to be a moribund part of the city which I had never before visited. Once there, I was led by my father into an old and dilapidated parsonage inside of which there was hardly any furniture anywhere, save for a few rickety chairs. The priest himself resembled a pauper in appearance; old, wizened, thin and of anorexic demeanor. Having been ushered into the spartan entrance hall, my father and I were invited to sit on two wooden chairs. There we remained for some short while, sitting in subdued silence in the half-light thrown from a dim bulb. For some unfathomable reason I experienced emotions of overriding and overwhelming guilt. This had commenced in the car journey, and now it intensified, I wanted to cry. The door of the priest's study creaked – and then swung open – at the touch of his fingers, and I was summoned by him to enter the office. To add to my anxiety, my father still did not utter a word. Inside his office, the priest proffered a solitary chair facing his desk upon which I could sit. I did what I was invited to do. Meanwhile, the priest sat behind his desk opposite me. My eyes glanced over the desk, which was simple, wooden, and had the appearance of something you would choose to reject in a garage or jumble sale. The priest seemed haunted, garbed as he was in austere black robes, with an accompanying somber mood pervading his presence. The whole thing evoked thoughts of penury, destitution, and threadbare age. Not waiting for him to ask, words gushed from my lips as I emoted the eerie events transpiring at night in my bedroom, still clutching guilt tightly to myself. Framing words in halting cadence, my voice was weak and tremulous, not just from the terror of my lucid descriptions but also from embarrassment. I did not know what was wrong with me; with the world! With that delicate and lovingly decorated room, my bedroom;

in the House of my Father.

The priest, however, seemed strangely unconcerned. And incongruously (to me) inquired, "Have you got a boyfriend?" I couldn't believe it! Even in my extreme naiveté I realized the priest put these manifestations down to things sexual, when I sensed – knew – they were things spiritual. As for sex, at the time I wasn't even interested in boys in the sense of physical attraction. I must have been eighteen or so, so this lack of desire could have been described as some sort of sexual retardation in modern terms, I suppose. But the priest didn't even ask if I was going to church or receiving the sacraments. And when I suggested, with fear in my voice, "I think the room might be haunted!"

He retorted immediately and coldly, "Only people are haunted."

This terrified me – and simultaneously made me wonder what on earth he was on about. I mean, I'd heard of haunted houses, but haunted people? I was stunned. I assumed that he must have thought I was evil. This frightened me even more, which was why I didn't say anything else whatsoever. I could only stop breaking out in a cold sweat by reassuring myself that his explanation didn't make sense, given I was praying to God all night. The interview was a horrible experience. But now, many years later, as I reflect back on this encounter with that poor man in those purgatorial surroundings, I feel no sense of the humiliation, despair and even anger that welled up within me then. Just sadness; grief, almost. At the poverty, the loneliness. Just that priest in isolation in that dark, bare and memorably chill room. Nothing but God to help – and not even God – because there was the sense of aloneness. Darkness. What he needed was a good meal and a family, a warm hug and a dog lying in the hearth. Maybe then he would have heard a genuine cry for help from someone who had just a spark of the infinite burning within them, like we all do! A spark! But the priest couldn't hear because he was so desperately alone in his ministry,

so alone.

Alone in the dark night of despair.

Him.

Me.

My father.

All of us.

Anyway, the priest dismissed me from the room and summoned my father. I don't know what the two of them talked about behind the door that swung closed on me, because my father never again raised the matter. We just drove home in silence. I, crestfallen, ashamed; ashamed because there might be something 'wrong' with me.

I continued praying. A short time later, quietly and without fanfare, another priest, who the hell he was or where he came from I don't know, arrived at our house. He blessed my room. The entire premises. And left. That was it. I felt devastated but didn't say anything. I shut up and kept praying. This went on for about a year, during which I would be awake almost always the entire duration of each long and lonely night, using a rosary because the repetition prevented me from going to sleep. So it was a very effective form of intercession. *Fighting off these hairy demon things at times. Watching spools of energy like wasted souls. That was what I felt they were ...*

I was so scared the tiny hairs on my arms would bristle as I prayed. I had never known anyone go through anything like this; I was ashamed. These things were out to get me. And there was no one to confide in. I considered myself mad. I think the rest of my family thought that way a bit, too. Certainly my sisters. But we never openly discussed it. I did broach something once or twice with my mother when I sensed something atop a cupboard in her bedroom. I was actually imagining it then, and I knew. But I so desperately wanted to talk! She didn't! Instead she almost ran out of the room. I experienced that pariah feeling again. But I knew, I knew, I knew!

I had to pray.

And, still, later: *someone I knew, and voices of little children. And the woman was chasing these phantom voices. Whose voices were the voices of children.*

People: grown people reduced to worse than ashes, lost voices in a landscape. Disfigured souls that never can develop unless they break out of the web because they are chasing dreams; entrapped in a landscape of unbecoming. The ephemera and jewels of this world; the toys and hobbies and fascinations and interests that can obsess us and keep us from waking to who we really are. Spells cast, forming a worldscape of enchantment: the forests of the fairytales, the little boy who would never grow up, the little girl in wonderland. Myths, dreams and legends. This was where all this was coming from: from the underworld. The world of lost souls, of lies and sleep and dreams –

that turn into nightmares. And keep us. Keep us from becoming who we really are.

Many years later, also, I would switch on the radio and listen to a short story about a woman and her mother who seems to have been a witch. The story referred to the woman's mother keeping souls "trapped in a bundle". Souls – people – caught like flies in the vortexes of her spells. Of course, the story left me stone cold: horrified! I couldn't listen to the full descriptions because they revived my own experience. But at eighteen I had been little more than a child wrestling with phenomena I couldn't understand, except for spiritual intuitions that didn't seem to resonate with modern philosophy or psychology or everyday living.

The manifestations ceased abruptly.

Shortly after, on Christmas Eve 1971, I met my husband-to-be. I didn't even thank God at that point, or Our Lady to whom I had prayed so fervently for intercession. My ingratitude was something I later felt terrible about because then, and only then, I realized:

this was God stepping in.

How much better is thy love than wine!

Solomon's Song; kjv

CHRISTMAS '71

Romance!!! A word almost of things lost and forgotten in our present landscape.

My parents didn't like Michael. He wasn't good-looking, as we Ryans were, and he was even poorer than we were. Mike was from a family of eight, living at one time in a two up and two down with an outside loo. Of course, the children were born over a span of years but it was a cramped dwelling to say the least. A plus point was that Michael's house was a rented cottage; council was one down on private rental. Michael seemed a really decent person, and had dreams of traveling. He was very ambitious and was considered for Oxford, but becoming involved with me took a lot of his time and he didn't work hard enough to attain the grades needed. Michael was different from me in that he enjoyed his school years, although he did have some bad experiences. He would recount stories of a legendary monk, Brother Clarence, the headmaster of the school Mike attended, who would enthusiastically encourage all his top students to apply for Oxford or Cambridge: nothing less was good enough. Brother Clarence would invite Mike into his office and bring out a bottle of whisky (just for himself, Clarence didn't share it with Michael) and recount stories about his non-ordained brother who had gone to America and was making "pots of money". Brother Clarence advised everyone to go to America, and Michael thought he was great fun.

Michael's mum was a plump, jovial woman who seemed to take to me. Mike adored her, and would frequently tell stories of his childhood and of how his mum liked to get out of the house but couldn't afford holidays. So she used to take Mike on mystery bus and train tours, day trip stuff. Being more than a bit wild, he loved this. Little did she know that Mike and I would go on our own mystery tour, the greatest mystery tour of them all –

Fasten your seat belts folks

for

a bumpy night

and ...

A girl with Bette Davis's eyes

Night:
    You are entering
        Deeper and deeper into

The Dark Night ...
of the Soul.

Being in love, I became erratically wild and behaved atrociously at times, even more so when it became obvious Mum wouldn't countenance the romance. Besotted, I would buy wedding magazines, planning for that wonderful day when I would be married. I soon got the message and stopped. There would be no wedding, no beautiful white dress, no extravagant cake, no priestly blessing. Anyway, Michael had difficulty with his family and felt one or two members could become a little too boisterous on special occasions. So Mike wasn't keen on the formal wedding thing anyway. My dream frustrated, I became more and more problematic to deal with and was a ghastly example to my sisters, something I would later regret deeply. When my mother banned me from the dinner table, I became depressed and realized I had to escape: I wasn't wanted anymore. I don't blame my parents in some ways for their increasing negativity, but eventually I informed my family I would be leaving with Michael when he left Newport to go to university. It was all very unpleasant and distressed me for years after. The thing that upset me most was the sense of being excluded, especially from the dinner table. I don't know why,

or perhaps I do

now.

The odd thing was, that in a traumatized state the night before I left, I went round my tiny bedroom touching the walls, feeling them, sometimes with my eyes shut. Sensing the environment, the memories, because I was determined in a strange, mystical way I wasn't consciously aware of, to have the feeling and recollection of my family home imprinted indelibly upon my memory. Touching the walls *as if to imprint the memory of the experiences on my soul and psyche.* My palms flat against the raised patterns of the wallpaper. Seeing, *then sensing, then intuiting.* Walking round, sometimes eyes open, sometimes closed, my face wet with tears. *Hearing, sensing.* Touching with a determination to allow all this to be retained within my soul: the outline of the cupboard with its round wooden door handle, the cool almost damp feeling of the painted wood. Remembering, remembering ... embedding the tactile sensations forever so I would never, never forget,

the House of my Father.

The happy times, the sad times. The Christmases and Easters of my youth. The birdsong outside the window, the fields beyond. The days and nights of my childhood. The love and the tears,

the House of my Father.

Only my mother rose from bed to bid me farewell the morning I left, even Dad didn't come down to see me. Mum prepared breakfast, which jangled – and was unwanted – because it seemed phony; after all she had hardly cooked for me in months. I ate the breakfast because I was too distressed to protest. She observed me, a look of perverse maternal satisfaction on her face – as I swallowed the food in lumps, constantly on the verge of bursting into tears. Mum accompanied me to the railway station. Deep down I felt she was at it again. I was hers; her child. And this boy was taking me away.

Because of the trauma, and in anger, I decided to cut all links with my family: it was just too painful. I felt especially bad about not having a proper wedding. We did have a registry office wedding a few years on, but I would have liked to have been married in a church in white. That only happened many years later. Then it was just Mike and me, and a very spiritual lady called Clarie who stood as our witness. With a stained glass image of Thérèse of Liseaux looking down on us. I was always rather attached to

Thérèse (we had a statue of her in our house in Newport) though I could never really empathize with her as she portrayed herself in her autobiography; Thérèse was far too saintly for me to have anything in common with her. But I still visit that church where we made our vows, where they have that image of Thérèse, her enigmatic smile reminding me of her protection; a smile redolent of the fragrance of the roses she promised would fall from heaven following her death.

I became at times something of an emotional wreck, suffering both mild depression and chronic fatigue, without knowing what chronic fatigue was. I was so down on occasion that I would hint at suicide. I was really desperate, but not that desperate, thank heaven! (I know you have to be extremely careful with anyone who threatens suicide.) Emotive threats were my way of attempting to express how unhappy I sometimes felt. But it was disturbing for Michael and he would worry terribly. More usually, I was upbeat and a good cook and careful with my appearance. We entertained frequently, usually Michael's friends, and I prepared inexpensive meals of brilliant pies and gateaux. And we had a pretty, if faded, little flat which comprised the downstairs section of an old couple's interiorly dilapidated house, so we were blessed. When I see the way some kids live in rented places in Australia during their time at uni, I feel sorry for them. Many of the places near us make me wonder about the landlords who drive their Mercedes past and rent out: I mean, they're like slums.

All in all, I had a pretty bad self-image, which emanated from my being unable to cope with life as well as most young girls, perhaps twinned with a lack of confidence inherited from my father. But mostly Mike and I we were incredibly happy. Michael had taken a year off and worked as a drayman and laborer in Newport before starting uni, so at first we weren't too badly off. But as time went on, things became more difficult and we began to run out of money. Michael would often work all night in a factory and study by day so we could get by. Finding it impossible to get up in the morning, I took afternoon jobs, working in shops and offices. Generally, I found these mundane placements boring and didn't last long in them so I tended to drift from job to job. Luckily, employment was readily available.

For wisdom is better than rubies.
The Book of Proverbs; kjv

And the key to eternity

As time passed, and our savings shrank to zero, things became dire financially. We took a loan from my brother to pay the rent (by that time I had regained contact with some members of my family) and sold my beloved guitar to raise money. Michael was very upset about this, because he liked to encourage me to write songs and sing. In desperation I took a job at a local club, something I wouldn't have done normally because the place had a slightly risqué reputation and you had to dress in a ridiculous and, to me, embarrassing and demeaning uniform. Rather ghastly really; shorts, thick stockings and a high necked top. But the money was good, and I could work nights. The club had a restaurant and attached casino and I was given a job in the restaurant as a waitress.

It didn't turn out too badly, considering. But initially I baulked at the heavy make up that was required to compensate for the subdued lighting. Walking into the changing room that first night I was taken aback by the girls, whose vividly painted faces seemed at once lurid and strangely unhealthy. I had a momentary sense of being in a world reminiscent of Manet's painting, *A Bar at the Folies-Bergère*, a picture the mood of which so fascinated me I later wrote a short story about it. The employees of the club were a mixed bag. A few of the girls were university students, which made for intellectual conversation, while the rest of us came from all sorts of backgrounds. The club had an exclusive clientele consisting mainly of businessmen and their wives, legal people and professionals. The casino area would attract high rollers who spent a lot. It was here that the club's real money was made. The most affluent among the players were Arabs, who might spend thousands of pounds in a night, lots of cash for the late seventies considering it was only a small casino in an out-of-the-way town. As I enjoyed being involved with food and generally liked people, I found the work convivial and, after a while, even took on the role of union representative. This lasted for only a short time; perhaps because I was a bit stroppy at one meeting with management, because I was promoted and became a restaurant manager. This meant I could no longer be in the union. However, I was now able to wear a smart trouser suit instead of the embarrassing waitressing gear, and I also enjoyed learning how to flambé simple dishes like crepes and steaks. The only thing I didn't like was the authority I wielded, because I didn't enjoy ordering people around.

By now I was educating myself at home, reading voraciously in the areas of religion and philosophy. With more money to spend I indulged my love of books. The UK was a great place to be an autodidact, because books were reasonably priced, and there were a lot of good second-hand bookshops around. I was particularly interested in Judaism, Buddhism and European philosophy. I also wrote a short story that won a competition on the radio and was broadcast; very basic Christian stuff about Christ and the Resurrection and the whole Easter event. It was deeply spiritual, but I was increasingly becoming that way. Right after the story was broadcast I came under what I now realize was spiritual attack:

I remember waking up and coming under furious attack from devils. I could actually feel them, and they washed over into my waking consciousness.

It was horrible, and I put it out of my mind.

I would practice a form of Jewish meditation based on the mystical tradition in Judaism, the Kabbalah. I also felt very drawn to the whole concept of empathy with the environment, sometimes very prominent in Eastern religions such as Buddhism and Jainism, and would read texts from the mainstream religions. It was about this time *I had a vision of tongues of fire coming to the window.* It happened when I was lying on our bed relaxing and *these flames seemed to come before me.* I wasn't frightened but I was shocked. I was wide awake, of course.

Sarah, one of the waitresses at work, was a practicing Christian, and when I told her that I was fasting to keep my weight in check she suggested I offer the fast up to God. This seemed an intriguing idea. At another time Sarah was putting her make up on before work when she said, "I had a strange dream about you last night. I dreamt we were all sitting in a circle around you and you were in the middle of the circle dressed in white. And we were all covered in blood". Sarah was applying her make up as she spoke, but suddenly ceased what she was doing, a look of puzzlement on her face as she added, "I thought I had to tell you that". It was a really weird moment;

a moment out of time. A fragment.

Sarah and I were to become quite good friends, Sarah of the platinum-blonde hair and vermillion lips who might have been that girl at the Folies-Bergère, twentieth century primped. She used to love declaring that working at the club was, "The next best thing to show business". And since Sarah's previous job had been cutting up meat in a butcher's shop (I recoiled when she told me how they cut the cancers out) this was really something of a truism. I recall Sarah enquiring of me whether Michael and I were "thinking of having any children some day?" I replied that I couldn't face the idea of the pain, and regaled her with an account of my mother's descriptions of childbirth. Sarah was empathetic, but genuinely sorry. She just said it was "a pity" because Michael and I were "a nice couple". I picked up the ebbing sadness in her voice as her words petered out, the wistfulness that echoed in my soul that I could not quite feel. Yet.

The kitchen staff were so bloody strange I tended to keep a distance. The chef slept in a coffin, and there were rumors he was involved in witchcraft. However, one of the kitchen staff, Terry, became a friend when he was assigned to work as a bus boy. At parties the club periodically held for staff members and their friends, the conversation would sometimes drift to areas of philosophy, religion and spiritual experience, and we would talk till the early hours of the morning. During one of these conversations, Terry mentioned he had woken up one day being "attacked by devils". I didn't say anything about my experience, but thought the coincidence odd, and left it at that. Instinctively, I felt it unwise to talk about negative spiritual experiences. Terry's girlfriend was Liza. Liza was beautiful with long, dark curly hair and almond-shaped eyes set in a curiously compelling angular face that made it interesting to regard. Liza had Canadian Inuit ancestry. Mike and I invited Terry and Liza to dinner one night, and I cooked pasta with prosciutto as a garnish. Terry took one look at it and wouldn't touch it, saying he had worked in an abattoir and had seen his fellow workers torture animals before killing them. Terry's story horrified me because he implied the torture was routine, just for kicks. Mike and I stopped eating meat after that. My disgust was reinforced because I also watched the chefs in the kitchen at work tormenting live lobsters before killing them. This was viewed as a real laugh by the kitchen staff; something to liven up work time. It was also terrible to hear the lobsters squeal in agony as they were boiled alive. I became totally revolted by it all, and decided you didn't want to eat animals if you could at all avoid it.

Having lost faith in Christianity, and yet reading traditional scriptures like the Old Testament, the Koran and sections of Buddhist and Hindu scriptures, I started to ask the question, "Who's telling the truth? What is the truth?" I would do this fairly frequently. On one occasion I was lying down on my bed asking God to "reveal the truth", when I had another strange experience and I actually saw the words, written in a cloud,

"Love is the Key"

The cloud just appeared. It was like an explosion of energy in front of me.

I was wide awake.

One day I wrote in a Bible I have to this day the words from the Book of Proverbs,

"For wisdom is better than rubies;
and all the things that may be desired,
are not to be compared to it." (kjv)

All the things that may be desired ... are not to be compared to it.

These words became a guiding force in times of shifting sands.

So I was a mixed bag. I prayed a lot, my prayers all over the place, some from the Jewish Siddur, some from Hinduism, others from Buddhism and yet others from Christianity. I would ask God to, "Tell me the truth. Take me to my limit and really let me know who is telling the truth". At the time I believed that all religions and philosophies were relative, an increasingly popular idea, and was fittingly irreverent.

Anyway, life was better than it had been for a long while. With more money available, Mike and I were able to go on our first holiday. We plumped for Malta, mostly because it was winter and Malta would still be warm. Also, it was a good discount deal. On arrival, I quickly discovered a little church in Miellieha Bay displaying an icon of Our Lady attributed to St. Luke, (recently ascribed to the early medieval period). I would spend an hour or more in this church each day, just sitting and contemplating. It was really special, because the shrine displayed baby clothes from infants who had been healed through petitions to the Virgin. I loved it, sitting in that church; the stillness, the dim light, the tranquil, pervasive sense of sanctity: of Presence. A nun would come and open the church up and come back later to close it. As I was usually the only one there, she would have to ask me to leave. It was a wonderful, inspiring, mystical place.

Back home, I became more and more interested in the environment and food and health generally. As I said, I had been brought up to eat good quality food and look after myself and other people. Michael's mother was also something of a mentor in this regard. Our parents would go without to put nutritious food on the table; at least this was what it was like when I was little until my mother went to work full time and that took over a bit. Mum used to pontificate saying, "Rich people give their kids sausage and chips and have nice furniture while you get the best food I can buy!" Michael's mum was similar (although lacking the drama-queen flourishes) and helped us out a lot while Mike was in college, bringing hampers filled with all sorts of goodies, mainly edible. She was a wonderful woman.

I became vegan, eating no animal products at all. Following in the steps of mystical theology, I began to 'walk lightly' in the world, eating organic produce as much as possible and avoiding anything that involved exploitation. I also became more artistic in the way I dressed and would try to wear really beautiful clothes; floaty, long French peasant style skirts and dresses reflecting what I determined to be my 'bohemian nature', endeavoring all the while to refrain from looking like a hippy. (This didn't always work.) I also wore natural cosmetics. A rather incongruous hang-up was my attempt to resemble Marilyn Monroe, when I didn't look at all like the film star. To this end I lightened my hair and kept it short and tightly curled, which was aesthetically a disaster and didn't suit. Just looking in the mirror I intuited it wasn't coming together, and in an attempt to make amends, would thread scarves through my hair like complicated and intricate headbands, leaving tendrils of blonde curls to frame my face. It was quite effective actually; so long as I didn't remove the scarves.

Soon after I made up with my family, my mother came to visit. I made a real effort to look pretty and impress her and wore my most evocative and floaty dress of azure blue cotton. It worked; I could tell by the look on her face she thought I looked wonderful. Interestingly, at that point I hadn't joined the club and was quite generously proportioned. Not fat, but certainly not fashionably thin as I loved chocolate and would sometimes binge, usually on chocolate ice-cream. Anyway, because I was larger than deemed acceptable according to the conventions of the time, Mum concluded I might be pregnant. This rather depressed, and even bugged, me. A while later I decided I really had to do something about my weight when Mike's mum came to visit and gave me a present of a size twenty-two coat. The trouble was, just like today, people were really hung up on thinness to an unhealthy degree. I was only size sixteen, and tall, so it was absurd. However, just the sheer hugeness of the coat Mike's mum brought embarrassed me into dieting. Lord, it seemed to take ages to lose weight! But my chance came to crash diet when Michael was on holiday from uni and working at a bakery in Newport. So I ate only boiled eggs, a fashionable diet at the time. I lost weight in kilos by the week; it was mad.

After I started work at the club I built up courage to inform my parents. I knew it wouldn't go down too well as they were observant Catholics. Though, as it transpired, they were quite supportive. I think they were desperately happy I was back in touch with them. However, they must have been dismayed because I remember Mum enquiring if I was "pure?" This remark must have seemed so peculiar to me that it went over my head at the time. But after Mum left I began to wonder, "What was she imagining? Of course I was pure". I was occasionally naughty and might have a little flirt, primarily because I needed to be reassured that I looked nice, in the dizzy-daftness of my youth. But being unfaithful was not in my bones, not in my nature. I was blissfully happy with Michael, and realized how wonderful it was to have someone who loved you and cared about you, no matter what.

It was a happy time in many ways. Mum and Dad were closer than they had been in years, and my mother didn't go on at Dad so much about his lack of ambition. As a result my father's appearance and demeanor had radically improved. Dad now looked after himself and dressed really well, considering he wasn't wealthy. He still looked handsome, though his skin was lined. Dad had that wonderful Irish skin which sometimes doesn't last, flawless in youth but taking on the appearance of delicate and aged parchment in later years. On the other hand, my mother would drive me to distraction by persisting in enquiring whether I wanted to "leave Michael?" So it was difficult. Her possessiveness had the expected effect of making me want to get as far away as possible from her, though I loved her dearly.

By now, Laura had gone to study for her degree at Oxford, while Alice was doing a course in media studies at university in Bristol. I would go home to Newport every month or so and talk a lot about the spirituality I was studying when I wasn't at work. Laura was reading politics, economics and English and had become a socialist. But she also knew about the Liberation Theologians in South America, and I found that fascinating. I really admired these priests and theologians when I read about them.

Alice was delicate in appearance; porcelain skin and tiny bones, artistic and avant-garde. Now in her early twenties, she modeled, although in height she was only about five foot three inches. She wore her silky waterfall of red-gold hair up on occasion, and would do crazy things with it, like push knitting needles through that limpid languidity. For Alice such artistic extravagance worked. Yet it was a bitter day around this period when my mother remarked curiously, puzzlingly, of her daughter's rose-quartz quality;

"You know, I sometimes feel Alice is fey."

The opaque statement made me physically and emotionally tense, and I almost threw back the words with a searing, angry glare; "Don't say that!" Sharply, bitterly. Aware, with a tremulous fear, that such negativity was not wise.

My sisters would sing together. They were harmony with a capital 'H', extremely gifted vocally and musically. So things seemed to have settled down for us all, and life was moving in a fairly steady manner.

Around this time a really big vision happened. I was asleep, in deep, deep sleep and,

I was shot this picture:

it was like a picture being shot onto a pitch black cinema screen;

one minute total blackness and then this image. It was of me, sitting in a church. I remember I was wearing a white robe. There were other bits of the message, like a lot of these types of visions, because these visions often conveyed a message.

I woke up and thought automatically, "But I'm not even a Christian?" I was really rather shocked. And extremely puzzled. I told Michael and then put the visionary image out of my mind. I did not call it a 'vision' of course. No-one talked about visions.

But all the same, I started to become rather more intrigued and puzzled by these experiences. Having heard she painted, I even asked Liza at the club to draw some of the imagery from the book of poems I'd compiled years before. That poetry still troubled me; I couldn't make sense of it. Liza agreed to do some drawings, which was nice of her. I discovered one of Liza's drawings recently.

I was considered glamorous by Michael's friends because I did bits and pieces of modeling; 'county' fashion shows and things like in-store modeling, an unusual occupation for the wives and girlfriends of students we knew. To give his acquaintances a more balanced view, Michael assured them I could be problematic. It all seemed innocent back then ... I think we were quite naïve in a way. I mean, any cohort that could adopt pogoing as a dance form had to be naff! To my credit, I didn't actually pogo myself. But this strange hopping dance that made the participants look like human grasshoppers had a fervent, if transient, popularity. People living together, not bothering about marriage, seemed cool, unconventional. It was all totally laid back, a time when Mike and I would be invited to parties and hang out until the early hours talking about all manner of stuff. There were drugs about, but I never saw anybody take them, and thank God we never took them. Friends and acquaintances weren't even flirtatious really, and we respected relationships. But I was still a little wild, and remember getting drunk on occasion in the belief I had better experience the condition if I wanted to be a writer. As a result, I made a complete idiot of myself and passed out in a garden on the way home after one Christmas party. I remember being dragged unceremoniously to my feet by Michael, looking rather like a disheveled rag doll in my long, ruffled dress. I was later very unwell because – in my alcohol-fueled food frenzy – I had guzzled too many mince pies, a house-special of my favorite friend who hosted the affair. It put me eternally off mince pies, and I began to fret a little about the long-term brain damage caused by this type of alcoholic over-indulgence.

While I was studying in my free time, and writing bits and pieces, Michael took up photography as a hobby, and had some success with his pictures. He carried his camera everywhere, his forte being reportage. As I was interested in religion and culture, we drove to Stonehenge once for the summer solstice intending to publish an article about the event. It was cold and damp and the affair was uninspiring. I believed people's religions should be respected, and didn't think much about the negative aspects of druidism, which seemed to me some sort of archaic cultural ritual event with no real significance. We never got round to producing the article, but I did compose a macabre poem about the episode, and read it aloud at a dinner party to some friends who were, very correctly, bored and most unimpressed. And then, and later, I would sense a *dissonance. The negativity of the poem. As if I'd picked up an emanation from a landscape of darkness* –

I wished to God I'd never written it.

Our regular visits to Newport I continued to find an ordeal, painful memories of leaving home still fresh. But I got on well with one relative whom we all called 'Aunty' Karen (Karen was actually my mother's niece) and would spend time with her discussing religion; Karen was very spiritual. I told Karen I practised Jewish Kabbalistic meditation, a form of meditation associated with mystical Judaism. Aunty Karen seemed to confuse this with occult kabbalah practices, and I had to explain that the Jewish Kabbalah was practiced by Jewish mystics and saints. I described how, as part of the meditation, one contemplated the Holy Spirit, Jesus and the Divine Attributes. I also discussed my meditation practice with my mother. She was interested but cautioned me about not placing Christ "at the centre of your soul".

At times at home with Mum conversation would move to the past. My mother had memories of a woman in the family, a lace-maker, who, until her eyesight failed, made clothes for Queen Victoria and of how in the South of England, from whence some of Mum's family hailed, they had hoped for Napoleon to win and set them free from the tyranny of the aristocracy. This, I found interesting as – through history lessons – I'd always been taught to conceive of the Napoleonic threat in entirely negative terms. Mum also told me how her family had been forced out of their home in the Great Depression, piling their belongings into a cart after Granddad lost his antique business to a competitor. It had only been a little shop, but the loss ruined them. Destitute, Mum recalled the whole family of six children and two adults standing on Bristol station before wheeling their cartload of possessions along the railway line to get where they were going. Mum told me of her absolute terror of the future with her home gone, and of how Granddad in a rage wrote in huge letters on the wall of the railway line along which they were walking, "Thou shalt not covet thy neighbor's goods".

I understood more and more my mother's terror of poverty, and thus her driving ambition. So, I felt it was good that Mum was doing well, she really loved to teach. It gave her great pride in herself, together with the fact that she now had lecturing friends with whom she could play golf and sail; middle class pursuits like that. Because to be 'middle class' was for her very important. She longed, and dreamed, to be rid of the taint of the lowliness of being labeled 'working class', the denizen of a council estate.

Yet quite recently, long after her death. I had a vision of her. And she was crying, saying,

"Everything you think's important in this life's not."

I would study pictures of my mother as a young woman. In appearance she resembled Ingrid Bergman, with a prominent nose and strong features – except that Mum had dark hair and eyes. She must have been a striking figure in her youth, with wide shoulders and a slim, strong body which endured into old age. Mum never used much make up, just a little lipstick to emphasize her thin but well-shaped lips. I really loved her but was always torn. I couldn't handle the way she kept hanging on to me, it felt clingy and suffocating, and I knew she could be incredibly destructive in a psychological way. So I felt a strong need to keep a distance from her, for my own good and hers.

I wrote for a local magazine and had some poetry published. The manager of the club saw it and suggested I contact a major publisher, but I really didn't have the energy or drive for that. One of the poems was about Liza. A kitchen hand must have read the poem, because he made a suggestive remark that I might "be a lesbian"; just because I wrote something flattering about a woman, I thought it was really twisted to think like that. Of course, a few of the people at the club were homosexual. Or rather they were sexually promiscuous, because they were often bisexual in reality and free with themselves. With a small minority anything seemed to go, but I only became aware of this after I had worked at the club for quite a while.

Something that jarred towards the end of my time working at the club happened when I went to see Liza and Terry. Terry often talked about strange things, conversations which I mostly shrugged off. He was interested in dream states and referred to states of sleep like REM. Terry was also interested in UFOs and told us that, as a result of his flying saucer interests, 'security people' had come round to his flat and given him a hard time. I really didn't know whether to believe him, but as Liza seemed to be aware of the event I supposed it to be true; Liza always came across as level-headed. As Liza and Terry's relationship became fragile I think it's possible Terry started taking drugs. (I'm not sure about this.) Anyway, he became depressed. Once, I noticed some slightly jarring pictures of children on the wall of their flat. They could have been artistic, but something Terry said really worried me: I didn't like the whole feel of it.

Then my father became sick. There was all sorts of talk at first, but it transpired Dad had lung cancer, or rather silicosis, from when he was deployed to unload coal from ships while he was in the army during the war. It was odd. I knew people who had died; a friend, some relatives: people like that. But I couldn't accept, even contemplate, the idea that he might die. Dad came to see us and took Mike and myself and Mum to a lovely restaurant near our home. Dad was so sick he sat outside the restaurant in the lobby waiting while we went in to eat and a kind maitre d', whom I've never forgotten, came over and talked to him. Dad didn't seem to want to even look at food. But I remember him saying to me that now he was sick, "Your mother and I are closer than we have been in years. It's like when we were young". Even while he was talking, I had this simply terrible feeling. I recalled how I'd become sick when I was young to gain my mother's attention and love. Of course, this was a harrowing recollection; was he in a way doing the same thing?

I remember a while later going home to see Dad. That hauntingly wonderful looking man. Now he resembled a Muppet. Michael and I walked into the dining room and it was just unbelievable, you could feel the suffering. It was so terrible Michael could hardly bare it. My aunty Mary visited from the Convent. Looking at him Sister Mary announced,

"This is the cross."

The cross. It seemed so true. It was just inconceivable that someone could be in so much agony. Even then I thought of *some sort of purifying fire.*

My father asked me to, "Smell my medicines". One had to have been morphine, I guessed. So there was this terrible suffering, and still, when you looked, you saw past that to his wonderful bone structure and those amazing eyes. Yet *at this point I felt something of his soul had already left this world.*

Alice cared for him as he became more and more ill. She was still at home. My mother would only handle Dad with gloves in case she caught 'it'. I remember standing in my old bedroom where Dad lay in bed, moving fitfully between sleep and wakefulness; skeletal, frail. There was a silence, and the sense of someone slipping from this world, falling gently away from us all. There were stars in the sky, and the snow was white, and I wrote about crosses in the sky; the *stars themselves were spangled crosses* against this black sky and the snow was a dazzling white. I can still feel that moment as I think back. The crisp cold of the sick room, the purity of the stars and the snow: and my father, the darkness ... and the light.

Later, my father said one odd thing to me. It was when he was downstairs in the living room sitting in his old rocking chair. I entered the room. He was so desperately weak he seemed to have to struggle to enunciate the words. And all he said was,

"I'm very worried about Alice ..."

Just a plain statement. And I remember thinking, "Why?" Why should he be worried about Alice? Although Alice was doing most of the caring for him, so that must have been very traumatic for her. She seemed a pure soul.

Yet those words; "I'm very worried about Alice ..."

A moment in time and out of time ... time standing still.

"I'm very worried about Alice."

The funeral was just awful. We were all in the most desperate state of grief; beside ourselves, barely able to walk into the church, barely able to stand. I felt a dim anger; I couldn't believe in a God who allowed such agonizing suffering. My father had been a decent man. He had spent his youth working in a lowly occupation to ensure his siblings had a good education, and devoted the remainder of his life to looking after his family. I couldn't take it in. He had no retirement. He just was born, he worked, and he died; that was it. Michael and I both really doubted the existence of God then. I mean, how could a good God allow such terrible torment? What was the point?

From that day on the whole question of the 'Why?' of suffering took hold of me. I really had to find an answer, and that fuelled a desire to study. Time passed, but everything was different. I lost a little of the crazy sparkle from my life. A little while following my father's death, my mother came to see us. She was torn apart by guilt. Alone with me in my bedroom she was on her knees as I sat on my bed. It was almost as if she was in a confessional because she went on her knees and confessed to me and to God. Crying and begging forgiveness –

Of whom?

Of me?

Of God?

Of Dad?

She wept loud, copious tears. Almost wailing the words,

"I didn't love him enough!"

I just sat there and looked. I don't know what I felt altogether. Mum was sobbing and sobbing and repeating the words over and over again; she was in a terrible state. I think she suspected Dad had taken his life in early 1979 so she could be relieved of looking after him and go back to work, which was so important to her. Mum's whole focus on ambition was a driving force in her life more or less up to that point. And all Dad ever wanted to do was make her happy. He lived, and she suspected, died for her. I think she knew then that she had made a terrible mistake. Only later, learning more about the grief process, I became skeptical that my father had deliberately taken his own life.

In the following months, Mum had two strange visionary dreams concerning my father;

in the first he appeared as if in absolute torment. Dad (she only saw his face) looked at her and said abruptly,

"Goodbye!"

Mum told me she woke in total shock.

Then she had a second dream.

My father was walking out of the house and into the light outside. His mother, who'd passed away years earlier, *was waiting for him.* Mum said my father was young again,

"Just as he was when we first met."

All those years ago. My father, who really wanted to be a priest. But he got married.

It was all becoming too much; I felt a need to get away, to escape. With the death of my father I couldn't work at the club anymore; I don't know why. It was very strange, I would call in sick all the time. Eventually they made me redundant because business wasn't too good, a number of staff were leaving. Michael had finished his degree and was offered a job in South Africa. It wasn't a place we really wanted to go, but we both needed to get out of Britain; we felt trapped. It was then I had another of those really big, strange visionary type dreams. It was the same again: *at one moment there was total darkness and then the vision appeared. As if out of beyond forever;*

it was my father. He was looking very stern. Dressed in a black robe; the kind of robe a priest in the Catholic Church might wear at a funeral.

He was a priest, an angel. And he was warning me:

"You must not be so proud."

The voice, his voice, snapped the words. As if it was an enormous effort for him to say them.

Then the vision was gone. I woke up, shocked because my father seemed so severe. I didn't think I was proud at all. In fact I concluded, "I'm not proud?" I couldn't understand it,

my father; warning me ...

But what on earth did he mean?

The wilderness years: wandering in Samsara.

The road from Jerusalem to Gaza is a desert road.
(Paraphrased from The Acts of the Apostles.)

"All night long on my bed
I looked for the one my heart loves;
I looked for him but did not find him."
(The Song of Songs)

Samsara implies endless wandering through existence. Kind of going round and round. And that's what it felt like we were doing. In a way, looking back ...

So it was. Jo'burg. Fall of '81. The music of the time, *of the mindscape*, might have been Pink Floyd's,

Another Brick in the Wall.

Because that's what I heard they were singing on the streets during the Soweto riots of the 1970s. And that's what it felt like, getting off the plane; the armed guards and guns: energy! Violent energy, the energy of the whirlwinds of change. A hip band would sing the song,

African Sky Blue.

The mindscape again.

African Sky Blue. This one song evoked the sheer beauty of the place, the vibrant effervescence that was South Africa. Yet the country was rocked by these violent eddies, while swirling within them were the dynamics of peoples of many cultures and religions, whirled round like leaves on some blustery spring or autumn day. The white company manager who came to escort us to our temporary accommodation warned me I could be raped on the streets. Mike didn't say anything, but I knew we both thought, "What on earth are we doing here? What have we run away too?" Fortunately the fellow was overly dramatic, but he scared the daylights out of both of us.

We ended up in Parktown, a suburb of Johannesburg. The apartment was modern and spacious, very light in atmosphere with two bathrooms, which was luxury to us. The complex itself had a good size pool and gymnasium with pleasant gardens and impressive security. Once inside the complex you felt very safe indeed, although the surrounding area could be edgy, dicey. We were situated quite close to an apartment block with a notorious reputation for residents committing suicide. We discovered early on that a lot of ordinary people carried guns. I couldn't imagine owning a gun, and initially felt insecure. But, as time went on, and the violence wasn't anywhere near as bad as we first thought, I became energized by the sense of a new beginning. I quickly garnered enough courage to take my pictures round the major magazines, and landed modeling work. I also enrolled at university. I had thought of doing anthropology as a major, but decided to start with courses in religion and philosophy because, on review, the material involved seemed fascinating. I worked incredibly hard and did well and enrolled to do a major in Judaica. At this point my path crossed with an amazing Jewish woman, Claire Cohen. Claire took to me immediately. She must have been around sixty at the time, but she looked fabulous, years younger, small and slim with a striking smile, determined face and real, amazing, chutzpah; her inner qualities seemed to imbue her with an energetic beauty that bubbled over into her looks, because she was by no means classically good looking. Over time she became something of a mother figure, collecting my photographs from magazines, encouraging me in my studies and generally doting on me. From

Claire I learned that great generosity of spirit that is true femininity, a wonderful spirituality. I learnt from her to try to build people up authentically and make them feel positive about themselves, while warning them gently about negative stuff; no jealousy about this woman at all. She was one of the most positive and inspirational individuals I have ever met. Getting to know Claire and her husband and children made the venture to South Africa worth it in itself, and I was very influenced by her family life, which exuded love and didn't undermine the dynamic characters her children and husband possessed. Claire only had sons, and they were in their early and late twenties, but they all seemed brilliant and funny and welcoming. She was not a strict, observant Jew but Fridays were really special. To be forgotten, or put aside, was any grievance any member of the family harbored. All her boys, and their wives or lady friends, if they were available, had to come to Shabbat dinner. Her home felt like a cocoon of love, away from the turmoil of the outside world:

the sense of the mystical Shabbat. The Shabbat candles being lit. The woman's reverent, very feminine presence as she prays over the candles and the family. The sense of belonging and simplicity. The mystery of the great interweaving love between God and Man, between husband and wife. The holiness of the family, and the Torah; the Shekhinah presence moving.

The Song of Songs itself expressed in the breaking of bread. And the wine passed round from hand to hand in the dim, mystical

light.

This, to me, was what life was about; about God speaking to us in intimate relationship. Family, friends, food and wine. Not power or prestige or some fancy job:

I now know this, yet I did not know then; this was why I felt so drawn to Judaism.

So along with studying the history of the Jewish people, I found it even more difficult to understand the irrational hate Jews often inspired. I became more aware of the way Christianity had been partisan to this, legislating to force Jews into disreputable areas of work such as money-lending, burning their sacred books, instituting the ghetto, forcing Jews to wear the Star. I also read about the pogroms and race hatred, all happening across cultures and time zones with no rational basis. It was also in a way a learning curve for Michael, who made a great friend in a Jewish guy named Jacob Silbowitz. Jacob was funny and loyal, and even got Michael out of serious trouble on one occasion when Michael's car broke down in a remote and dangerous location. In desperation, Michael phoned Jacob who dropped everything to drive hundreds of kilometers to get Mike out of trouble. And yet, like quite a few Jewish friends we made in South Africa, there was an edginess about him; as if he was only too aware at any time, anywhere, it could all happen again. I learned, from the rabbis who taught us, this was one reason why the Jewish people kept the focus so intensely on the Holocaust. Because it wasn't the only massacre, the only incident. But perhaps to them – and to me – the Holocaust seemed almost something else; a kind of turning point, a gyre of history. What the hell had gone on in Germany, not only a Christian country but one of the most cultured civilizations on the planet? What had happened to ignite that insidious, irrational but unfaltering hatred?

It didn't stop there! I even recalled one of my relatives, for no apparent reason, confronting a Jewish boy she knew. Just telling him straight, "I don't like Jews". I don't think my parents would have believed it; a Catholic who worships God born a Jew, making this statement.

Claire and I would go to a Jewish women's group, and we attended shul with Jacob. I obtained a new copy of the Jewish Siddur and used prayers from it. Not only was I continuing to practise Jewish mystical meditation, I was now studying Halakhah, the Jewish Law. Indeed, I became so fervent that at one point I hesitantly mentioned to Claire I was "thinking of converting". Claire was taken aback. She said it was difficult to convert and reminded me of the history of the Jews; the never ending hatred, the danger. I decided she had a point. "Oh dear," I thought, "I'll take a rain-check on that one". Being gassed, or otherwise persecuted didn't seem an inviting option. I decided I would just aim to be a 'righteous gentile'. And left it at that.

On the gentile scene, we also developed a lively circle of friends. Michael had been introduced, via work, to Dave and Susan, a successful business couple. Dave didn't take to me, although he got on well with Mike. However, I got to know Susan fairly well. Tall with dark hair and burnished skin, she adored expensive clothes and jewellery and was quite stunning; always with perfect, luxe nails and hair, usually so primped she might have walked out of a beauty salon or off a fashion page. Susan was from a wealthy Italian background, her family being well-known in social circles. She was born a Catholic, but would come out with the odd, strange remark about people's religious practices; I presumed, perhaps, aimed at me because I was studying religion. Yet I was quite taken aback when Susan told me about people she knew who would "make pacts with the devil" to obtain wealth and prestige. The fact she seemed to know about Satanic groups I found even more unusual, as even at university they didn't come into the spectrum of study. Since I was rather unaware this went on in modern society, I couldn't help wondering how Susan obtained her information.

Being primarily a business relationship, after a time our contact with Dave and Susan pretty much fizzled out. But I recall one odd experience I had when they were around.

In Johannesburg the modeling scene was much more high-powered than the one I had been involved with in the UK. Here girls would get jobs in other countries and become internationally successful, so there was much more money involved. During the period Mike and I were friendly with Dave and Susan, I was modeling in a big show, compered by – as it transpired – two rather nasty people. Rich and glamorous socialites, these guys were media celebrities. The couple were generally so awkward everyone became unnerved as nobody seemed to be able to make up their minds what was required, and so we were constantly rehearsing and reworking. To compound the stress, there was only a mixed changing room and I had to hide behind a hanger because I didn't want to be seen in a state of undress. The whole thing seemed too close to selling your body for lucre for me, and I couldn't handle it. I just wanted to get the show over with and, as there was wine available – which was unusual – I was so stressed out that I had one or two glasses on an empty stomach to help calm me down. As a result, I became slightly tipsy. The whole thing was an ordeal for all the models as things went wrong. Even the stage collapsed, so the show had to be moved outdoors. I got really wound up and was glad to get home, the glamor flaking at the edges.

Back in the apartment, feeling exhausted but relieved, the intercom situated near the door buzzed. I went over, picked up the receiver and heard strange voices repeating, *"We've stabbed Michael! We've stabbed Michael!"*

I put the phone down and then picked it up again. The voices repeated the same words. I felt quite panicky; this was really odd! But of course, Jo'burg could be violent. The doorbell rang again. Now I picked up the receiver to hear Dave's voice telling me he and Susan had come round for a casual visit. Given the circumstances (they hadn't done this before) it was fortuitous. When they arrived at our apartment I invited them in, and in some turmoil, told them exactly what I'd heard over the intercom. Dave, who displayed ornamental sabres and replica weapons on the walls of his house and had casually informed us, "I sleep with a gun under my pillow and carry a revolver everywhere" was, I presumed, adequately equipped and prepared for the situation. He immediately went out to search for Michael, who had gone for his usual recreational run.

Feeling shaky, I sat down and tried to talk about something else to calm myself. So I told Susan what I'd been doing, giving details of the hassles of the modeling show and the dreadful atmosphere. I mentioned the name of the couple who'd choreographed and compered the show and Susan responded matter of factly,

"They're into Satanism."

I was taken aback. I didn't ask how she knew. To be honest, I sure as hell didn't want to know: I was in a bad enough state anyway.

We talked about other matters, and somehow Dave must have found Michael because shortly later Dave and Michael walked through the door. I was obviously extremely relieved. Of course, Mike was perfectly okay, and we all had a brief conversation before Dave and Susan left. I didn't mention the occasion again, even to Mike. To put it mildly, I felt embarrassed. The whole thing fazed me; I had definitely heard the weird voices. I wondered at the time if it was kids mucking about, yet it didn't sound like kids, the voices were too high pitched and squeaky.

We continued to see Dave and Susan. One of the last times we met up was at their place, when Susan gave me a pack of tarot cards. Apparently, she didn't want them because they "felt evil". I didn't like to refuse the gift because I was gullible enough to feel embarrassed about being rude, so I took them home. I remember looking at the cards and thinking the images were sinister; bloody macabre actually. I knew a bit about Jung and his study of the tarot, but it wasn't something that held much interest for me, so I put them aside.

I got rid of the tarot cards quite soon after, probably ditched them in the bin. I did puzzle over why Susan had given them to me; I mean, it didn't seem a terribly nice present, given her concern that the cards seemed 'evil'. I heard later Susan had joined a quasi-Christian group, very fundamentalist but without the Eucharist; they had some weird reason for not taking communion. Interestingly, Susan herself, whom I was to meet up with from time to time in the course of our travels over the years, is hyper about having anything she considers dark or evil-looking anywhere in her house or near her family. Almost to the verge of phobia.

I was doing really well at this point. I'd dropped the modeling and was working in the media while still studying. On a high, I was disappointed when Michael unexpectedly and unpredictably announced he wanted to "leave Johannesburg". As my job looked really promising it was very depressing, but I knew Michael's work was becoming extremely taxing, especially as he had to travel a lot. Only later did Michael explain his reasons for leaving Jo'burg more fully. Apparently, he'd felt on the verge of some sort of breakdown at that point. I found this interesting years later when I had more experience of the dynamics of spirituality; those evil voices I'd heard. *That sense of attack* and then Michael talking about being "near to having a breakdown …"

We moved to Durban. I remember writing to my mother and mentioning Claire, remarking how wonderful my Jewish friend was. My mother phoned, pestering me for Claire's address. She seemed, again, both possessive and disturbed that I was really fond of Claire. (It was strange; I never heard from Claire after that.) In Durban I managed to continue studying and began doing research, talking to all sorts of people about religion and looking particularly at Buddhism and Hinduism in South Africa. I also developed a strong friendship with Francesca, a fellow student whom I still contact; a very brilliant girl. (I was rather envious of her actually, as her grasp of sociology far outshone mine.) Francesca had this wonderful short, but thick and glossy, blonde hair cut into a bob. She looked rather like Wanda Ventham – I think that's her name – a very successful actress in the UK at one time. Studying together, chatting together, we had memorable times, so it made up for the loss of my job in Jo'burg.

In Durban, I had another experience that really stands out. It happened when I was invited to a Buddhist meeting. A Tibetan monk had come over to South Africa. I remember one night beforehand having this really odd dream, I *was walking into this old house and found myself sitting next to an elderly lady. We started talking, and I was discussing my course and what I was doing.*

A few days passed, and when I attended the meeting I got a strange feeling; the house looked similar to the one I had dreamt about, although I had never been there before. I sat down and an elderly lady came and sat next to me. We chatted, and suddenly she looked distinctly nervous, even shocked, and remarked abruptly as she shot me a worried look,

"We've had this conversation before."

I felt distinctly uneasy, but felt it better not to say anything. Maybe we did have the conversation before. But the conversation happened in a dream.

The mood of the meeting became even more disturbing as time progressed. The monk came in; he was a Gelugpa, I think. (I didn't write down the name of the Buddhist order he belonged to.) The monk commenced the session with a traditional chant, while we all sat and listened. The chant was guttural, deep and unpleasant;

as I sat there I literally began to feel my body vibrate. It's something I've never felt in the same way since. *It was as if the molecules of my body were vibrating and moving, and so the sound itself was producing an intense vibration.*

I had a sense of spiritual dissonance.

I sat through the talk, uneasy now, and came away with a distinct feeling that something negative had occurred.

At that time I met up with several teachers from major Eastern religions. I was very influenced by the Jain respect for life, an aspect of Jainism that influenced Mahatma Gandhi. I was also studying and researching Islam for quite a while, being interested mainly in Sufism. From Islam I picked up the sense of deep reverence for God, for the "Beautiful Names of God". The attitude to women I found more negative. As time went on, I discovered that in very conservative sectors of major religions women can be marginalized in one way or another. When this happens, the women concerned often assume a position of compliance, and may try to rationalize the situation, almost as if there is an inner struggle going on. Their arguments can sound superficially persuasive, yet I got the idea that this was a way of legitimizing the oppression; because it often does amount to that. Sometimes, what I felt was going on was that they couldn't extricate themselves from the situation because some underlying psychological or emotional issue kept them there. Often, of course, the women really are stuck, and leaving the religious culture puts them directly in the way of violence, perhaps they might be injured or killed. Ultimately, it would come down to issues of power and control. Indeed, as I progressed in my research I became wary in a broad sense about these issues. Power and control in religion and ideologies can have very negative effects on both men and women, causing them to become intolerant, and opening the way for them to do and think very weird and evil things.

It shook me a bit, and I became concerned and vigilant in spotting these negative tendencies. I also became increasingly careful about negativity at every level, realizing that moving towards positive, life-affirming positions, was both healthy and tended to avoid problems. Even so, I frequently got it wrong. But at least I was coming to a point where I would question actions I felt weren't thought through, or weren't positive. And I would apply this rationale to myself, though not always entirely consciously, asking;

"Now why on earth did I do that?"

Ultimately, this way of approaching life has had such an effect on me that I question why I do something if it's not entirely positive. I don't like destructive behavior.

I visited one new meditation centre with Peter and Sally, some new acquaintances who were interested in the therapeutic value of meditation. This particular style of meditation had been introduced to the West by some swami or guru in the fifties or sixties. I thought the South African hosts who were into this particular practice looked distinctly, if amiably, drugged-out. But they had a lovely house with the most beautiful grounds, and we were served all sorts of teas in wonderful pottery cups (my love of pottery again). Anyway, this uber-chic pair – and they dressed with élan being fashionably slim and attractive in a casual and laid-back Ralph Lauren style – showed interesting videos, which I never got around to viewing, of white-robed practitioners levitating; sort of skimming like human hovercrafts through the air, all the while maintaining the lotus position. Stills from the videos were on the wall of the entrance hall to the house, but I found the idea puzzling. I thought about it, and even later couldn't quite work out the uses for doing this unless, as I mused in daft whimsy, you could really pick up speed and so obviate the need for public transport. Maybe also it would be useful for putting in light bulbs in high places, and cleaning windows in skyscrapers, that sort of thing. The trouble was, it seemed to be rather a transient manifestation of psychic power. (Someone hinted at trick photography, which I thought rather spoiled the mystique.)

We weren't at the house for long, but if the practice had a positive effect on one's health, I thought it might be worth a go.

More interesting, were the frequent visits I made to another retreat centre which used to attract well-known Buddhist teachers, mainly from the Theravada tradition; the Buddhist tradition that is widespread in places such as Burma, Sri Lanka and Thailand. I found Theravada Buddhism more engaging than the Mahayana tradition practised in Tibet and elsewhere. That definitely had too much iconography for me, I couldn't handle the deities. On a very basic level, I thought these looked nasty to the point of appearing grotesque, even menacing. The garish color combinations didn't help either. Ultimately, the idolatrous and shamanic elements involved made me distinctly uneasy. Still, I respected the Dalai Lama for his pacifism.

The route to this sea-side retreat centre was potentially dangerous. The Africans in rural areas sometimes practised witchcraft, and if you broke down, the possibility was that you could be murdered for your body parts. Good transport was a pre-requisite. I didn't know that much about indigenous or primitive religions, it wasn't one of my areas of specialization, but I was cognizant of some aspects. Later, it informed my suspicion of New Age stuff such as Goddess worship and the modern take on shamanism where the emphasis is entirely on positive aspects, such as the idea of a harmonious relationship with the environment, but with a complete disregard for any negativity involved; really nasty stuff such as ideas of ritual sacrifice and, perhaps even worse, the spiritual and psychological hold these individuals can exert on people.

Our time in Durban was drawing to a close. It was a beautiful place, but Mike found the employment opportunities restrictive, so he was looking for new openings in Johannesburg. I was again sad to be leaving, especially giving up my friendship with Francesca. Writing and telephoning's okay, but it's nice to sit down and chat over a coffee. On a more positive note, towards the end of our stay we started to go down-town where a famous musician hung out on Sundays. He was white, an incredible dancer, and he and the Zulus would dance together. So the street would be a sea of black faces, with Mike and I and only a few other solitary white people listening to the music, and Mike taking photographs. Most other white people wouldn't go there, but it says something about the relative safety on the streets in the early eighties in South Africa. Memory blurs, but the music of the time I recall most is Juluka singing,

Scatterlings of Africa.

On the streets; the vibe in our minds, in our souls;

the music of the mindscape.

We returned to Johannesburg and moved into an apartment block where Peter and Sally (of the levitating meditators) had also moved. They were a gregarious pair, and we rented an apartment on a lower floor. The couple were full of life, and very sociable, with a wide circle of friends to whom they kindly introduced us. Sally was a brilliant cook, and loved throwing dinner parties and organizing get-togethers. But some of the crowd that became part of our wider circle now were a different kettle of fish. There was a general moral loosening up, with married people having random affairs that eventually turned into a really damaging scene – emotionally and financially – for everyone involved. Basically, it seemed that more and more people were getting themselves into a state.

At uni, my lecturers were mainly theologians, pastors and religious of various Christian denominations and rabbinic authorities. One rabbi I remember particularly was both pious and brilliant, while another I encountered appeared more negative in his attitude; I guess he found it strange that a gentile girl, a 'goy', would want to study Torah and the history of the Jews. Anyway, it was an illuminating, exhilarating time for me.

On graduating, I was invited to teach as a junior lecturer. Only part-time, which was just about all I could manage as it involved early morning rises. I really loved the academic environment, but

I wasn't that reliable towards the end, and used to skip days when I was fatigued. The lecturers in the department were incredibly inspiring. People assumed all Afrikaners were bad, that seemed the general perception in the UK at the time. However, I was blessed knowing some really good Afrikaners; it made me conscious never to demonize an entire race. One professor, an elderly Dominee, influenced me in particular and became something of a mentor. Another person I found inspirational was an American woman missionary. But the place was peppered with such people, and it helped enormously that it was a mixed race university. The major lesson I learnt from these theologians was to look at a person and see not just what they were, but also to encourage their talent, their potential; to envision what they could be, and open up the opportunity for them to get there.

I had my own tiny office, with a blackboard in front of my desk. For some reason one day I wrote on it the first line from that well-known poem by W. B. Yeats, *The Second Coming*. I don't quite know why I wrote it, but with a mixture of injudicious pride at being able to intuit the tenseness in the air, and a contrasting somber melancholy, the words mesmerized me in a way. So I would work and look up at the quote and ponder,

that sense of fragmentation, of disintegration; of things falling apart ...

The universities in South Africa then were edgy. One professor's office was fire-bombed by white extremists, and there was a lot of support for the anti-apartheid movement here and there on campuses, so life could be risky for academics. Even innocuous research papers might be classified and banned. My time there had its moments of truth in other ways, and I well remember one rather jovial African theologian – whom my theological mentors affectionately referred to as "Professor Banga" (thus shortening his difficult to pronounce Khosa surname) – who mused,

"Soon we Africans will be sending Christian missionaries to Great Britain."

And we would go out to the bush with African Christians, and listen to Bible readings as they worshipped God with dance and singing. Evoking the soundscape of the *African Sanctus* from the film *If*. I can almost hear the music in my soul; now! Resonating! And envisage – once again – another (but this time physically blind) African prophet from a Christian group we attended, waving Michael and me farewell as we left his Sunday gathering in the veldt. The sounds of Africa, and the remembrances of things past …

I was writing on religious affairs for a highly respected newspaper, with Michael doing the pictures. To give you a sense of the mood at the time; people were so nervous about journalists and academics, that at a dinner party at Sally's, a male guest seated next to me turned and remarked completely out of the blue, "If you're a spy and you report anything about what I'm saying I have friends who will deal with you". It was so barmy I didn't bother to respond, and Sally almost choked on her pudding. But that was the hypersensitive atmosphere under apartheid; guns under the pillow were pedestrian, as were suitcases carried to work with loaded rifles alongside work documents, a granny with a pistol in her purse. We thought if it ever got to that for us, we'd be out of the place.

The event I perhaps remember most of all during this time happened one weeknight when I was working. Michael had set up his own business and had a sparsely-decorated office in our apartment, while I had another equally spartan room where I kept my books and papers and studied. We weren't that well off, as my salary wasn't much, and Michael's work began to dwindle as the economic and political situation declined toward the end of apartheid. It must have been about seven-thirty or so at night and there was a knock at the door. Two men in black were there and introduced themselves to me, saying they came from a local Christian group and wanted to talk about Christianity. For some reason, I invited them in (Michael was in his office). I ushered them into my study, and they started to discuss Biblical teaching. I can't remember exactly what part of the Bible they were discussing, and I don't think I even gave them a cup of tea (which I thought later was very bad form on my part). But I got this really peculiar desire to swear at them, *I could feel little pointy burning things – like arrows or needles – hitting my arms, it was vague but quite noticeable; and I had this terrible urge to swear.* It was weird, they were pleasant gentlemen and not at all pushy.

I remember they came twice. The second time was a week or so later. After that they didn't come again. I recall going downstairs to Sally and Peter's apartment, and asking Sally if anyone had called on her. Sally looked perplexed and replied,

"No."

To this day, I actually feel that in some way or other those two men were some sort of angelic visitation. Those men would become to me then, perhaps, and in the future; *'Banga's angels'.*

It sounds strange, but that is how it seems.

My family started ringing more frequently, informing us that the press in the UK was reporting on the deteriorating security situation and increasing violence in South Africa. Generally, my family seemed keen for us to pull out for our own safety. At the same time, Michael's business was becoming more and more difficult to keep going. With great generosity, Alice promised us her flat when we returned (of course, we didn't own a property in the UK). I was pleased my family was so concerned about us, and, too hastily perhaps, we decided to leave. I applied to two top universities, and submitted an application for a very prestigious scholarship for post-graduate study. I was on a high, considered quite brilliant.Under African skies …

(A bit of an egoist, really.)

That last night in South Africa I had another dream: *it was of a group of people, evil people. They were outside an empty and ruined church and they were led by a short, dark-haired man. They were chasing Michael and myself.*

The dream had disturbingly ominous overtones.

Stars

(real stars)

in the night

because along with *the crosses*

I saw that night my father was dying ...

were

stars ...

and shooting stars ...

but

hang on folks for a bumpy

Night.

Chiaroscuro

★ *chiaroscuro*
　　★ *a woman's glance*
　　　　★ *shattering crystal*
　　　　　　★ *champagne*
　　　　　　　　★ *and splinters of glass*
　　　　　　　　　　★ *darkness and light*
　　　　　　　　　　　　★ *the story of a woman's soul*

+Bette Davis eyes

Fire in the night.

Reminiscences, evocations of Africa. A Black African Bishop holding back a crowd that would have burnt alive a man with a flaming tyre soaked in petrol. Hannes Van der Walt and his beloved wife, walking along the shores of the beach at Uhmlanga, the purple-night waves crashing against the sand. Hannes' father, who told me so much in one sentence about the importance of keeping a language alive for a people;

"Language and culture are intertwined; you lose your language, you lose your world."

And Hannes' sister, whose bravery was evinced when a rock thrown at her car by louts took her eye. Just a rock, and a moment that changed her life.

The blind eyes of that African prophet, seeing and not seeing.

Michael and myself looking out from Durban beach; Michael pointing far across the dark waves, his hand outstretched in air which seemed almost to ripple, so sodden was it with moisture,

"Over there, the next major landfall is Australia."

(Yet I didn't think on the dreams of my youth.)

Coming back to the UK proved problematic at first. My mother still lived in Newport, while Laura had married an amiable, uber-suave businessman named Robert Moore, who worked in the arms trade. Laura herself was doing incredibly well. After completing a Master's in media studies, she'd embarked on a course in journalism, and landed a plum job as a stylist-cum-fashion editor for a magazine. From letters from my mother, I learnt that Laura had worked for a short while in PR for a fashion house, and attracted the interest of a designer who liked her style, her clothes, her hair and – most particularly – her attitude. So much so that she became his muse. From that point on her name was out there, and she was head-hunted and snapped up by someone from an international publishing group. Yet, I would find Laura herself always downplayed her success and never mentioned much about what she was doing, who she knew; that sort of thing. Laura never, ever name-dropped. Alice suggested this was why Laura was so popular with artistic types; they trusted her. Anyway, Robert and Laura now owned a townhouse that was elegantly furnished, rather Laura Ashley and chintz but with eclectic edges. It was all very glamorous, symbolic of their success. Laura was uber-thin, and wore wonderful designer clothes. Alice, meanwhile, after two difficult relationships, was now production assistant for a film company. That also seemed exciting, and Alice regaled us with hilarious and bizarre stories about film personalities with whom she worked. She had become involved with Mark Lanson, an emerging enfant terrible of the British film industry. Mark had recently completed directing the filming of a European art-house movie which was rapidly developing a cult following.

We stayed with Laura for a few weeks. Robert seemed to tire of having us in the house rather quickly, which was understandable. It became embarrassing for us, as we had very little money and couldn't afford to go anywhere like a hotel, while staying with Mum in Newport was out of the question; London and the surrounding areas were more buoyant work-wise. So we really overstayed our welcome. While with Laura I was accepted at the universities I applied to, but only received a scholarship for a year's study. Reluctantly, I decided to take what I felt was the second best option; I didn't particularly want to live apart from Michael for any protracted period, and it would now be problematic raising funds sufficient for a PhD which might run for three years.

At last we moved into Alice's flat, this was pretty wretched. I felt very sorry for Alice having had to live there. Even the road the flat was situated in was dark and dingy; there was a mood even when the sun shone of half-light and gloom, and Alice was such a sweet thing to put up with that! But Mark had hit the big time and was making an awful lot of money, so he and Alice had moved into a country residence in a very elite area. I was happy for Alice, but it was a really dire time for us, and money was very tight.

At about this time, I had another visionary experience;

I was asleep at night, and an angel dropped fire into my heart. I didn't see the angel, but the experience was of an angel flying high above. And then I felt the flame light in my heart.

The sense of my heart on fire.

For just a few seconds:

the fire of love.

I woke up.

Later, there occurred another visionary dream that seemed unbelievably strange:

the vision was of my family's house in Newport. In the vision I was lying on the floor of the living room, the window of which looked out onto the front garden. There was suddenly this old oak tree in the garden that wasn't there in reality. The bare oak tree bloomed purple lilies. Then it moved forward with a staggered, halting motion. It came through the window and wall of the room – without causing damage to them – and moved over me. The roots of the tree dragged across me, dragged over my soul as if to drag away my baptismal robe.

I couldn't make head or tail of this.

But the message of this dream was that it was some sort of Druidic or Celtic curse.

Life went on. I bought a magazine, and there was a competition for a cover girl with a twist; they wanted someone different, someone a bit edgy with an interesting résumé –

I knew immediately I'd win if I entered.

So I did enter. I wrote some blurb about myself, and sent it in with a picture Mike had taken of me some years earlier. In the meantime, Michael and I managed – by an extraordinary effort – to purchase a one bedroom flat off a plan. The flat was in a good area, and when it was completed, we moved in. Michael took on work while I finalized some research for the university in South Africa. I won the competition, and it was all gloriously glamorous. We finalists were flown to Paris, and after settling into our hotel, were escorted with a large entourage to a fashionable restaurant. It seemed amiable enough, but there was obviously an underlying tension. I became chatty with the girls; there were eight of us. Strolling back to the George Cinq where we were staying, I struck up a conversation with one of them. This girl seemed interested that I was studying religion, and started talking about religious practices in English villages, relating stories of children being born into Satanic bondage and about pervasive child abuse in these places, with people living their entire lives in a state of fear. She seemed to know an awful lot about it, and was extremely distressed, apparently it was all done in secret. I'd never heard anything like it, except for seeing this sort of thing in rather far-fetched English TV productions, and thought, if this were true, it was unspeakable. I really didn't know what to make of her. It occurred to me she might be drunk, but she didn't seem so, or maybe slightly deranged, though she was involved in a prestigious profession – she worked out of a village somewhere. All I did realize was that I didn't know how to react except with dismay. At one level, it occurred to me that she might be reaching out for help; the girl seemed terrified of something, and wanted to go out with me after the meal. She kept trying to persuade me, and suggested a nightclub, which wasn't my thing and we all had an early morning call to boot, so I declined.

Other things jarred just a bit. A fashionista named Veronica involved in the shoot remarked, "I had a premonition you'd win". Of course, I didn't really pay much attention to this. Veronica was hip with an edgy way of dressing; apparently she was never seen in the same outfit twice. I talked to her quite a bit as she was involved in another of the shoots I took part in. Back in the UK, about a week after the final shoot, Michael and I went for a light meal to a restaurant in town popular with media types. It was really odd, because I looked across the tables, which were almost joined together, and sitting nearby was Veronica. But she was wearing a wig, which put me off talking to her. I thought it was a bit of a coincidence, and almost spoke to her when she glanced across at me (I presumed maybe she hadn't wanted to be recognized). Veronica spoke quite audibly, and started going on about "the next meeting of the coven", which she was looking forward to. She said pretty much the same thing a few times. I didn't look at her directly again, I just thought it was all a bit weird.

Mike and I got up and left without acknowledging her, and I put it out of my mind.

It was a good time in some ways, rather calm; indeed, happy. Mike and I went to Alice's rambling mansion. I remember beautiful froufrou silk curtains and expensive leather sofas. The house was only partly furnished, but charmingly disheveled; elegance windblown. Alice had bought these feisty little poodle pups that ran round like wild things, racing up and down the staircases, scampering through the dining room, running chaotically up and into the bijou film studio, before darting out through the open doors and onto the expansive gardens. When the poodles got hungry, Alice would throw roast chicken on the floor of the kitchen for them to pile into. It was a time of craziness. Alice and Mark seemed to live on champagne and God knows what else. We hoped they weren't into drugs, because Mark bragged he went "for days without sleep", which is always a bit worrying. We knew a few people who seemed to be into drugs. Indeed, all the people surrounding my sisters were hip and cool and glamorous, but sometimes looked ever so slightly dubious. It was all media and film, rock and roll and vogue fashion.

Even I had my own little claim to fame when the magazine came out, and there I was; on the cover.

I remember – particularly – a party at Alice's. Alice, petite in flowing blue silk with those blue, blue, eyes, my father's eyes; and that trademark slick of amazing long, red-gold hair. Fluttering porcelain, delicate hands with tiny, pointed and exquisite nails defining and describing Mark's film, and the struggle he endured to "get it together". Storm-clouds of weird looking celebrity types, louche and sometimes in need of a shower and an air-brush. Mark playing guitar and singing his own songs in a corner to whistles and applause as he ended; applause perhaps a little too rapturous and sycophantic. Typical successful movie producer relaxing at home. He didn't look dirty so much as in need of a spruce; hair in his eyes, his face screwed into intensity as he talked hype with a cigarette dangling from his lips. Young men in loose white shirts and baggy trousers hanging out on those leather sofas. Girls posing in denim and jewels. All sorts mucking about in the film studio. Revellers – traipsing and dancing – round the English country garden to speakered stereo music, hand in hand, glasses of Moet or Mumm spilling over gorgeous dresses. Nobody seemed to eat much in those days, it seemed, I never recalled much food going the rounds. Perchance, because the most horrendous social crime of all was to be fat. Laura, discoursing in a corner cornered, gasping "Absolutely!" A word used ubiquitously – and often indiscriminately – at the time; rather like a meme, about how fabulous or vile some fashion show had been, or how absolutely, indescribably, beautiful a new model was. A model they'd all but forget in a soon-to-come tomorrow.

Laura, the model maker, memorable as a summer's day. Long strands of pearls dancing in homage to Coco (Chanel) across a severe blouse. No-one would pull one over on her; or so you'd think. She gave orders now, orders no one failed to obey! Laura, who knew exactly what she wanted. Traces of megalomania and decadence; a fragile insubstantiality about it all. Such was the zeitgeist of those few short years.

Mike and I, in the bar of the Dorchester, our favorite haunt, for a glass of Chablis on a Friday night, with the pianist tinkling the music from Casablanca,

As time goes by.

A glass of chilled wine, and a small selection of edibles to nibble. And I would perfume my hair with Nina Ricci – or something French – with the elegance of romance and the grace of fine lace ...

Discerning at a charity bash where mediocre models staggered, stoned and even more dishabille than was meant to be suggested. Diana, the enchanted Princess, everywhere in the media, the sharp sword of fame ready to tear her to pieces, Madonna being material. And the supermodels swathed in dollars, primped to improbability. Only the odd, lone voice of a Welshman warned of an impending "curfew of fear" as the gibbet of unemployment cowed the British people into obedience.

He was right! We really would be better not being young, or falling ill or getting old, as his impassioned voice declaimed. Neil Kinnock was ridiculed, of course, as all true prophets are. For we really were beginning to live beyond our means, and dreams, because, in a city made of cardboard underneath Waterloo Bridge, we would chat to the fall-out from this cataclysm of hedonistic consumerism huddled in his or her box;

this was exactly where you ended up if things went wrong, in a box; under a bridge. Or in a doorway on the Strand,

the Yuppie era: Thatcher's materialism.

Laura disclosed she was "still socialist", but didn't tell anybody except 'us'. Laura, fallen lucky, spiraling to success and now surviving on ferocious energy, coupled with driving ambition, a witty pen and fabulous face, a talent for spotting innovative design with a feel for the mood and texture of a coming season; an ability to create a montage of ambience and designer, a face and frock positioned in an evocative location that put her just ahead of the rest of the field. Everybody Laura worked with came from the upper classes, from the milieu of Oxbridge, of public and finishing schools, abetted to get where they were by word of mouth and friend of friend. Laura was really an interloper. And in a luxe job everyone wanted, so everyone was out to get her if she failed to meet the deadline; the expectation. Experiencing something of the frenzy in her soul one evening she exclaimed – just a little desperately – in her elegantly engineered and timbred Sloane (Ranger) voice,

"I want to eat! Nobody's going to give me a free ride or a free meal."

Laura, steely determined. I was informed by my sisters, rather as an aside so their refined, upper-class spouses didn't hear, that the housing estate where we'd been brought up was now a "rough zone". Notorious apparently. You really didn't want to let on where you came from.

So it was. London, the late Eighties. Laura and Robert and Michael and me. In Robert's black Mercedes, cruising Kensington High Street. Making an entrance. I, in staggering heels and height through the swing doors of a restaurant dressed with media and celebrities, scoured furtively by paparazzi hiding out for a picture of someone; not us! We weren't quite there. (Though Laura was, but didn't let on.) Laura in the front seat of Robert's car, in her new Chanel coat. Robert playing one of his favorite cassettes,

Bette Davis Eyes ... For Laura. Because he had spotted that Laura's eyes were Bette Davis's. And I looked; and they were:

she has Bette Davis's eyes.

The music of our times, the music of the *mindscape*.

And the shop lights of Mayfair and Harrods dazzling us with bright lights in the darkness as we cruised past Harvey Nic's, which had the most fabulous windows in town. And, maybe, the music on the radio would be the soundtrack from Mark's film. Or if not, maybe one of those songs of the time, Bryan Ferry, evoking the mood of the beautiful people of London town, and the ambience of the airbrushed glitterati,

"*Oh yeah. There's a band playing on the radio.*"

The uber-chic soundscape of Roxy Music. So we would hang out in a hip wine bar. Laura, evocatively drawing on a cigarette, crossing her elegant slim legs under her regulation Chanel couture black (with the buttons) and flats. And Robert, tall but small boned, splendidly urbane, with his fashionably tousled red hair; inevitably impeccably dressed. Regular, trademark, middle class English features. Robert always so proud of being British. Again, we didn't drink too much, or eat too much. It wasn't cool, it wasn't chic. Laura, fluttering her long lashes as she assayed the crowd, Bette Davis eyes glancing. Something really perturbed her one night, and she pulled her cigarette from her lips – that were like Mum's – and snapped,

"What happens when it's not 'our' time anymore?"

She meant when we're not part of the 'in' people.

Laura's words from those red-tinted lips. Her mouth a mouth from a Warhol print.

Words,

tumbling down time.

How long ago that all seems now … over twenty years.

"There's something funny about time," Mum would muse, in her strange, convoluted and fiery wisdom. As she cast a glance sideways, her head tilted, evoking more of Joan Crawford than Bette Davis; throwing a look at me: as if she expected something. And I could not answer, because I did not know – then! I remember all of this with very mixed feelings. We had 'done good' for three girls from a council housing estate.

Mum also found it exhilarating, and would come up to see my sisters especially. She couldn't stay with us as the flat was way too small, but she had a room in Laura and Robert's Mews residence in Kensington. At other times, Michael and I would go to see Mum in Newport. Once, at least, we went out with her and Michael's parents to a lovely restaurant. Away from us, Mother seemed lonely now; lost at times. We girls had moved on. Still, Patrick and Genevieve and my Aunty Karen were near. I have an image of Mum from when we used to visit. Standing at the door of our house, waving. Or, later, at the window of her apartment; a portrait: a study in loneliness; a face at a window. One of many. What do we trade in return for ambition and fame and fortune?

The window shatters and the glass shatters,

broken glass and shattered dreams.

What was Mum thinking then? As she stood at that window watching us leave. Maybe of the time when she first saw her wild Irish boy, with the unbelievable face and those eyes, and that madness of love? Her husband who dazzled her with his purity, in the days of their youth. A man who wanted to be priested, but also wanted a wife, a family. That purity and beauty and truth. A heritage of freedom, now just fragments. And a face still traced by memories of loveliness, at a window.

... Jealousy is cruel as the grave.

Solomon's Song; kjv

Prior to these events I'd attended an interview at university. The meeting with the Head of the Faculty of Anthropology, Professor Franco, was peculiar to say the least. The man spent a good deal of the time complaining about his marriage and the way his wife wanted to work, while almost nothing was said about the research I was to embark upon. "La de da. La de da!" I thought to myself as I exited his office when this down-beat, downright discouraging interview concluded, tossing my head defiantly and then unleashing my hair from its constricted bun. I'd put my hair up, and chosen a spinster-boring, boring, brown suit with matching flat shoes to channel 'academic-unattractive-dowdy'. Now, shaking the dust off my feet, I reminded myself I'd chosen this university to do my research with the eminent Professor Kasza, a world renowned authority in the field of Buddhist meditation. So, what the hell! I wasn't unduly concerned; I was a cum-laude scholar, this shouldn't bother me;

um ...

Dear me! From that point things went from bad to worse. Franco turned out to be a twisted piece of work. He was an ex-Catholic priest whom, so the rumor went, Rome was 'after' for some reason. Still, I must admit his lectures and the notes he gave were exceptional; Franco really knew his stuff. But this undoubted academic brilliance was marred by the way he would occasionally break off to make remarks of a disturbing nature about certain women ex-students. Franco even bragged about driving one woman to a nervous breakdown. He seemed to find it funny; this was misogyny in a power position. At another point, when I told him I'd received a scholarship he enquired, "Who did you bribe?"

I tried to see this as a joke. When a new woman student came into our class to begin study (following her late enrolment) he enquired of us, "Do we really want this woman in our class?"

There was silence. The men looked embarrassed, their muteness gushing a substantive weakness. The woman student herself seemed bemused. There was only one other woman in the group and I blustered,

"Of course we do."

It went down like lead. At other times Franco was quite charming, though not to me. Just chatting generally, I had the distinct impression that university life here was all about money. People were quite open about it, and our value as students was discussed in one lecture in financial terms. You didn't rock the boat, this wasn't the seventies. Very few students received awards to study, so the majority had invested a great deal in their courses; it was expensive.

Franco made it apparent he was going to personally supervise all our research projects. Finding this unsatisfactory, I went to see him and, as tactfully as I could manage, requested that Silviu Kasza supervise my project. As the subject matter of my research was not in Franco's area anyway, I hoped there wouldn't be any problem; (I was a very determined girl in those days, and I thought I knew where I was going).

Franco was furious and pronounced abruptly, "I could ruin your career."

There was a pause before he added, "That is not a threat."

I wasn't totally convinced. Anyway, I succeeded in changing my supervisor. My new supervisor, the afore-mentioned Silviu, was a Buddhist. Silviu also ran a group practicing – what I presumed to be meditation – at the university. Although only a short man with a plump, round face, bald pate and stocky build, Silviu had a certain charisma; derived mainly from his style of delivery. During lectures he would walk, even pace, the room instead of just sitting or standing. And talk thoughtfully, pensively, chewing over his statements. His manner had a touch of the raconteur about it, even theatre. Sometimes Silviu's insights were penetrating, though he tended to digress. The class had forty or so students, which made it larger than my other classes. For a short period things seemed to settle where Franco was concerned. Then this changed.

One day, about twenty minutes into the class, Silviu abruptly stopped walking. He stared over at me and said he needed to "have a word" with me; slap bang in the middle of the lecture. It was downright strange and unnerving. I followed him out of the classroom – and into his room – which was nearby. Silviu started pacing up and down, looking very agitated, and snapped –

"You have an enemy Mrs. Kennedy."

He repeated this and then said again, "You have an enemy, Mrs. Kennedy."

Only stopping to caution me by saying, "This is very, very serious."

As if this wasn't enough to clarify the situation, he then exclaimed, "I cannot stress how serious this is!"

He kept repeating the words, "Very, very serious."

Silviu appeared terribly worried. I thought it was a bit rich; indeed, I though it sounded quite mad. After all, I had only changed supervisor, which I presumed to be the problem. Anyway, this went on for some while, with Silviu pacing and repeating that I had "an enemy" and so on. After about fifteen to twenty minutes, Silviu stopped. I followed him out of the room and we went back to the class. Nobody said anything or asked me anything about it, it was as if nothing had happened. I assumed nobody wanted to become involved. Of course, the episode caused me some mild angst. But I continued to keep on as if nothing had transpired, just thinking people were "acting a bit strange".

I would go regularly to discuss my dissertation with Silviu. His was a small office, rather cramped, with a desk near the window where he would sit with his back to the flooding light. There was a floor to ceiling bookcase filled with academic works on the right wall as you entered, and various religious artworks on the left wall. However, he would never sit at his desk to interview you. The routine was that we would sit in front of Silviu, who would have his chair to the left of the door, facing the window. There was a small, rectangular table to his right where he would keep pen and paper. Directly in front of him were three chairs placed one behind the other backed up to his desk. As each student took their turn to discuss their work and then departed, you would move forward into the vacant seat in front until you arrived at the chair facing Silviu. Unfortunately, he didn't seem that interested in what I was doing, and his input was flimsy. More and more he would say things to me out of the blue such as,

"You're not a bad woman?"

He would repeat this, which was obviously puzzling. It was as if he were trying to make sense of something. Another phrase he used to repeat was,

"Mary Magdalene was a great sinner. But she was forgiven because she loved much."

He seemed to be talking about me, not so much about Mary Magdalene. There was that *edge* again. And then more light heartedly;

"Ah! Chanel! You're wearing Chanel."

Oh God! I thought. "Where do I go from here? All I want to do is earn a living. Give us a break …"

(And the perfume was Body Shop.)

Meanwhile, in Franco's lectures, things were chugging along. Then, one afternoon as Franco was delivering his notes, he rose from his seat to walk around the room. We were a class of about eight, seated about a large rectangular table. Franco walked behind me and as he did so tugged hard at my hair, pulling some out. I half turned to look at him; I felt I ought to remonstrate because it felt deliberate, but thought the better of saying anything. Franco moved on and returned to his seat.

With Silviu I began to grow nervous. His comments really began to undermine my composure; I definitely felt I was under some sort of vague threat. It reached the point where I decided to go and discuss my unease with a student counsellor. That didn't go so well either. To encapsulate the conversation, I informed the counsellor I felt I was being "intimidated and undermined". The counsellor responded by making remarks about me 'being attractive', and enquired playfully, as if he was toying with me and it was all a bit of a joke,

"Would you like to go out with me?"

I thought him absurd, the filthy beast. And decided I'd just keep my head down and shut up after that. A while went by, and I began to feel more at ease, though the whole course of study had lost its lustre. I really just wanted to successfully complete the thing and get out of the place.

Also odd was the way Silviu, who was supposed to be a Buddhist, actually seemed to make fun of Buddhism, as if it was all nonsense. Silviu once openly referred to Buddhism as, "A load of shit". He would sometimes smoke in lectures, and his cigarette dangled loosely from his fingers as he made the remark. Then he recommenced puffing in between sentences of monologue. What was peculiar was that Silviu didn't seem to be joking.

Some time later, Silviu was walking around and talking as he always did, when he abruptly stopped. I remember him looking at me, and then putting his right foot down sharply,

a bolt of energy hit me; striking halfway centre bottom of my right foot and running up my leg until it exploded at the centre of my chest, somewhere between my breasts. I looked down: shocked. A button of my blouse had popped where I felt the full force of the energy.

I did the button up as surreptitiously as possible as Silviu continued talking. Then he stopped again;

his right foot went down:

another bolt of energy.

It ran up my body and hit, again. Dead centre of my chest.

I was puzzled and informed Amalia, a friend with me in the class at the time. She just looked and remarked curiously,

"I've heard Silviu is something of a yogi."

"Do you think Silviu is a Holy Man?" I enquired. Amalia seemed wary,

"I don't think so. He smokes a lot. Not very spiritual, that?"

Her comment puzzled me; it wasn't what she said – it was the way that she said it. Amalia had spent some years at the university and knew many of the lecturers personally.

At home – more and more – I began feeling there was a lot of 'interference' when I was meditating; *a lot of stuff at the subliminal level*. I put this down to meditating in a city. But I had meditated in cities around the world before, so I was puzzled; this seemed different. Normally, I would sit and relax and bring my mind to focus on my breath, noting the sounds around me, the movements of my body and thoughts. A sense of peace would prevail as I moved into a state of tranquility, deep relaxation and heightened awareness. Now, with regard to the sense of disturbance, it was rather like tuning in a radio;

picking up a lot of noisy static, a jangle of stations all colliding. A jangle of discordant moods and emotions.

I was well aware that during meditation the body and mind can move into altered states of consciousness. Sometimes this begins with a state which approximates the juncture that occurs just as one is falling into sleep. It is then that mental barriers may melt away. But now, instead of a sense of serene awareness, it was as if I could feel and sense *an unease.* In a mental dilemma, I tried to tell myself it was just my own psyche, but I really felt that I was also picking up;

a pervasive negativity in that area of consciousness we have come to name the 'collective unconscious'.

With a mind functioning at this level of heightened awareness, something was causing

dissonance.

Later, with Silviu, I was waiting my turn as usual in his office. A fellow student was in front of me talking about something. I heard the student remark,

"The most powerful black magician is a Roman Catholic priest."

The comment didn't have the ring of truth about it;

there was a distinct sense of something wrong: a jarring negativity. And strangely, the dim sense not only that the remark was untrue, but that it was intended for my ears.

I wondered where this student and his remark were coming from. It took my mind momentarily back to that period in my early teens where I'd picked up those works of fiction that touched on Satanism and the occult. But you couldn't expect truth to come from the occult, from Satanists, from people who deal in lies …

When it was my turn to discuss my work in progress, Silviu made an odd remark;

"We will trap you with your love."

His words were so audible I looked round; I don't think the other students sitting behind noticed. Silviu repeated the phrase. He seemed almost depressed.

Then again, "We will trap you with your love."

I presumed he had been drinking; I'd smelt alcohol on his breath before when standing close to him, but this time I couldn't smell anything.

Silviu went on, "Soon you will be in my house."

I didn't know what on earth he was going on about, I had no intention of going to his house. I was convinced he was barmy, another one of those mad professors you read about. I noticed the Tibetan Tanka on his wall from a book of visions of one of the Dalai Lamas. I looked it up later, and I believe, (I didn't take a note of this) that it was a Tanka designed to ward off evil.

Another thing that was odd, was that Silviu kept asking me my age, and persisted in repeating the question. I knew I didn't look my age, but that was beside the point. Indeed, he would sometimes ask several times in a ten minute session. And there were other seemingly perversely inappropriate enquiries such as,

"You're not thinking of having children?"

Indeed, this questioning became stereotypical of my interviews with Silviu.

I talked to Michael about the trouble I was having, the feeling of being in some way threatened, to which he responded in his usual common sense manner,

"Look, you come across all sorts of people in life. Just ignore it and get on with what you have to do. There are all sorts of screwed up individuals out there, that's life!"

He paused, and looked at me, as if implying I was a little too ingenuous, before concluding,

"We all have to deal with it from time to time; not everybody's nice, get real."

I took his advice. I found my research fascinating, so that helped enormously to keep my mind off any negativity. I put my interest in religion and spirituality down to the rich heritage of my ancestors, some might even say it's 'in the genes'. Indeed, the search for truth and for God was, to me, the fundamental point of existence. And yet I was now encountering people who just might be going the 'other way'. This latter suspicion did enter my mind, but only in a vague fashion because, I mean, where the hell did they think they were going to end up? I mean, who the hell would want to go to hell? You've got to be crazy! So, I couldn't seriously take this into consideration. Yet doing my research I had one peculiar, if transient, encounter with a rather strange young man. The event took place at a rural Buddhist retreat centre in the UK. It was the only time I would visit the centre, and for some reason this man gravitated towards me,

immediately I felt it. This man felt like he was surrounded by filth. It was like feeling coal dust floating around a person's body. The thought immediately came to my mind,

"This man's a witch."

The young man introduced himself, and enquired of me why I was attending the centre. I replied that I was a research student. He looked and said,

"I'm a witch."

It was darkness visible.

Many waters cannot quench love, neither can the floods drown it.

The Song of Songs; kjv

Landfalls beyond normal consciousness

I finished my studies and we went abroad again, this time to South-East Asia, where Michael was offered a three year contract. I was planning to continue post-graduate work at a university there, but work on my project was curtailed when we were moved to an island off the coast. The religious situation here was varied and animism was prevalent; animism being the belief that natural objects and all things possess a soul, an energy force that can be influenced, perhaps controlled, for various ends. Even white ex-pats might wear charms to protect themselves from the evil manipulations of local practitioners of the black arts, something I found difficult to accept, because you don't fight evil with evil. But that was a very vague summation at the time, an intuitive sense, and I didn't dwell on the topic.

In the jungle they were logging trees. A Westerner was helping the indigenous Indians who were fighting the loggers over land rights. I remember seeing a stretch of forest that had been cleared by the logging company. To put it bluntly, it was as if the earth had been raped. Human beings were destroying the very world that supported their own lives: there was no other way to put it. This, with the presence of the sense of a strange spirit world, and the existence of a very primitive form of Buddhism just at times, and in certain places, gave the island a mood of half-life, of verging on an unhealthy un-becoming; not quite non-being, but of being in a dreamscape: a landscape of dreams. The atmosphere was so pervasive it must have affected me more than I realized, because I wrote a short story about the land crying out to a shaman, saying it was dying.

We moved again. We were supposed to be based in one major city location, but because Michael kept being moved my research became impossible. My frustration at this was mitigated, however, because I ended up in a lovely apartment on my own for a while, blessed with the most glorious gardens. The colorful beds of exotic flowers and expanses of lawn and tropical trees, influenced me so much I developed a love of gardens for ever after. I fell in love with the color and vibrancy and beauty. So much so, I would sometimes wait for the afternoon monsoon rains, and go outside to feel the warm drops of liquid cascading down, brushing the flowers, tossing them about with what seemed to be God's tears of love: it was unbelievably beautiful! And I cared not about my wet hair, and the streams of water splashing past my cheeks and lips and eyes.

Otherwise, feeling thwarted but trying to make the most of this disruptive interlude, I worked on translations a renowned Chinese monk was making of Buddhist scriptures. Meanwhile, Mike was dispatched to a remote site in a jungle area. The conditions on site were not good, but he was able to come home every second weekend, whereupon I would feed him up. Food was basic, and in short supply, at the construction camp and Michael started to cook for himself, using vegetables and doing stir-frys, because the cook on site wasn't too competent. The local workers considered Mike very wise doing this. They were Muslim, and Michael got on well with them and spoke of them as being "generally a most charming people". I think they developed a soft spot for him also.

I went to an art exhibition with Michael on one of the weekends he was on R and R. It was quite odd when I stopped and looked at one painting and thought, *"This is a tree spirit"*. I went and looked closer. The small printed description with the details about the artist said precisely that: the picture was of a tree spirit,

I wondered how I knew.

Anyway, it was just before I moved to be with Michael in a house in the jungle near the construction camp, that I had a strange vision while I was wide awake. It happened one afternoon when I'd relaxed in a chair after finishing some work on a Buddhist text. I saw, with my eyes open, an image of Silviu;

Silviu was there in front of me, as if seated in God-like majesty above the world. The message of the vision was that Silviu was encouraging me to look at the Tibetan tradition.

He had his hands stretched out holding a cord between them. On the cord hung three triangles. The triangles seemed to have been made of paper.

Without real reflection, *I interpreted these triangles as being the three major traditions of Buddhism: Hinayana, Mahayana and Vajrayana,*

and Man become God.

Of course, I continued to suppress these occurrences, and because of this I couldn't, in the final analysis, make head or tail of them. Now I am aware that you have to be very careful with all visionary events. You don't know where they are coming from. Yes, reality may be opening up; but what reality?

Are you opening up to God?

Or Satan?

Or merely your own imagination?

But at that precise time I didn't evaluate in these categories, and so I couldn't penetrate to the deeper meaning of what I was experiencing.

Relocated to be with Michael, I moved with him into a house in a village in the jungle. The local staff were accustomed to the area, but generally life for the ex-pats was difficult in many ways. They were isolated and their wives, if they had them, couldn't take the harsh conditions. So except for Michael, and an American whose wife I befriended, the men were on bachelor status. To compensate for the loneliness, heat, difficult and sometimes dangerous working conditions, many ex-pats drank heavily. Some visited prostitutes. Michael and I chatted about this, and before I moved to be with him in the jungle I had enquired of a local girl what she thought about the prostitution, which seemed to be little more than rampant exploitation and abuse. The local girl was matter of fact,

"Film stars do it all the time on the screen. No-one makes a big deal about that. They just make more money doing it."

I admired her forthrightness, but I thought it was a hell of a lot less glamorous than Hollywood. Here local girls might be abducted and put to work in brothels or bars. Others were taken from desperate parents who received money, sometimes believing their children would get jobs in the city, when the reality was they ended up working in bars and clubs as prostitutes, often in squalid conditions. At other times, and most often it seems, beautiful girls were sold into prostitution. I asked a Buddhist monk about it; I mean, why didn't the monks "do something"? The monk just turned away. It was an awkward moment. Apparently, many of the local men hated the way their women were sold for money. I found it difficult to reconcile that men would come from all over the 'civilized' world to take advantage of these poor women. I wondered what the hell was wrong with them. This was sexual slavery; you had to be a stinking grub.

We would go to a nearby city to pick up supplies. On two occasions I had really weird experiences I was unable to explain. Both happened in a hotel in the city, once in the reception area in the hotel where;

I turned round and saw a Chinese man smiling at me.

I blinked and he was gone.

On another occasion, but at the same spot on a lower level in the car park,

I saw a man running at great speed.

One minute he was there, the next he was gone; he had vanished into a wall.

It was as if he was running through another dimension.

All of them wearing the sword, all experienced in battle.

The Song of Songs

The glass beginning to shatter.

It was about this time that I had repeated dreams of flooding. Everywhere there seemed to be rain.

And after the rain we were in a hotel room watching the flood waters.

We were given excellent references from other ex-pats regarding a Chinese lady who might prove helpful as our housekeeper, on a part-time basis, as I couldn't speak the language. The idea was that Woo would provide assistance with matters such as the failure of the electricity supply or the water being cut off. Woo Chong was a highly intelligent woman, a brilliant linguist who could speak several languages, having picked them up working for foreigners in the area. We had long, interesting, conversations together when she would sometimes become impassioned by circumstances and events, which I liked because I sensed she genuinely cared. I recall one discussion during which Woo informed me that babies in the area were often born with holes in them due to pesticide residues. She was most upset about it, and wanted to know if Western babies were born with holes in them? Woo felt the locals were being treated as guinea pigs, and warned me not to eat the local produce because, no matter how much you washed the vegetables, you couldn't get rid of the sprays because the pesticides were absorbed into the tissues of the plants.

The monsoon rains came. The house was flooded. We held out on the second floor which was just above the flood level. The electricity supply failed, and it took three days before rescuers could reach us. Then boats came to ferry us to safety, after which we were driven to a local hotel. This was the first time there had been such flooding in thirty years or so.

From the hotel window I looked out, and remembered the visionary dream;

the flood.

This Asian land was very beautiful at times, and we loved driving round on Mike's days off. One incident I remember vividly was the sight of a refined and beautiful Muslim woman in an elegant skirt and blouse, her head lightly veiled, stepping delicately across a muddy road; a vision of loveliness in the shimmering heat. At other times we would stop and watch the rice workers in the paddy fields and sense the meditative stillness, the timelessness, across the tropical, steaming landscape. There were days when the sun was so huge it resembled a Chinese lantern. As we stood one day watching the workers throwing the rice seed, Michael turned to me and said he felt he could sense "the presence of God in the beauty of the landscape".

It was a moment when time stopped, and the hand of the grain thrower was as if stilled;

"See, God's painted us a picture."

Michael said in tones of unusual softness, inspired by the mystical nature of the scene. And we looked, as many people who have loved have looked. And recognized something of the beauty of God in the drawing of a landscape.

Alone in the house in long days of solitude I was writing. When I wrote, I frequently used to hold up my right hand to feel God's protective grasp.

I raised my hand one day and,

I couldn't feel the grasp.

I felt real panic, real dread; and wondered if I was imagining it. Then I told myself sternly, forcefully, to calm down.

While abroad we decided to apply to emigrate to Australia. We put in our application and were taken aback to hear that it would take around two years, possibly longer to process. This meant we would have to return to the UK.

Here I had another vision,

Shot into the darkness of sleep:

the fireplace in my father's house;

a fire is burning. In the centre of the fire is the holy water bottle my saintly aunt left me.

It does not burn.

On it are the letters IHS.

It was the trial of faith: the trial by fire,

gold in the crucible.

Lecturing work in England was hard to find. So I swallowed my pride, and went back to see Silviu. I had decided to go to another university to continue my research, but I needed references. Silviu suggested I work toward a doctorate at the university with him, and that he would undertake to be my supervisor. Naturally, this didn't appeal. But he was persuasive, while still displaying that almost insane perversity of discourse that made me understandably uneasy. He enquired if I was,

"Thinking of leaving the country?"

If I was,

"Thinking of having a baby?"

I told him I wasn't, in both cases. I thought it was terribly odd. But I'd come to the conclusion they were all crazy; mad professors. I was grasping at straws. I really didn't want to go back there, but I didn't want to give up my dream of working at university and researching either, and I needed to earn a living. Silviu sounded sad as he repeated yet again,

"You're not a bad girl?"

And added,

"You will not be going abroad?"

Again! He sounded disappointed. Sad. As if somewhere, deep within, he wished I were going abroad. The interview finished with Silviu telling me to contact him. As I was about to leave he repeated, enigmatically, what was becoming almost a mantra,

"Mary Magdalene was a woman who sinned much, but was forgiven. Eh? Because she loved much."

What was the matter with him? What was he talking about? Was he talking about her? Or me?

Silviu requested I bring a research paper I had written while abroad.

The telephone rang as I left. And I heard him say;

"Ah, Fifi! Fifi! I have been waiting to hear from you."

"Fifi!" I thought,

"Only cats are called Fifi!"

From the lions' dens and the mountain haunts of the leopards.

Song of Songs

The weeks passed. Trying to get to see Silviu again proved difficult. He was so evasive and problematic to pin down, I became increasingly frustrated. Deciding to throw the towel in, I telephoned with an excuse to extricate myself from any meeting with him at all; I was fed up. Surprisingly, Silviu appeared panicked by this and abruptly made a definite date for our meeting. It was to be at three o'clock the following Wednesday afternoon. Though now not at all keen about this course of action, I arrived punctually as requested. On entering his study and greeting him, Silviu responded to my words by just sitting. Smoking, and looking at me pointedly in a manner which could only be described as intimidating, but without saying a word. It was disconcerting, and I didn't know what to do. This being so, I mumbled something and handed him the paper he'd asked to see. Silviu stared at me as if he was, at some level, concentrating. I was standing directly in front of him having given him the paper,

then what seemed like a volley of tiny arrows hit me.

Not exactly me, but some area surrounding me. The sensation was quite distinct and totally dramatic and could not be denied;

I was being assaulted by some kind of invisible arrows or darts.

It hurt, I felt I had been almost physically wounded.

The arrows kept coming. They burnt.

My gut feeling was to get the hell out of there. So I just made an excuse. At first Silviu had no expression. Then a faint, unpleasant smile traced across his lips. He put out his hand for me to shake –

but I was gone.

The sleeper awakes: each with his sword at his side, prepared for the terrors of the night.

The Song of Songs

(The terrors of the night.)

Now the visions began in earnest:

shot into the darkness of sleep –

I see the image of a figure on parchment.

The figure is clothed like a rabbi. Or, more accurately, a priestly figure from the Old Testament. His left hand is raised with the index finger pointing upward, towards heaven, towards the sky. There is writing in Hebrew, as if on stone tablets, on either side of the figure. But I cannot recall the lettering.

The tablets and the writing seem to be the Ten Commandments.

The image was there one minute, gone the next. As if it had been directed into my mind. Again, like an image shot onto a screen in a dark cinema.

I awake, *to feel I am being cursed. Something about cutting my connection with the Ten Commandments?* Yet it was even stranger than that; because the garments the priestly figure wore resembled clothing I'd seen on statues from ancient Samaria or Babylonia in the British Museum.

But I put it out of my mind ...

A few days later I see another vision:

dark water rising.

And my dreams are changing. Mutating. To become strange and sinister premonitions. Dreams of foreboding.

My consciousness circles a table. A group from the university are meeting and discussing,

I intuit their words as if I am listening in to their conversation;

"Three people are to go down to hell."

A friend of Laura's offered Michael the chance to establish a new firm. It looked promising at first, though Michael explained we were making preparations to migrate to Australia so, for us, it couldn't be long term. Michael agreed to initiate the project and see how things went. A man called Andrew Mainstone became involved as co-director and, as Michael was going abroad, Andrew moved into a position whereby he took ultimate control. Andrew was odd, to put it mildly. The first time we met at a function to celebrate the establishment of the new company, Andrew turned aside to me and said,

"I am going to make Michael's life hell."

Just a statement with no emotion at all, except that of threat. And the words were enunciated with such nonchalance I couldn't quite believe what I was hearing, and so didn't react. Andrew, with no real expression on his face except perhaps dislike and disregard, repeated the words before casually turning away and commencing conversation with someone else. I was totally non-plussed; it seemed bizarre for someone to be so openly threatening. I can't remember telling Michael immediately; perhaps because I felt embarrassed by my lack of response.

I resumed writing and an agent expressed interest in my short stories. Meanwhile, I'd booked a holiday for us in a residence near Assisi. The description in the magazine advertisement described this destination as a collection of holiday apartments in a building that had been used by monks as an annex to a nearby larger monastery. Much of the building dated back to the fourteenth century, and so I thought it would have character. I rang the lady in Italy who owned and rented the apartments and her description fueled my interest. It wasn't expensive, moreover, it sounded atmospheric, out of the ordinary; just what we wanted.

We were excited about going.

More strange dreams.

I see the figures of Chinese gods racing towards me from far off.

I wake.

The figures seem to penetrate my consciousness.

Rudy and Anna, the owners of the converted building where we were to stay, met us as we parked our car in the garage. The couple appeared pleasant enough people, Anna looking slightly older than Rudy, being perhaps in her sixties. Warmly welcoming, the couple chatted as they escorted us away from the garage and along a cobbled path to the main house. This was a well maintained two-storey villa at the front of a complex of buildings. Rudy left us and went into the house, leaving Anna to show us to our suite of rooms, which took the form of an apartment in an adjoining annex. This was reached after a short stroll along a simple cobble and dirt pathway at the side of the main house. Dimly lit in the dusk of early evening by a single electric lamp, the entrance to the apartment was through a huge and beautifully restored old door. This opened at the turn of a heavy key, and Anna flicked on a light to illuminate the lounge with its impressive vaulted ceiling. My eyes moved to the large picture window at the far end of the room overlooking the Umbrian countryside, and Anna turned to me. With a wave of her hand she explained,

"This entire complex is our home. So it isn't impersonal, like a hotel …"

To the left of the lounge as we entered was a smaller – but still impressive – wooden door opening onto the bedroom area,

I felt a slight but definite disturbance in energy; a sense of unease, of spiritual disquiet.

Anna again located the light switch, and flicked on the light for us to see. Even so the bedroom was dimly lit, the main item of furniture being a simple double bed with a wooden headboard and non-descript linen. Oh! And there were some bedside tables. As I looked round I tensed at the sense of gloom. Anna led the way as we followed, descending a short staircase from the bedroom to reach the kitchen-cum-dining area. At the end of this room there was a small window overlooking the countryside. Beside the window was a door leading to what turned out to be a patio area. Right of the kitchen was another old door of dark wood, but this was quite small. It led to the bathroom which housed an ultra-modern shower. This was in what looked like a sort of grotto, so the effect was incongruous, reminiscent of showering in a cave where a fairy or nymph could jump out. Or a goblin. Rather weird.

Having shown us round the apartment Anna withdrew, leaving us to our own devices. I walked round, taking stock of the place. In the dining area there was an impressive rustic wooden table of antique appearance, while the walls of the apartment were of some sort of rippled concrete or plaster with stellar symbols at points. These symbols, however, were small and didn't register immediately. I touched the walls, feeling something. And closed my eyes;

what was it? What could I feel here? I tried to focus, to concentrate.

Michael interrupted my reflections, he was hungry because we had travelled all day and hadn't eaten much. As it was early evening and the light was dimming, we took a quick trip to a local village trattoria Anna had recommended. Here we ordered pasta, proclaiming "nienti carne" when making our choice from the menu, (Anna had advised us to do this on hearing that we were vegetarian; apparently in Umbria they often put bacon or meat in vegetable dishes to flavor the food). Finishing our meal quite quickly, we drove back to our apartment, Michael complaining about the erratic driving on Italian roads.

It was dark, so treading very carefully on the uneven footpath we made our way past Anna and Rudy's villa to our rooms. As Mike put the incredible and huge key in the door-lock he looked at me, not too happily. I didn't ask why, and at first he didn't say anything. As it was pitch black we had to fumble for the light switch. There was the slightly damp smell of a very old building. As the light flickered on Michael shot me a glance and then almost barked in irritation,

"O.K! What's up? What's got into you now? Come on, tell me! Out with it."

I wouldn't respond truthfully at first, and just shrugged the question off. Then, when he wasn't looking, I rather guiltily touched the walls again. I wasn't quite sure why I would do this, but I seemed to feel – to sense even – through my fingers; an awareness I was able to intuit,

what I would feel later was a tear in the fabric of our reality, a rippling out of the energy of existence from somewhere else. Another reality breaking through.

Or, as if I was walking through the walls of our House of Time and into another place.

Anyway, I only did this momentarily as it might have attracted Mike's attention – which I didn't want. And also because it made me feel uneasy. *Something was wrong.* But after the wine and the food and the excitement of it all I wanted to enjoy myself; we were on holiday for heaven's sake. So I turned to follow Michael through the door and into the bedroom. By now we were both very tired, Michael more so than I because he had been driving. Mike immediately disappeared downstairs to wash and clean his teeth. On returning to the bedroom area he said a cursory goodnight, mumbling he was "tired". Mike then got into bed and seemed to fall asleep immediately. (Which is not unusual.)

I went down to wash and remove my make up. Even walking down the stairs,

I felt the spiritual unease increasing.

It was not a pleasant experience at all. Michael had left the kitchen light on and there was a light in the shower room, but it was so poor I could hardly see my face in the oval of glass that was the bathroom mirror. There was a chill in the air which had the effect of making you feel as if the hairs on your body were starting to stand up; not just a normal chill, *a spiritual chill*. And again, that increasing sense of the presence of something; *an uneasy spirit*. Even as I over-hastily applied the olive oil I used to remove my make up and attempted to brush my teeth I realized,

something was looking over my shoulder, something I could almost see.

Disturbed, I didn't bother with mucking round and exited the bathroom as speedily as possible. Returning hastily back up the stairs I found Michael still sleeping, his gentle breathing and presence reassuring. Feeling disquieted, I turned off the light and got into bed.

Darkness. Very dark. No light from the surrounding countryside flickering in. There it was again. Even as I closed my eyes; stronger now,

just below the level of normal consciousness. Images. Of medieval life.

I panicked, and by shaking his shoulder, tried to wake Michael up. I was scared and wanted to talk about it. Mike woke abruptly. Of course he didn't want to discuss anything one little bit; he was on holiday and he was really, really tired. He articulated this, sounding distinctly nasty. I felt bad about having disturbed him and shut up. We both settled back. Still feeling uneasy I drifted off to sleep. I can't remember what time it was exactly but;

in the middle of the night I woke. I was totally awake and still. Beside me I could feel what seemed to be a six foot pillar of dirt. It stank of decay like rotting vegetation.

I was frightened and shocked. I lay quite still, trying to control my fear and analyze the situation,

I could smell this thing. I could feel this thing. It didn't have the same solidity of, say, a person. It seemed to be half and half; half in one reality, half in another.

I was wide awake, and I could feel and just about see it:

a huge heap of dirt covered in decaying vegetation that seemed like bits of leaves.

I froze, but as soon as I had the courage I got out of bed and without even thinking, made the Sign of the Cross for protection and deliverance before searching for the light switch. Switching on the light had the effect of waking Michael and he was really, really annoyed;

"Switch the light off," he barked, half asleep and grumpy as hell. I responded,

"It's an old building and it doesn't feel right."

I really didn't want to say any more.

But, of course, that did it. Mike roused himself and forcefully demanded I tell him exactly what was wrong. (I was glad he was awake actually, because it made me feel better. I know this sounds selfish, and I really did feel guilty after having woken the poor guy up.) Rattled and ratty, Mike pressured me to explain even though I didn't want to. Eventually I gave in and told him,

"I can feel a presence." In fact, I could still just about feel it, "Something's not right here."

I added, "There's a disturbance," pathetically hoping this really odd remark from a twentieth century woman did not sound too barking mad.

"Oh my God! Go back to sleep. For Pete's sake, woman; can't we get some rest? It's been a long day."

Mike, of course, was fed up and totally exasperated and added in annoyance and irritation,

"I knew from the moment you walked in the door you'd been spooked."

He enunciated his purported conclusion pointedly and accusingly, as though it was all my fault. Marital harmony disrupted anyway, I told him what I felt about the place. And the "tree Spirit", as I automatically defined it.

"Tree spirit? What the hell's a 'tree spirit'?"

"It's about six foot tall and covered in leaves and filth and seems to be dark brown in color. It smells, too, of this awful rotting vegetation, like decay." I couldn't stop now, "It's awful in the bathroom. I just got out as quickly as I could. It's really, really bad. I looked in the mirror and I could see this thing staring over my shoulder, looking at my reflection."

I said I felt "It" as soon as I went in there. That "It" was a sort of odd, damp cold. I exclaimed, "There's something there!"

I elaborated that this "It" in the bathroom was more like a being of the anthropomorphic type.

"Oh, fuck me dead!" was the response I got.

Michael was horrified. Borderline furious, he proclaimed in no uncertain terms that he was not at all happy to have his holiday spoilt in this way. Furthermore, why wasn't I like every other wife coming on holiday? Yada, yada, yada ... And why did he have to end up with a wife who picked up ghosts and ghouls when he could have married a "normal woman?" A secretary or nurse or something. Perhaps even a lawyer who made pots of money. In fact;

"Any normal woman."

And so on and so on. I let him run with the flow, until his anger assuaged by exhaustion and the need for sleep meant the flow stopped, and he finally ordered,

"Switch off the damn light!"

Which I wouldn't. So we slept through the night with the light on. Luckily, the wattage was low.

The next day we were out and about, joyously whizzing through the Umbrian countryside in our little car, stopping off at villages and walking cobbled streets and visiting churches and shops, generally doing holiday things and eating a bit too much. When we arrived back late at night after supper, sleeping was achieved in fits and starts with the light being switched on and off as Mike slept and I switched it on, and he woke and switched it off. This became pretty much the routine for a day or so, and was only broken when Anna and Rudy invited us for a late supper in their place. Forgoing the outside eating area with its pizza oven, Anna and Rudy instead entertained us within the confines of their neatly compact rustic kitchen. We had pasta and salad, accompanied by thin red wine that burnt slightly as you swallowed, sourced from a vineyard belonging to one of Rudy's relatives. As the evening progressed, and talk moved from life back in England and life in Italy to religion and spirituality, I mentioned that I meditated. Anna looked at me and enquired,

"Have you got down to 'alpha'?"

I must have appeared nonplussed because Anna repeated the question; actually, I wasn't sure how to respond. I knew a bit about changes in brainwaves during meditation, but I wasn't used to meditation outside the traditions of Judeo-Christianity and mainstream Buddhism and Hinduism where 'alpha' states of consciousness weren't generally referred to or even discussed. So I had no idea if I was getting down to 'alpha'.

After dessert, Anna and Rudy invited us on a tour of their house. This was not particularly memorable, save that the building was very old. But the rooms were pleasant enough with slightly worn furniture of the frayed country-chintz variety; nothing extraordinary. Until, that was, Anna opened the door to reveal her meditation room. This was quite something in that I had never seen anything like it before, the room itself being large with a sort of raised, bed-like square dais. Over this was a huge and elaborate white canopy with flowing white curtains falling to the floor on three sides. It looked almost regal, like something a queen of some sort would sit within: a kind of throne – it was extremely odd. I reflected very quickly about sitting on that dais, with the long white filmy curtains falling around me, pondering the ultimate effect. It was certainly different from sitting on a chair or in a pew or on the floor, the usual position adopted in meditation practices with which I was acquainted.

Anna offered me the use of the meditation room, and the dais, for my own meditation. She said it provided a good centre. I politely declined the invitation and, after a few moments of unrelated discussion, we exited the room. (With some relief on my part, I don't know what Mike thought.) For some reason, I guess it was the few glasses of wine that loosened my tongue, as we moved through the suite of rooms forming the villa I remarked I was "picking up images" as I touched the walls of our apartment. Anna seemed surprised. I also told her I sensed "a presence" in our apartment; notably in the bathroom. Anna went pale, and remarked they had a world-famous Indian mystic staying with them some time before who'd said the same thing. But the Indian mystic said the presence was benign. Anna added that they had a lot of other people staying in our rooms, but they hadn't noticed anything. Anna went on to say I should get some herbs and do a little 'ritual' thing. I informed her,

"I bought a cross in Assisi."

I didn't want anything to do with herbs in our rooms. I instinctively felt that messing about with herbs wasn't a healthy idea in the deep, spiritual sense of disposing of restless or negative spirits. And, as well as the cross, I had obtained some holy water from a church and, using these sacramentals, had prayed and performed an exorcism. The atmosphere still wasn't good, but it was a lot better than it had been, and I hadn't felt the pillar of filth quite so tangibly again.

Anna regaled us with a story about this renowned Sadhu. Apparently, he had an ashram people from all over the world came to visit. It was vegetarian, and there were a lot of animals. Anna remarked that the Sadhu was "amazing" and that he'd visited Assisi because of St. Francis. She also said the Sadhu could "release energy". Anna had seen him throw someone right over the top of a car. This was what he could do, just touch someone and throw them into the air. Anna thought it was incredible. I thought it was amazing too; but it didn't sound very holy – throwing someone in the air for no particular reason, you could injure them for one thing. I wondered what the point was, throwing people round like that.

Of course, I was acquainted with stories of this sort, mainly arising from our time in the Far East, and sometimes also connected with traditions of martial arts. And I was also aware of gurus who were reputed to do fakir-like tricks, such as causing piles of sand to appear in places. The sand appearances, particularly, I associated with a guru Woo had told me about. Woo found it fascinating, and this person was popular in the area we had lived in and was renowned for producing piles of sand in various locations.

Really, something about all of this and the way Anna and Rudy talked made me wary. Now I recalled the markings in various spots on the walls of our apartment, symbols of moons and stars that reminded me of ancient religions and astral cults. All rather way-out, and adding to the spiritual unease generally, because symbols, especially symbols of a spiritual kind, have a quality of being able to open up reality in that they provide foci and an opening for spiritual energy. Since the complex had a history of being attached to a larger and quite important monastery, it all seemed peculiar; holy places feel holy. They feel spiritually *good* to be in, in the sense of feeling positive, warm and evoking love, reverence and peace. In short, a sense of being in the presence of God. By contrast, this place *didn't feel spiritually good*. While I was distracted along these lines we continued the short tour and were shown into the library. Here there were books on various topics, and from a cursory glance I noticed quite a few that could be categorized as New Age. Passing through the lounge area on the way back to the kitchen, Anna showed me a small table where some interesting looking crystals were placed in a dish. Selecting one she suggested,

"Feel this." Adding, "I use the crystals for meditation purposes."

I took the proffered crystal. It didn't look particularly unusual, but there was a sort of weird energy, *rather like static*, emanating from it. I felt over a few. Each one had a slightly different resonance, a kind of *auric sensation*. (I am trying here to articulate in the best way I can a subtle phenomenon.) Anna gave me a crystal to feel that she said was "special", describing the crystal as being "part of a meteorite that fell to earth". I felt the crystal for a few seconds before replacing it, without comment, among the pile in the dish.

Conversation continued as we made our way back to the kitchen, with Mike attempting to switch the subject to everyday matters without really succeeding. Once back in the kitchen, Rudy remarked he couldn't understand the Sadhu's interest in Assisi. Rudy looked puzzled and said he "felt nothing" in Assisi. By then it was very late. Instead of coffee, we were offered some greeney liquid made from herbs to drink in rather quaint and cumbersome earthenware goblets. I wasn't fond of greeney with herbs, and neither was Mike (we don't have to discuss these sort of things having been together for yonks), and I was dubious in the extreme about all this 'herb and crystal stuff'. So we politely declined the beverage. Just as we were about to leave, Rudy again asked me about our room, referring to the remark I made about the room being haunted. I explained,

"It's in the bathroom." (The "It" of the anthropomorphic variety, that is.) And added, "It feels as if someone's buried in there."

The words sort of popped out without my thinking about them. Again, possibly the effect of the wine because, as you know, I don't usually discuss spiritual intuitions except with Michael, and not too much with him because it worries him. Anyway, to cut a long story short, there are times when I really feel one shouldn't drink; and this was turning out to be one of them.

I had had a weird vision of a man being violently murdered as if to silence him, to stop him from talking.

The intuition took the form of a dream of someone long ago being attacked by several men down in the living room area of our apartment. They'd stabbed this person in the throat while he struggled and fought desperately for his life. The assassins forced the man down on a table, which seemed to be the sort of living room table you would have dinner on. It was really terrifying, and most disturbing, because I could feel this man's horrendous terror as he fought, unsuccessfully, to save his life and fight off his aggressors.

Rudy went pale, rather as if his jaw should have dropped open. His look rounded the night off on a peculiar note.

Back in our apartment we prepared for bed. I still didn't like it in the bathroom, and Michael wouldn't go in there now after dark so I must have spooked him quite badly. I gingerly enquired,

"Don't you want to use the bathroom?"

To which he replied, "No, I brushed my teeth in the kitchenette. I'll hang on till the morning."

"But will you be alright?"

"Don't worry about me. If it gets bad I'll go out the front and find a tree."

"Oh!"

"It'll probably damage me irreparably. But I'm sure I can hang on until the morning. There's no way I'm going in that bathroom after dark, thank you very much! You've fixed that now for me, haven't you?"

I didn't feel I should say any more. But Michael wouldn't go straight to sleep as usual. Instead he harangued me for some while complaining,

"While you look okay on the outside, it's your brain I'm worried about. Thank God you've got me for a husband. No one else would put up with it."

I remained silent, but he wouldn't stop, "You're all a bit strange in your family. Good looking alright, but strange. And you're a bit too clever for your own good. Our lot are okay, normal people. Just your average normal people. We do normal things and have normal problems."

"I'm sick to death of you criticizing my family," I responded, finally fighting back. "I come from a family of very ethical and well-educated people. I'm very proud of them. Some of my relatives are brilliant, brilliant! Free thinkers and extremely religious."

"You're all bloody mad. And you all look Germanic to me; you're all Germans, if you ask me. A bit of the Kraut in all of you. Look at your brother. He could have been in the S.S. It's frightening! And your uncle looked like Gestapo too. You're lucky you've got me to stabilize the mad genes in you."

"Huh! We trace our heritage to the Low Countries," I said deliberately and proudly emphasizing the words "our heritage". "And my father's family came from around Cork, just like your family. A hundred years ago our families might have even known one another."

(That was telling him, I thought!)

But Mike got the last word in:

"Heaven help the poor buggers if they did."

That night I had the weirdest visionary type dream;

it began with music. Strange music. All taking me way, way back. To medieval times and images of villagers living in poverty, in countryside sparkling with sunshine. The music was strangely evocative, almost other worldly. It continued throughout the dream. And the colors were so vivid, they were more intense than the colors of life itself.

Then the dream became disturbing, and so I struggled to wake up. When I did, I wondered what had been going on in this ex-monastic establishment; this really was not good stuff at all. The whole place was like a time warp. I recalled another thing I had seen while wandering through an unused part of the building,

a chalice at the window, to catch the morning sun.

The dissonance again. *The atmosphere of unease, of disquiet.*

A hole blown through time: the past now present;

like a spiritual atomic bomb.

Things had happened here that shouldn't.

It was like a rift in the fabric of reality,

a gateway,

to another House of Time or reality.

I wanted to get away. Michael had a good time, he loved Umbria. But he never again wanted to see that particular holiday residence,

"Just book a nice, ordinary, hotel next time, dear. Somewhere normal so I can get some blasted sleep …"

Why should you look upon the Shullammite, as upon a dance before two armies?

The Song of Songs; esv

When we returned to England, I was stunned to see a picture of Liza (ex the club) in the newspaper. Liza had a lovely singing voice and had studied speech and drama during the years we were in South Africa. Now she was on stage in a musical, I thought this was amazing! We went to the theatre concerned when we were up in town. One of the guys in the stage office gave me Liza's telephone number, enabling me to contact her. Liza also seemed excited as we talked on the phone, and we agreed to meet outside a tube station in North London. Michael suggested we go to a nearby restaurant with a reasonable reputation.

Liza had her hair colored a vibrant red. She was very complimentary, pleased to see us and said I "looked beautiful". I returned the compliment, Liza was still Liza and she still looked wonderful, and, as we both liked compliments, (an uplifting remark on a bad day keeps the word turning) we were both happy. My appearance had improved, as I'd let my hair grow to waist length. I'd also relinquished my over indulgence in the dye bottle for health reasons, so I was near my childhood shade. Because I wanted to look nice for the meeting, I was wearing one of the designer copies I'd purchased in the Far East. All the seamstresses required was a picture taken from the catwalks of France or Italy or somewhere similar to run up something spectacular, without a pattern; brilliant really. And the garments were incredibly inexpensive. I didn't even get made-to-measure but bought off the peg as I was a small size, so that was even cheaper.

Liza was carrying a huge briefcase, which she placed on the seat beside her in the restaurant. I placed my bag on the floor near my leg, *feeling quite definitely that it was going to be stolen,* then dismissed the idea as slightly irrational, just glancing down now and then to check the bag was okay. We chatted for a while and I told Liza I'd been doing research in religion and writing, but was at a bit of a loose end otherwise, and didn't seem to know where life was taking me. Liza responded by saying the stage "didn't pay" and so she was getting by working in restaurants. She appeared depressed over this, and it came as a surprise as Liza was playing a fabulous role for a woman in a production staged in a theatre bordering the heart of London theatreland, so one would think it was very prestigious. Liza went on to tell us the sad news that she and Terry had split, and that she was going out with a new man. Then Liza said Terry had "got back into the witchcraft again" and that it had become a "heavy scene".

"Oh heavens!" I thought. It was a pause moment; a kind of "Oh!" "Um!" "Where's the exit?" kind of moment. We were taken aback but tried not to show it, having no idea that Terry was involved in the occult. It seemed bizarre.

Liza continued, saying things had got "really bad" in the relationship with Terry, and she didn't want to talk about it. There was some arrangement with Terry whereby she could phone him but he couldn't phone her. Liza said it was the only way she could handle the situation, and that Terry had a new lady friend, a very dominant personality, as Liza described her. We talked for a while about old times before I glanced down. Someone had taken my handbag. This brought our lunch to a rather quick and unfortunate conclusion.

A few days later Terry himself phoned me out of the blue, saying he had obtained my number from Liza. Terry said he was re-training as a plumber and seemed very upset over the split with Liza. He talked about the arrangement of not being able to contact Liza, and our conversation halted. Stuck for something to say, I mentioned I had a headache. Terry replied this was because he had "dropped something in the kitchen". Terry chuckled; which I didn't think was funny. I guessed what he was getting at; the witchcraft thing. I'd heard or read about sympathetic magic when I was in South Africa. Terry went on, sounding somewhat spaced out, saying he'd heard I was "very beautiful now". I asked him if he was okay, because he sounded odd. The whole thing, indeed the whole conversation, was disturbing. Terry didn't answer but asked,

"Have you still got that headache?"

I quickly changed the subject, saying things seemed a lot different in Britain to the way they used to be. Terry replied that people were disillusioned. They'd come to expect a lot, and found out their expectations hadn't been met. He chuckled again, a rather weird chuckle, and added,

"They're being got at. It's all subliminal. We're undermining the entire country. It's subliminal perception; weird, man."

I thought it was very weird. And there was something else; this guy was frightened. You could just pick it up. We talked a short while longer before I managed to get him off the phone; Terry was too strange for me. I talked to Liza again shortly after, but that was it. The conversation with Terry didn't lead me to want to contact either of them again.

We were doing very well, though we were still living in our tiny one-bedroom flat, and Michael's co-director Andrew was making Mike's life difficult, causing him increasing stress. Although Mike's job was prestigious, his salary was not terrific. Still, we lived life to the full and would take time out to liven things up, eating out with friends at the local cafes – which were good and reasonably priced – spending lazy afternoons in art galleries and, less frequently, indulging our love of theatre and the opera. On grand occasions we would head to our favorite bar at the Dorchester for a cocktail or glass of wine; this I loved! For I liked, just sometimes, to get dressed to the hilt and do something of a promenade in the European fashion, making the most of those haute-couture copies I'd purchased abroad. One night after an evening glass of Chablis at the Dorchester, we were just in time to hear Pavarotti singing "Nessun Dorma" in Hyde Park. And we stood in the rain, hand in hand, unconcerned about getting drenched, as the incredible aria reached its dramatic finale; the tenor's incomparable voice ringing out across the city of London in the dusky evening.

With such evocative intermittent intermezzos life ticked along smoothly. With me writing away and meeting up with my literary agent, my great hope for the future.

Something of a hiatus came when Laura rang out of the blue. I didn't hear much from her now, she was very busy. Laura had been appointed editor of a prestigious international publication, and was working long hours making frequent trans-Atlantic trips; that incredible energy and drive of hers. Anyway, she asked me to do something in the way of research for her as there was a major couture and fragrance launch to cover, and she had to draw on key staff. Laura knew I was interested in alternative medicine, and asked me to fill in and travel to Southampton and visit an exhibition,

"Just bring back a progamme and some bumph so Lucy, one of my staff, can be freed up to help me. With your help she can still get something out in the way of a short review."

Laura had been so good to us, I was only too happy to oblige.

After a difficult train journey I rocked up at the exhibition, which was on alternative healthcare and associated issues. Outside it was a bit sparky as a group of fundamentalist Christians were touting banners and shouting that New Age teachings were "evil". Despite this, the demonstrators seemed rather pathetic and non-aggressive and wouldn't faze anyone. Inside the hall where the exhibition was held there were stands of various kinds, some advertising health food products, others more whacky displaying items such as runes and crystals. I walked round, rather bored, noting the tarot readers and fortune tellers along the way.

I meandered aimlessly before coming to an area that was cordoned off where people were being healed by a group of spiritual healers. Here individuals of varying ages were sitting in chairs, having hands laid over the tops of their heads. The healers themselves were men and women, generally quite young, in their late twenties and early thirties; at least this seemed interesting. I paused to watch for a moment, wondering how this healing thing was supposed to work. One of the healers, a tall, heavily-set fellow, glanced across and stopped what he was doing and came over to talk. I just stood there while this man (whose name was Roger according to his name badge) expounded the wonders of this particular healing group. I'd heard the name of the group before – on the radio, I think. As he talked Roger kept prodding me on the arm, my left arm. It was extremely irritating. More than that, it was painful.

I wanted to get away. But for some strange reason I stayed; it was almost as if *I was rooted to the ground.*

One of the women healers stopped as he was talking. She also came over and joined in the conversation, which was really a monologue, with Roger discoursing on his brilliance as a healer. As he continued, I wondered about the people who were left sitting who wanted to be healed that these two had abandoned. Continuing the monologue, Roger told me he was sending out "healing vibrations" to people, and mentioned the name of a famous actress stricken with cancer.

Meanwhile, he persisted in prodding my arm. It was a burning pain. I had a strong urge to move away: again, *it seemed as if I was rooted to the ground.*

I listened for as long as I could, without being able to get a word in edgeways, with Roger becoming repetitive on the narrative of his "great healing abilities". Yada! Yada! Yada! He certainly seemed to be on an enormous ego trip. But even as I got away from him, I felt my arm again; it was sore where he had prodded it –

and that jarring sense. The intuition of spiritual dissonance, of something not being quite right, something not right about the whole thing.

I picked up a handful of leaflets to dispatch to Laura and went back to my daily routine. But things changed. Now I noticed that every so often, sometimes in the daytime, sometimes at night, I would suddenly feel that burning pain in my arm;

as if the healer was there in the flesh, prodding me again. It was so noticeable I would get the urge to clutch my arm. It was in the same place I had the childhood vaccination that nearly killed me.

And I would see the healer's face; almost as vividly as if he were standing there.

Obviously, this became disturbing. That wasn't all. I'd other problems; I had become ill. It started as thrush. Indeed, while we were abroad I'd developed a fungal infection of the fingernails which I cured myself by cutting down on sugar and lacing mineral water with lemon juice. This now recurred, so I presumed my immune system was down. I went to the doctor and was given an anti-fungal medication. This worked for a while, but when I stopped taking the drug the thrush returned. The doctor was reluctant to re-prescribe, and suggested I cut out sugar and take a pro-biotic. It was no use arguing with her; she seemed to wash her hands of the whole affair. The regimen did not work, and I became more and more ill until I found it difficult even to get out of bed. I now had a whole spectrum of symptoms, allergies and problems with my nails and digestive system. Because of all this, and especially because I wasn't digesting food properly, I began to lose weight. Having given up on my doctor, I decided to take matters into my own hands and try to solve the problem by contacting some top naturopaths, but only by telephone, so as not to incur horrendous medical bills. Luckily, I received very good advice from some excellent naturopathic practitioners, and found a lot of literature on what is called Candida, systemic thrush. Following expert advice, and taking handfuls of supplements, I eventually recovered. But it took time and at one point I was extremely sick.

It was one morning following my recovery that I was listening to the radio (I am an avid listener when doing boring household tasks like cleaning), when a spiritual healer was talking on one of the channels. My ears perked up when I heard he was attached to the group I had come across at the exhibition. He was discussing the subject of spiritual healing, about healing yourself, and the healing power "latent in every individual". Even as I listened I felt the burning pain, and reached for my arm. The burning was in the position where the healer had been jabbing me with his finger.

Something worried me about all this, so I decided to do a bit of investigative work and telephoned one of the healing group's centres in Manchester. I was put through to Malcolm, yet another healer. I told him about my experience at the exhibition and how, following this, I'd developed a serious and debilitating illness. Malcolm responded by saying Roger must have,

"Damaged your aura." Adding, "He must have been a bit rough."

I was becoming suspicious now, but explained again, "I wasn't there for healing. I didn't even request healing. I was just talking to Roger. And all he did was poke my arm. What puzzled me was that it hurt, it actually burnt."

Malcolm seemed a little embarrassed, but I didn't push him. Instead, I let him explain. He said I needed to "understand the theory". Malcolm told me about the aura.

I replied impatiently, "I've heard about the theoretical idea that all living beings possess an aura."

This didn't stop him because he expanded, "The aura forms a protective shield around the body". I nodded as I listened. I had indeed met up with someone during my time at university in South Africa who was working in the field of Kirlian photography, Kirlian photography being a technique developed in Russia in the 1920s or 1930s, sometime around then. My contact in South Africa was a top medical scientist, and his research interest was discovering methods of diagnosing disease in the aura prior to its physical manifestation. What the aura actually was, an energy or electromagnetic field, neither this South African scientist nor anybody else seemed to know at the time.

By way of explanation, Malcolm now informed me that Roger had "punctured" my aura. This sounded peculiar; and I wanted to make sure of what I was hearing, so I put the question;

"Roger damaged my aura and I became ill?"

Malcolm agreed it was "possible."

Bloody hell! There was a sinking feeling in my stomach. I thought not just of myself, but of all the other people this guy Roger had been healing; people who might have been really, really ill. But Malcolm continued unabated,

"What you need to do now," he went on insistently, "is to shop around and find a healer who understands these things and your sensitivities, and can work with you to repair the damage."

This I found a totally ridiculous and downright stupid idea; the guy must have thought me an idiot.

I responded dryly, "I am better."

But Malcolm continued, trying to persuade me to get in contact with one of "his people" to let them do some "more healing work" on me. I didn't allow the conversation to proceed any further and curtailed what he was saying and replaced the receiver.

I couldn't believe it! Malcolm actually expected me to go back for more. *The burning sensation returned.* I grasped my arm. *I could see Roger's face.* This was bloody peculiar and not at all funny; in fact, it was scary.

My thoughts turned to the actress Roger had been sending his 'vibrations' to. She had recently died.

Spiritual healers who could make you sick!

Blasted witches running round.

Heaven help us! I thought;

the world's gone mad!

What would Mum and Dad make of this?

This has got to be some sort of modern lunatic asylum.

But it got worse ...

The spiritual flood waters rising.

We would go to France for short holidays rather infrequently, sometimes by train, sometimes driving. We usually stayed in small, inexpensive hotels in Paris and its environs. Driving through the countryside of northern France past the cemeteries we would stop at the graves of soldiers from the First and Second World Wars to say a prayer, give thanks, and marvel at what they had done for us; it cost them everything so that we could be free. This made Mike and me both sad and grateful at the same time. To us, northern France was always a poignant landscape, torn by war. And, in the churches, those dark Gothic cathedrals, the statues of the mysterious and mystical warrior saint, Jean d'Arc; The Maid of Orleans ...

The vision again:

dark water rising,

a sea about to become turbulent.

I wake

to a feeling of foreboding.

A psychic came on the radio one night while I was waiting for Michael to come home. The psychic was not even in the country, but she suggested we all try to start up something that wasn't working,

"Something electronic or mechanical, a clock or wireless or something," the psychic suggested.

She would then give "the signal" and we would just press the button or whatever and see what happened. Mike and I had an electrical unit in the flat that hadn't worked for ages. I thought it sounded interesting and worth a try. I checked the unit wasn't working and then, when the psychic gave the signal, pressed again; eureka! It worked: the motor started.

Gosh this was mind-blowing, I thought. I mean, that human energy could do such amazing stuff; human energy. Imagine the possibilities ... All sorts of people rang in to say something like a watch or a clock had started ticking again. I was so gob-smacked I rang the program and informed them what had happened; I was actually elated. But only briefly, because Michael came home a few moments later, whereupon I excitedly informed him about the events that had transpired that evening. His response was totally unexpected. Michael went pale and reacted by hastily making the Sign of the Cross. He said automatically,

"Witch!"

I was really shocked; it was a sort of joke I told myself – but I didn't like it. It was horrible, I felt terrible about myself. I mean what an awful thing to say to someone who was so serious about seeking God. But Michael wasn't messing around. To explain my actions I told him it was just human "energy" and that,

"All sorts of people were ringing in." Words began to fail me as I started to think ... To tell the truth, now I was beginning not to like it at all; what had I done?

Michael went on to repeat, "It's not right. I don't want to discuss it." And added,

"It's not normal to start up a motor just by touching it."

I felt appalled, even ashamed, for some strange reason. Michael was damn right; of course! My conclusion made me feel even more wobbly. In fact, I felt more disturbed about the event the more I pondered it; I mean, the implications. Anyway, I pretended to force it out of my mind and we had supper. Yet now when I think back my heart sinks ...

Odd things continued to occur.

Strange fluctuations in my field of perception.

A little while later I picked up a mirror to paint my lips, stared into it to see;

myself? Or someone else? The impression was that someone was trying to reach out to me.

Several faces appeared, swirling in and out of view; I could see a circle of people. I couldn't believe it: it was like some sort of telepathy. I wasn't imagining it. *And I felt a distinct presence of evil,*

it was horrible.

At the same time I was meditating, pretty much on a daily basis. As I said, it didn't feel quite right anymore, which puzzled me. I used to extend my practice by maintaining an attitude of wishing happiness on all beings and all creation. This, again, is a very common technique among Buddhists, but I've also read some 'Christian' literature along similar lines. So, since I always wished well on everything and everyone, a sort of spiritual positivness by way of attitude, I couldn't really understand what I was experiencing. That feeling of

unease

which I couldn't fathom.

So, there I was. Wishing love on all creation.

You cannot imagine how dangerous this is spiritually.

So I will digress here. Beware of spiritual directors or meditation teachers of any kind or persuasion who encourage you to, "make friends with your demons". Even in a flippant manner. Evil is real. It hides behind masks and lies. One of its most alluring strategies is to take the truth, up to a point, and then subtly twist it. You climb the Spiritual Mountain and on the way you encounter the phantasm, the hand that offers the apple of subtle deception; just make friends, chase your dream of ambition, of wealth, of women or men or boys or cars. And it will be okay,

"Come this way …"

But I was not of this persuasion yet. I didn't realize how duplicitous, how hollow-souled, some of the most famed names of world mystical literature could be.

On an everyday level, Michael was having increasing problems with Andrew; this guy seemed to go out of his way to be perverse. Of course, I only too well recalled the words Andrew had spoken sotto voce, about making Michael's life "hell". I thought he must be really weird; bad news and downright nasty. As regards family, we caught up with Laura and Robert less frequently now. They were hip. Laura was incredibly, almost painfully thin, but had those lovely bones. I remember wonderful experiences, like Laura talking about being at a ball with Princess Diana where she danced next to the beautiful, but ill-fated, Princess. Later, I was at Laura's place at a party. There were a lot of people involved in the arms industry, which didn't seem too good. Anyway, in a way Laura and Robert seemed to have tired of us, so we kept a bit of a distance; Laura could be like that, you could sort of go in and out of fashion, rather like clothes. And I knew Laura was incredibly busy and I had made the faux pas of ringing her up one day about a triviality, which I regretted because it had interrupted her, so I'd probably cheesed her off. Alice and Mark were also tied up now with things in the movie world.

Anyway, despite this, life seemed to be good for all of us.

About this time Alice rang. It was difficult to get through to her as Mark was always busy with important people in LA. I remember we chatted about a lot of things, including the research I'd been doing. Alice asked me if I had, "tried witchcraft"?

I was a bit taken aback and replied, "No."

Something jarred. I also remembered one or two other incongruous remarks Alice had made; but we'd been brought up as Catholics: you didn't mess with this sort of thing.

Alice quickly changed the subject. I didn't hear much from her for a while after that.

Laura gave birth to twins, a boy and a girl. Michael was asked to be a godparent, and was very pleased. The baptism ceremony was in a little Catholic church. It was moving, and everyone was so elegantly dressed and the babies were just beautiful. I remember going round to Laura's place a while later and holding the two babes, it made me feel maternal for the first time in my life.

The voice of my beloved knocking.

Canticle of Canticles; d-rv

About that time I think, I can't be that sure because I didn't write down the date, the leaves were falling, the summer had ended and a chill wind was blowing; or so it seems now. A chill wind blowing, not only through the world but also throught my soul. Anyway, it was toward the end of the year when something happened that was only odd enough to note just then. Later, it would leave an inarticulate grief that was a wound in the soul, a stiletto thrust, invisible to the eye;

it was a vision of Alice, my sister.

The visionary image was in stark black and white. One moment it was there, another it was gone. Shot into my mind from somewhere. Like a screen image frozen from a film at a critical juncture.

(It is terrible for me even to write this.)

One minute total darkness, and then the door of the film studio thrown open to reveal Alice standing on the platform outside. Bound in bandages from head to foot like an Egyptian mummy, with only slits for her eyes and mouth.

Alice was a hostage,

she was in spiritual bondage. The mood was of utter desolation: her personality had been sucked out of her,

she had lost her soul.

Even as I write I remember my father, struggling pitifully as he drew near to death. Struggling, as if with all the available strength he could muster, to utter,

"I'm very worried about Alice."

That moment, *in time and out of time*. Again, visions have different sources; you're caught between God and the Devil. I pray for Alice always. Hopefully this was a chimera, a smokescreen, a lie. Something to deceive me. But it was a sleepless night.

Michael noticed. I just said,

"I had a dream."

Dear Alice. I was perplexed, yet it was only a dream …

A dream is a dream. That's what I told myself; that's what we're all told.

During the early months of 1991 a different sort of dream began. These were not so much visions as nightmares,

images of devils and dead people, ghosts and shadow beings that had their existence in an underworld perpetually in a state of semi-darkness.

At first I managed to dismiss the nightmares, telling myself my imagination had become disturbed. Why, I didn't know. And there were other 'dreams';

Michael and myself building our house on sand, on a beach where the tide could wash our house away was one dream that seemed important.

It was only towards March, as the nightmares became more frequent, that I grew worried. I checked literature sources on psychology and dream interpretation, but couldn't work it out. Still, the nightmares grew more disturbing, more frequent. Now I wondered if something was undermining my health. As Easter week approached the dreams were simply terrifying. These were nightmares the like of which I'd never experienced before in my life. I was visited by demons that taunted or attacked me. There were goblins and fictitious creatures inhabiting mythical worlds. There were violent dreams and sexual nightmares;

there were dreams of tarot cards being read.

In one particular dream, which had a dramatic visionary quality that was becoming more and more frequent, it was as though my consciousness was circling, watching,

tarot cards being shaken. Against black felt cloth on a table in a dark room.

(I write it as it was.)

The hands throw down a card that lands against the black felt cloth. Behind the hands is a curtain, as if whoever is reading the cards is in a room with a curtain behind where they are sitting.

I had never had a tarot reading, *but I knew that whoever was reading the cards, they were reading the cards for me.*

And the card thrown down was the fool.

The fool.

And there were terrible dreams concerning Alice. I hadn't heard from Alice for a while. But when I asked about her because I was becoming really concerned, Laura dismissed my worries nonchalantly, reassuring me Alice was "fine". It was just that she and Mark had an answering machine on their telephone day and night because Mark had important people trying to contact him. So you couldn't get through to Alice …

There was a visionary image of an angel flying over the tops of houses, painting doorposts with blood.

It was coming up to Easter,

Easter 1991.

> See! The winter is past;
> the rains are over and gone.
> Flowers appear on the earth;
> the season of singing has come,
> the cooing of doves
> is heard in our land.
>
> The Song of Songs

I was becoming more perplexed, having less and less sleep. I began to pray, convincing myself the nightmares would cease at any moment and life would revert to normal. By Wednesday of the week before Easter Sunday, I was becoming so seriously affected by fatigue I would not only pop back to bed to rest in the morning as I always did, but I also had to sleep in the afternoon in order to function at all. I was off my food and pale. Michael was worried.

On Good Friday,

I had a nightmare in which I was being attacked by demons. The nightmare washed over into reality. I woke up, fighting the demons off.

Michael enquired what was wrong. I just replied,

"Nothing. I'm okay, it's nothing."

I didn't want to worry him. But I was aware that my voice betrayed my nerves. Mike suggested he take me for a drive to the West End to cheer me up. We would often drop into Westminster cathedral when we were in the city; we liked to stop and say a prayer. This time as I walked through the doors of the cathedral I felt immediately better. The effect was startling,

I could feel there had been a darkness around me. A tangible, coal-colored blackness, a dirt that drifted away and dissipated as we entered the doorway.

We stayed in the cathedral for a short while. I lit a candle. Then we went outside. But I didn't want to leave.

We drove past the designer shops I loved. Michael was interrogating me, asking what was wrong, insisting,

"I think you ought to tell me."

So I began to tell him about the dreams. I mentioned I wondered if I was "going crazy" and suggested,

"Do you think I'm having a nervous breakdown?"

"You're not nervous," he replied in his joking fashion. (This is typical of Michael, and I knew he was doing his best to cheer us both up.) We decided to buy a thermometer. Michael thought I'd better see a doctor. I responded in a low voice thoughtfully, anxiously;

"I really feel I'm under some sort of evil attack ..."

By Easter Saturday we'd purchased the thermometer. My temperature registered normal. Yet I was now fatigued by nightmares so vivid that every time I closed my eyes the images would come;

it was like being in a cinema with a horror movie of unprecedented terror running endlessly. The images were real as life and in full technicolor. There were men and women talking. Men and women I'd never seen. And weird beings.

The nightmares now almost always had a visionary quality. I closed my eyes to see spirits floating wraith-like around the ghostly ramparts of a decaying castle. And then deformed demonic creatures would rise up against me.

I found it hard to sleep Easter Saturday night. I dozed and then got up and went back to bed again. Michael was terribly worried about me, and also slept fitfully. The atmosphere in the small flat was tense. Early morning of Easter Sunday, seeing I was back in bed following the disturbed night, Michael asked,

"Is it okay if I go for a walk? I really need to get some fresh air."

He left, and after about an hour I decided to get up and wash. As I put my foot on the floor a terrible physical weakness took hold; I could hardly walk. My legs shook and trembled. I had to push myself up with my arms and crawl to the bathroom. I just about managed to get myself into the bath to sit under the shower. Limp, apathetic from terror, I could only allow the water to wash over me. But the water didn't seem to make me clean. I prayed and began weeping.

I got out of the bath-tub and started cleaning my teeth, then suddenly threw up in the hand basin; the vomit was green bile. I couldn't believe it even as I saw it. I said aloud,

"Oh, my God; this can't be happening to me."

I thought I was having a nightmare; I'd never been physically sick like this with green stuff before in my life. Something from a horror movie I'd read about came to mind where a girl is possessed and vomits like this. Naturally, I began to panic; all I could think was that I had to survive, I prayed to God to survive! In a not so bizarre way I thought it might be a brain tumor. I managed to get dressed and even tried to paint my face to make myself look better, but my hand was shaking so much I couldn't make a good job of it. I went into the living room with a towel wrapped round my damp hair and lay on the floor, praying for Michael to come back. I felt alone and frightened. But outside it was a nice day. Through the window, fringed with pink curtains I could see sunlight;

sunlight.

It was totally, weirdly, incongruous; it was as if the world had ended, but outside everything was the same.

I tried to lie still, but my body began to writhe, to convulse; again I couldn't believe it. I repeated aloud (in an attempt to stabilize myself mentally),

"This cannot be happening. This cannot be happening."

But my body continued to writhe, to twist, to gyrate. I thought of scenes of shaman in trance I'd seen on television in programmes on anthropology: the shaman were possessed. I thought, again, it was a nightmare; at any moment I would wake up. My God,

"My body is convulsing."

In an attempt to get a handle on the situation, I spoke aloud saying,

"My body is jerking up and down without my having any control."

I couldn't believe it; it was a nightmare, but I was definitely awake.

There was a pain, a physical pain, *between my eyebrows as if waves of energy were being directed there with force.* I remembered bits of information I'd read about the pineal gland, the third eye of the mystic or psychic; sometimes you see this portrayed in icons of Christ and the saints.

Again, I attempted to analyze what was happening and spoke aloud to reassure myself. I reflected, "I'm not a bad person?" I mean, I'd never murdered anyone or done anything physically like carrying out a violent act or committing adultery. I only occasionally lied. I always tried to help people and to be loving and kind. I told myself I could stop the energy moving if I tried. So I tried, and it stopped. But it was still there; a kind of energy running round and through my body. My mind shot back to the unit in the kitchen, to odd bits of information I'd heard about the phenomenon of channeling energy. Channeling? But how would that happen? I tried to think, to rationalize, and wondered,

"Could energy be channeled *at* a person if they were receptive?" It seemed crazy. I grabbed my arm.

I could feel a terrible, unearthly chill coming from my left side. And I could see the face of the healer.

I heard the key turn in the lock of our front door, and a few seconds later Michael came into the room. I told him what had happened, and by an enormous effort – my arms had become strangely weak like the rest of my body – managed to force myself to sit up. Michael looked concerned and offered to make tea and breakfast, and we tried to talk about other things. After a cup of tea and some dry toast I managed to get myself together enough to suggest we go to church. Going into the bedroom and attempting to get ready by combing my hair, I again began to cry. It took longer than usual for me to dress, but when I was ready I followed Michael out of the flat. At this point our neighbors, a Canadian couple, emerged from the flat opposite. Realizing I looked awful I sneaked back in and shut the door. Only when I heard their footsteps descending the stairs did I emerge. I went down and walked to the car park and got into the car beside Michael.

We drove to London with a sense of impending tragedy, of despair, in the air between us. All the while I was telling myself to "calm down", to "hold on", and I kept thinking of the effect on Michael if anything happened to me. A terrible indecisiveness took hold as I considered I might be losing my sanity, and I mentally reprised key events that had unfolded over the years. Maybe, just maybe, as my sensitivity told me, there were things beyond normal vision that most people could not see.

As we walked through the doors of the cathedral I immediately felt better;

it was a feeling of being cleansed, of dirt and darkness flowing away from me, flowing behind me and away from me and out of the door.

Above, centre aisle, hung the great crucifix. I reassured myself, as I made the Sign of the Cross with fingers still damp from holy water, that I would be "okay now". A Mass was ending, people were filing past us and out, I felt better; there was hope. We prayed in the chapel of the Blessed Sacrament. But as soon as we exited the cathedral it became really bad again:

it was as if demons attacked as I passed through the doors. I could almost see a whole squad of them flying in formation through the air towards me: black things.

I touched my forehead, between my eyes, feeling the pain.

There was the stabbing in my arm, the arm inoculated with that deadly vaccine years ago when I was a child; in the same place. In the same place the healer had poked me, *burning me – as if the point of that injection was a physical or metaphysical weak point; a point where my psycho-spiritual body was vulnerable to Satanic attack.*

It was all so unbelievable, I kept trying to rationalize the situation. But, of course, I failed.

That Easter Sunday night the visions of hell really took hold. The attacks grew worse and, as dark fell, it was as if I could feel huge movements of energy coming towards me, waves of energy increasing in force,

like an ocean of energy, a great sea.

And I was terribly tired. It was about eleven o'clock when we collapsed into bed. Michael, as usual, literally passed out.

The assault began in earnest. I entered the underworld, a place that seemed to be beneath the earth and populated by evil spirits and demons. Each time as I tried to close my eyes the visions were there. I was not asleep; I merely had to close, to blink, my eyes; my entire inner world was alive.

I tried to persuade myself I was ill. I longed for sleep! It didn't stop! It was around three o'clock,

around three o'clock Easter Sunday night, 1991.

A massive bombardment of evil entities and devils began. I lay back, too weak to fight, trying to convince myself that, 'this is a hallucination, and is not really happening. It will stop; there are no such things as evil entities, everyone knows that. *But I could hear them. They had voices, insidious, taunting,*

"We've got your sister."

I lay back. This was a massive hallucination, and I was going to let it blow over me. What wasn't real couldn't hurt you.

I could hear music now. An odd instrument that seemed to be out of Middle Eastern music. Chanting and drums like some occult ceremony. A pulsing rhythm. Strange voices using my name. Only my married name, with my maiden name included. And I could feel the presence of someone amid the chanting; someone I knew but could not quite discern:

but this all had to be an illusion, I was a harmless person.

There was the sensation of my foot being rubbed. Of a cord being tugged to unleash my unconscious. That psychic cord I'd felt before which seemed to link me to Silviu that I'd disregarded. Running from my foot up through my right leg to the centre of my chest between my breasts. A psychic connection; an energy link.

"Why hadn't I heeded the warnings?" I thought. Telling myself at the same time, "This is crazy; I mean, this isn't for real. This sort of thing doesn't happen in real life."

So I let go. And as I let go so I let all of hell in. My body, my entire consciousness was swamped by evil;

a dark sea entered my soul, swirling and rushing. A filthy smoke rushing up from hell, in and up through my body until it completely filled it and then burst out through what seemed like an invisible hole in my head. I could feel lines of energy within my body being filled with this dark, Satanic energy; like energy meridians. At the same time energy centers in my body seemed to be whirling around absorbing this dirt. Energy centers, particularly along my spine, whirling in motion.

I still couldn't believe it;

and I heard voices: voices chanting my name.

I could see the doll, a doll like a voodoo doll, wrapped in bandages.

The music gained intensity. Then the music stopped;

the darkness seeped swiftly around my body, pouring and cascading. Caking against my skin, so that I could feel it as tangibly as if I was spreading dirt over and beneath my flesh. A layer of dirt encrusted around me. Then I felt what was like a stitching all round the outside of my arms and legs,

as if someone was stitching up, or had stitched up, a doll. At some point in time –

and I was now becoming that doll.

I thought, "If this be God's will?"

I was beneath that sea I had seen in the vision of the dark sea rising; I was drowning in the unconscious.

The sea was the unconscious;

becoming conscious.

The sea of evil was around me and over me. I felt thin channels of a burning energy reaching down into my legs and through my arms.

The painful sensation of my foot being rubbed increased; I was fully conscious, but in utter horror and suspension of belief.

The chanting of my full name (curiously – again) with my maiden name recommenced,

"Hannah – Ryan – Kennedy."

"Hannah – Ryan – Kennedy."

What on earth was happening? This was unreal, it was impossible.

I was buried beneath the unconscious so that I almost seemed not to exist anymore; I was in hell. The cross-like stitching continued down my arms and legs. I again thought of voodoo. And I could hear the voices, see the terrible doll; totally stitched up. The chanting stopped again. I heard the words,

"We've got her."

Who's voice? I recognized someone.

The drums stopped.

I saw a knife trace across.

It was as if I was in several places at once.

It was around three o'clock. Easter Monday morning. 1991.

A long way off? Somewhere a way off? Far or near?

I remained totally paralyzed, stricken with disbelief.

Nightmare! Delusion! Hallucination! I closed my eyes. *There was heat; a devil from hell swooped. I did not see it, I could sense it.* I told myself again and again and again and again,

"I am hallucinating."

My entire interior reality was hell. A closed in world, a shut off world where there was no life. I did not just see this, I felt it. There were vast vistas of ice.

Desolation. Loneliness. Lack. Ruin. The absence of God. A terrible aridity. The doll. My mind whirled ... an unbearable reality with no exit had closed around me; somewhere beneath this reality I still existed. But I was drowning, drowning in an underworld of the subconscious; it would not be long before it was not me.

"Save me, O God
for the waters have come up to my neck.
I sink in the miry depths,
where there is no foothold.
I have come into the deep waters;
the floods engulf me.
I am worn out calling for help;
My throat is parched.
My eyes fail,
Looking for my God."

Later, these words, and similar passages from the Psalms, would resound,

the Psalms of David;

the Psalms of our God.

But then it was sheer terror. I felt someone who looked like me, talked like me would exist; someone who had lost their freedom of will. I would be washed away, lost forever in the dark sea of nothingness. Being would become non-being, I would be in bondage; that deathly loss of human freedom: total submergence of individuality beneath the will of evil. I would be under some sort of telepathic control,

I would do whatever I was told to do.

THIS IS HOW LOVE DIES,
this is how love dies …

The Voice of Evil. Of a Satanic, black witch. Of the emissary of Satan himself.

"This is how it happens …

We will suffocate the love out of you; squeeze it out day by day. Year by year. You will never know love again. You will never feel again,

this is how love dies."

Cold. Dry. Fear.

Ice.

The voice of evil itself.

"This is how love dies. We will eat you alive. And nobody will ever know what happened to you, Hannah-Ryan-Kennedy."

And then, *"We've got your sister."*

The devils screamed. And the chanting went on. I'd had so many warnings. Why had I ignored them? Across the years. The psychic attacks, the visions, the premonitions. The vision of my soul being ripped away from me in that Druidic curse; of my father warning me,

"You must not be so proud."

"Hannah – Ryan – Kennedy." The chanting continued,

"Hannah – Ryan – Kennedy."

The angel warned me, why hadn't I paid attention? Now the flood had come. Two people grinding corn, as the New Testament says. One taken, one remaining …

Across the empty expanses a wraith-like entity floated. Something like a soul, but a soul with no shape. I opened my eyes, looking out from the sea of darkness. The knife far off, terror all around. Fear is not just within us,

fear is an entity; a thought form, an energy from hell: fear is real and evil.

A terrible smoke was writhing out of hell. It seemed as if I was tuning in to something dying in terror. As if I were aware, at an existential level, of some Satanic ceremony going on some distance away;

the smoke was terror, it was the smoke of Satan.

Fear has form, it is an energy.

I was beside myself. I prayed weakly, "Oh my God. Oh my God. Oh my God."

And writhing in the smoke, coiling from the depths of hell itself, winding its way securely around my spinal column was the serpent.

I went completely crazy. And cried out insanely like a mad woman;

"I'm going to live forever!"

(The words just came.)

I couldn't believe I'd come so close to evil. Evil: *existential evil.*

I seemed to quieten. I thought of Silviu, and cried out,

"He's stolen my soul! Oh God; he's stolen my soul!"

It just seemed horrendous, *I was in hell,*

but my body was on earth.

Michael had woken to my cries. He was exhausted himself from worry and stress, but had been trying to calm me down. *I seemed at once far away and yet close; in two worlds at once.* And I was almost shouting now,

"Oh God, he's stolen my soul!"

That was the feeling; the terrible feeling, as if my soul had been viciously ripped, eviscerated,

excised, from my body:

I had been spiritually gutted,

a fish, gutted.

And those words repeated in my mind,

"You will be in my house."

Not the House of my Father … but the House of Satan.

That was where this was taking me.

And I could hear a voice, as I had dimly before. The voice of a person confidently repeating the words,

"We've got her under telepathic control."

And the feeling of being surrounded. As if some group had been watching my movements, stalking me; psychically stalking me. And now they'd closed in for the kill,

it was unbelievable. Those faces in a mirror … and,

oh my God! Oh my God! This was absolutely horrendous, I was not even in a fight for my life; *this was a fight for my soul,* for my freedom. The freedom to think, to act, to exist as a free individual;

this was to put me in bondage forever. (There was an image that sprung to mind I cannot repeat here because it is so terrible; an image from the future and from now, and I do not want to go there –

the Abomination of Desolation.

A human being become the impossible ... the unbecome:

"When you see the appalling abomination set up where it ought not to be (let the reader understand) then those in Judea must escape to the mountains; if a man is on the housetop, he must not come down or go inside to collect anything from his house ... For in those days there will be great distress, unparalleled since God created the world, and such as will never be again." (njb.))

And later would come the words from the Book of Exodus in The Old Testament,

"I am the Lord your God, who brought you out of the House of Bondage."

That this could happen was beyond human comprehension or witness or belief, but I was aware now that it could. Still, I could not give in to evil. The conception was against the very essence of my being. But the sheer unbelievable reality was, this was actually occurring,

in the twentieth century.

I am a twentieth century woman, evil entities do not exist. Hell does not exist (or else it's a state of mind). But this was real, this was a place. The Biblical resonances didn't really strike me because I was too distraught, and my knowledge of the Bible was not really clear. Only later would I find them, those Psalms I might have read in the past but never understood. Especially the many verses relating to the spiritual floodwaters,

"Dark waters have entered my soul."

The waters of the underworld, the waters of chaos; the waters of death: the waters of hell.

I was having visions of hell – *more than that; I was actually in hell.*

A moment between moments, a moment *out of time*. A moment of realization:

I

on earth and in hell. In two places at once, between worlds and sinking; sinking fast, drowning;

drowning in the waters of death and annihilation. This was *the Biblical Flood:*

floods on the land, floods in the psyche. The psyche of humanity erupting under the cosmic force of evil. Human evil, ontological evil … tearing apart … rupturing … floods and fires and earthquakes …

And then there came the voice,

calm,

angelic,

telling me to,

"Call on the mercy of God."

Many waters cannot quench love; rivers cannot wash it away.

The Song of Songs

I can't remember how I endured the remainder of that night; but endure it I did. When I rose I was still seeing the terrible visions,

vistas of ice with the destroyed souls lost there. The sense of eternity opened up. I was swooping over cavernous ranges of ice; mountains, valleys and landscapes of ice frozen eternally ... and unending, ceaseless despair ... the landscape of the forever lost.

I managed to get up. Michael had gone into the sitting room, distraught with anxiety. I remember looking in the mirror, seeing myself disheveled, my hair strewn and tangled, stuck to my cheeks in places with tears and sweat. And I again heard a small voice. This time the angelic words were,

"You will be a witness to the truth."

Truth! Yet now there was confusion, disbelief even. I was trying to pull myself together, to resist being submerged; swallowed alive,

Jonah in the Whale.

I was in the belly of *the Whale of the Unconscious*, of the Sea of Evil. And all I could manage was to wander the tiny apartment in a state of utter desperation and despair. I had a small cross my father had left me, one of the few things I had from him after he died. It was made of cheap metal, a gold cross on a black background. My father had kept the cross on his key ring, and I now held it pressed firmly to my forehead, at the area between my eyebrows. It helped deflect to some extent the ferocious waves of energy engulfing me. The feeling was so penetrating that the area between my eyes was one of intense, almost excruciating pain; something akin to nerve pain, an agony.

I recalled a favorite picture that we used to put up sometimes in the flat. It was a photograph that had become precious to us, a photograph Michael had taken of the stern of a boat, a vessel called the *Golden Apples of the Sun*. The name of the boat was on the stern with a clearly readable section from W. B. Yeats' poem, the *Song of Wandering Aengus*. It is taken from Yeats' collection of 1899, *The Wind among the Reeds*. And the poem runs –

"Though I am old with wandering
Through hollow lands and hilly lands,
I will find out where she has gone,
And kiss her lips and take her hands;
And walk among long dappled grass,
And pluck till time and times are done
The silver apples of the moon,
The golden apples of the sun."

This poem had become special for us; an evocative image, so we had the photograph of the boat framed. But my God! Now it had this terrible, incredible, and totally horrific resonance; the connotation of the loss of self: as if something terrible can happen to people; something far worse than physical death.

"Where has she gone?"

Those plaintive words;

the loss of free will.

What would become of me? Where would I go? Who was I becoming or turning into?

I was being washed away beneath the ocean of my own iniquity.

Did this happen to other people out there? Did they know? Or did they somehow suddenly subtly change? Have a total breakdown? Go mad? Just become ever so subtly evil?

Or commit suicide?

Totally unexpectedly?

Was it like this for others? Or did I just experience it in a very profound existential way? Did others experience it differently, so cut off are we from our real natures, our real selves as spiritual beings, not merely physical beings? These are questions that ran through my head; then. Even today,

the questions don't stop.

I thought, knew! That if I was taken to a psychiatric institution they would sedate me, but the torrent would be so powerful I would at some point suicide. So that was not the way to go –

I had the strong sense of a suicide cult.

Something I'd never heard of … Something I have never heard of.

So what was I to do? I was in a quandary.

I just knew I was under intense spiritual attack. I also knew I was on a knife edge. Which way to go? The problem was I was now so traumatized I was having difficulty stringing a sentence together.

I couldn't handle long delays and explanations on telephone lines with people who might think I was unhinged and slam the phone down,

what to do?

So I got Michael to ring the Anglican Church. It took quite a while before he got through to the right person, and I thought I would go mad with anxiety as he was transferred from one person to another, in the usual type of telephone phone-tag delay. I don't quite know why I chose the Anglican Church, the obvious thing would have been to contact the Catholic Church. But I guess my experience years back of trying to talk to that Catholic priest played into it, and I knew I needed to receive Holy Communion; the body and the blood of Christ. I knew only Christ himself could get me out of this, though I couldn't articulate it; this was evil, existential evil. Who else could deliver me from hell,

except the Son of God?

The faith buried in a tomb, a tomb of my conditioning of denial and secularization.

So I hung on.

The terrible visions continued.

Easter Monday, 1991.

It was also April Fools' Day –

April Fools' Day! I recalled the negative vision of the fool. It was me in the vision, that was the sense of the vision at the time; and it had happened. I, as the fool of the occult tarot, the vision had been a reality; more than reality. Real time: I had picked up an evil prophecy from the landscape of consciousness;

it was as if a pit had been dug.

A pit. And yet another memory, a memory of one of those strange quasi-visionary poems of my youth. A few lines of which I recall inaccurately, because I have yet to retrieve the short manuscript from amongst our stored belongings. The poem runs,

"Stay! From the pit he cried,
for I am tired and cannot climb
These slippery walls.
Whose sides enclose my being:
Stay do not pass unseeing!
Your laughter is my tears …"

The fool … the pit … the tarot …

My mind raced …

The tarot? Jung was interested in it, but what I was discovering, yet did not realize at that point, is that consciousness is better understood in terms of

a landscape.

And that the division of conscious/unconscious is a heuristic construction with no ultimate reality in any sense whatsoever. A hypothetical construct which has probably done more to obfuscate our understanding of the nature of our own souls, our psycho-physical being, than to illuminate that understanding. But I was still in horror then, so much so that I continued to find it difficult to believe what was happening.

The Anglican centre Michael contacted told him they would send a priest, but the priest was currently conducting a funeral. So it would be a while. Michael was having difficulty now in maintaining his composure, and was nearing tears. When an hour or so had passed Mike called the Anglican centre again, his voice increasingly unsteady. He was once again reassured that,

"A priest is on the way."

Hours ticked past, during which I felt a little as if I was drifting in time,

drowning and rising as the currents of energy came in waves.

Michael paced the flat, made tea, wandered in and out of the lounge and then, as we sat together, just held my free hand in his. Speaking gently and trying to reassure me, his voice almost cracking, repeating several times over the space of the hours,

"Hang on. Please hang on. You know how much I love you ... I don't know what I'd do without you."

At times he would loosen his grip a little and just sit with his head in his hands, not knowing quite what else to do. It was just a few brief hours, yet seemingly endless. Eventually the doorbell rang. I still had the little cross glued to my forehead, my hand perspiring, holding it fixed and steady. I felt I could drown at any point; that it was touch and go. Michael answered the door and welcomed the priest before bringing him into the sitting room. As he did so I rose shakily from my chair.

Canon John.

A tall, well-built man in late middle-age stood in front of me. He was dressed in somber black robes and had a large, black satchel slung over one shoulder. Relief swept through me, through Michael, and through the apartment. This was salvation come to our house and I was going to get out of this horrific, this unimaginably terrifying situation –

I could feel this man; this priest was surrounded by a sphere of light. It was quite tangible.

Again, most people refer to this as an aura, which my dictionary defines as a subtle emanation proceeding from a body and surrounding it as an atmosphere. *But to me it felt and seemed more like the perimeter of his soul; this priest felt holy.* I, on the other hand, felt really *dirty*. So it was a wonderful and uplifting experience and a terrible and diminishing experience at the same time;

I was spiritually polluted: dirty.

We sat down. Canon John was calm as a rock. He appeared concerned and compassionate, yet not the least disconcerted to see me looking a total mess – and desperately intense – with my hand pressing my father's cross to my temple in an attempt to assuage the energy waves; as if he saw this sort of thing every day of the week. Because the Canon felt *clean, holy*, I wanted to cling to him. Of course, I didn't. I just sat down across from him. He announced calmly,

"I've brought communion," and requested of Michael, "Could you possibly set up a small table so that I can put the vessels on it and conduct the Eucharist?"

Michael looked round and found a footstool that could be converted into an altar; and I felt a momentary twinge of embarrassment that we didn't even possess a coffee table. Mike then placed the footstool in front of the Canon. As he did so, John drew out a cloth of plain white linen from his satchel and placed it over the top of the footstool. Then he took out a black rectangular box, made of what looked like leather, from which he extracted a plain silver paten and a rather beautiful chalice, also of silver but with delicate filigree work. The Canon placed the paten and the chalice on the improvised altar.

"We will need some water", he said, looking round.

The very way he spoke, the calmness, the sense of the holy in the way he handled the chalice and the paten and the cloth; and, indeed, the way he handled himself; his self-composure and kind demeanor, was grounding; calming and stabilizing. The Canon took a small crucifix from his satchel, placing this also on the improvised altar. Meanwhile, Michael dutifully went into the kitchen, and I heard the tap run. He returned with our best cream jug full of water. The Canon took the jug and poured the water into a small silver container before placing it on the altar. I was sitting on one sofa, while Canon John sat on the sofa adjacent. Michael stood, but when the Canon requested of me, "So. Tell me the story". Mike sat down next to me.

I didn't look at Mike. Instead, with my eyes fixed on the comforting sight of the altar and the saintly Canon, I related a potted history-cum-confession. Bits of my whole life, with as many details of my time at the club and the university and other events I felt were relevant. The fact that this priest felt like a walking church helped defuse the situation; which was one of me in a sort of existential agony, *between worlds*, rocking back and forth, and Michael relieved but spaced out and confused, as if he couldn't take it all in.

As I finished, the Canon produced two small prayer books, handing one to Michael and the other to me,

"So that you can follow the service," he explained. "It begins on page 119 where you will find the confession."

The Communion began with the words I now know so well,

"The Lord be with you."

To which we responded, "And also with you."

So began the confessional prayer. As it finished the Canon pronounced a General Absolution on both of us. The form of the service was almost exactly as I remembered it in the Catholic Church of my youth; the familiarity, the beauty of the liturgy came flooding back;

as if I had never really forgotten.

Missa Solemnis

The priest as Elijah. But something greater than Elijah is here. The priest brings fire to the earth.

Teshuvah; repentance. The most wonderful feeling as the burial bindings fall away, and you walk out into the light. And the soul that is the crystal castle of Teresa of Ávila ignites, coruscates, in divine energy. As through the veil torn we stand both here, and there. In time. And in eternity. We see, for the first time; we really, really see,

who and what we are meant to be. We enter, on this earth, the Kingdom of God,

the Kingdom of the free.

That is the Resurrection. And the way (and the early Christians were known as the people of the Way),

the Way is through repentance.

Every Mass is Missa Solemnis.

To whom, then, will you compare God? What image will you compare him to?

The prophet Isaiah

So the Mass was said. In our little flat. A moment in time, and forever in eternity. And there was the sense of the coming of the holy; of God. And of the coming of forgiveness and redemption;

Easter: Christ Risen.

I took the bread and then the wine, the body and blood of Christ.

And the darkness was literally driven out as I did so. The devilish screeches and screams driven out, silenced, by this incredible inflowing holiness. This unbelievable spiritual fire that could not be stopped. I seemed to be – right then witnessing – the Resurrection. I felt the serpent untangling from my spine, the stitching all coming apart.

Canon John asked me to drink the remaining wine from the chalice,

and far off I heard the sound of shattering glass; of glasses, or containers, shattering ... as demons were released ... something I cannot properly articulate, and have never understood.

At that exact point the telephone rang. The time was near four in the afternoon, Easter Monday, 1991. Canon John told Michael to answer the call. Michael picked up the telephone, and seemed uncertain; it was Terry. Michael held the telephone receiver tentatively as he spoke Terry's name, as if he was unsure of what to do.

I quickly uttered, "Terry was the guy I told you was supposed to be a witch."

I was numb. It was, of course, months since I'd heard from Terry! Now, I felt I'd come under Satanic attack and had *somehow tuned in to some sort of Satanic rite*. The events of the previous night flashed back, still horrifically vivid. The Canon told Michael to cut Terry off, and Michael made an excuse by saying I was "busy" and replaced the receiver.

I haven't heard from Terry since.

"I felt I'd had my soul ripped out," I told the Canon. My voice was weak.

"They can't do that."

(He knew! He somehow knew; how?) He handed me the times of the Eucharist at his church, adding that he would telephone later to ensure I was okay. The Canon had a group of prayerful people he said he would ask to pray for me. St. Aidan's, Canon John's church, was little more than a stone's throw away, so it was all amazing. This priest was one of the Church of England's specialists in the Ministry of Deliverance, and he was right on our doorstep. (I learnt later there were only a handful of specialists in exorcism in the Church of England in the United Kingdom; perhaps seven or eight.)

"What's important now is to get your spiritual defenses up," the Canon said, looking at the cross, which I now held in my hand.

"It's my father's," I explained, reluctantly allowing the cross to pass from my fingers into the palm of his outstretched hand.

Canon John took the cross, closed his fist around it, and shut his eyes. He had a round, rather chubby face; a strong face, but kind and sincere, the face of a man of deep compassion; the face of a saint. He rubbed his fingers over the metal, still with his eyes tight shut; just the way I sometimes touched things. And I knew he was *feeling the holiness.*

Touching an icon, feeling *the sense of the holy, of purity and love;*

an opening to the infinite Good. After a few moments he handed the cross back to me. I took it, and we talked about how I felt some sort of occult group were involved. I didn't express the feeling that it was a *suicide cult,* it seemed too weird. But, as we were talking, the Canon remarked that he was worried about the suicides in the area, especially over the Easter period. (I later heard him mention one local woman who had thrown herself in the river around this time. John seemed particularly troubled, and his brow furrowed when he mentioned the death and the woman's name. Yet her name, often quite unexpectedly, comes back to me on occasion. And I wonder and pray for her. And perhaps for many others; and for all of us. Because in primitive societies suicides are often connected with sorcery; with witchcraft of all kinds.)

"It feels like I've been targeted."

I thought this sounded pathetic. But the Canon responded showing no surprise and without emotion,

"They probably wanted you dancing at one of their ceremonies."

Oh my God! Yet really this explanation didn't even register, I was far too relieved to express horror, disgust or feel sick or anything else; it was all too much for me to take in – I was numb from a kind of spiritual after-shock. As I said, the experience had been almost as if an attempt had been made *to spiritually 'gut' me.* The sensitivity was exactly that. Yet this experience was far more horrible than any sort of physical gutting; unbelievable though this might sound: it was incredibly terrible, a concerted attack on my psyche; my mind, my body,

my soul.

So as to rip out my entire spiritual persona and replace it with something else, or to make it feel so much like that that you would cease to exist in reality as an autonomous individual,

because of the fear.

That unbelievable; horrendous – fear.

I found this almost incomprehensible. Yet I'd heard so many things about primitive or pagan spirituality over the years. Trying to make sense of this now, the terrible ethos of the pagan, my mind sifted through my life and experience. Of course, this was all easier to understand in regard to so-called primitive cultures, because I'd heard stories from actual witnesses. But more difficult in a country such as Great Britain where the ritual murders, the human and animal sacrifices, the stories of the Wicker Men and possible Peat Bog murders in Celtic pagan cultures such as Druidism, were more problematic to verify. Just stories. Though sometimes suggested by archeological finds. These are oral cultures, remember, possessing no written history. And the ceremonies are often secret; you wouldn't want to keep a record of ritualized terror, especially if you wished to resurrect it or perpetuate it. So I just intuited: an ethos of the past resurrecting in modernity like a nightmare vision of the future; entire civilizations moving backward into Satanic bondage: the doll, the stitching, the spells. The power of the occult tapping into the subconscious, which has now been marginalized. Augury of the future, dressed up and prettified for sale to modern people out of touch with their psyches and souls. Mass marketed to individuals who have largely forgotten what life was like for those outside the freedom brought by the Jews and taken up by Christians. Messianic peoples – hated by everyone – because they gave us the One who would save us from our sins. This all flashed through my mind,

rather like shattered glass re-aligning, a kaleidoscope reforming a picture of reality;

what life might be like for that terrified girl I met at the magazine shoot; for people I'd heard missionaries talk about, in absolute terror of the witchdoctor or the shaman. But again, we don't have those do we? Witchdoctors, I mean. Or have they just been re-named? You can't sell death unless it's sanitized,

and that sense of being gutted?

To exist in such a state would have been worse than being one of the walking dead. The reality of this hit so deeply that for many, many years after if someone used the term 'gutted' the memory of the experience would flash back to me, so that I would feel physically sick, and sometimes would have to leave the place or room where the remark was made; to escape. The horrendous nature of this aspect of the attack I didn't discuss with anyone except Mike, and I don't think he really understood; of course not. No-one could understand, except someone who'd been there. This was just too unbelievably terrifying and evil to describe. How can you describe the indescribable? This was evil beyond anything I'd ever heard anyone talk about! Then. Or now. The thought that there was even a possibility that human beings could become involved in this sort of thing left me mind-blown: what had humanity come to? Descended to?

And there is more; but of that I cannot say, because the scenario was only revealed,

almost vision like. Of a truth so terrible, and lies so obfuscating. And of histories re-written ... and that might never have been.

But I am going to write something now that is entirely for you, my reader, to wrestle with because I find it difficult to come to terms with. I know that if you turned to God with all your heart you would get out of the situation. But I tried later to figure out how you would survive if you succumbed to such an attack. The only thing I could come up with was that you would have to block out the entire experience; you couldn't consciously face such an event. To survive, you would have to cut off part of your psyche. Of course, this would make you in the end unstable mentally and spiritually. You might, alternatively, become more and more cut-off psychologically as the inner psychic struggle continued. You might have to be medicated. An illness might be diagnosed. You might remain quasi-catatonic. One of those classified as severely mentally ill, who just don't react. Perhaps you would exist in an eternally mentally paralyzed state, with never-ending voices in your mind, in unceasing struggle against the constant chatter of the underworld,

but no one would ever believe you when you tried to explain.

And into the past ...

Other questions for you: how did 'Christians' count stitches as they knitted while the heads of fellow Christians fell on the scaffold in the terror of the French Revolution? How did 'Christians' turn their backs when dissenters were murdered in cold blood in the Inquisition on the order of Popes and rulers? How did the European wars of religion happen with 'Christians' murdering fellow Christians? How did some German Christians throw Jews and others into ovens? And on. And on. A Christian might be a soldier defending his country, or be forced to defend land and family. But to kill in the name of Christ? Or an ideology? You cannot do evil and call yourself, or be, a Christian; because you cannot break the Covenant –

but you can if you have been Satanized. Drowned. Spiritually gutted.

This scenario equates to a situation of human bondage with cataclysmic implications. Because if a person didn't become recognizably mentally unstable, then they might do terrible things and revert back to living totally normally, never quite acknowledging why they did these things; even if – and when – they were confronted with the facts. They would be in a sort of permanent existential denial of the horror and of their own evil; they couldn't go there. They would just cut off that part of their consciousness. Effectively, they would be nothing more than a puppet not ever quite knowing who, or what, was pulling their strings;

bondage. To a power group; an ideology, a belief system, a charismatic leader, a tribe perhaps. But ultimately, to Satan.

But I had survived! It was a lesson I learned: the whole world could turn against you, but God will never let you down. Faith in Christ is the most wonderful gift you can bestow on anyone. But to even attempt to take away faith, or erode it, is a most terrible thing because this opens a person up to human bondage.

All these things seemed to whirl through my mind, and so I was overwhelmed;

I was like dust. In a whirlwind. In the sandstorms of time. And only later would I realize,

God had intervened yet again.

Canon John was the right person in the right place at the right time. Not only was he a specialist in the area of spiritual attack, he was also a Greek scholar who'd taught at a seminary after spending time as a monk. I asked the Canon if I'd been "possessed". Obviously, I found the thought both horrifying and terrifying. He replied that if I had been possessed I would have tried to get away from him. He described it as a spiritual or (more narrowly and less accurately) "psychic attack". Canon John added that the Church of England had strict rules for carrying out an exorcism, and that a Bishop had to give his consent for this to be done. The Canon's position, anyway, was that the Eucharist itself is the greatest exorcism; the presence of God;

a presence evil can never withstand.

What I couldn't articulate; what puzzles me to this day, was the sheer level of the attack, the incredible ferocity. And as *a thief in the night.*

Every Eucharist is Missa Solemnis.

"I think you should go for a walk. Get out into the fresh air." John concluded before saying goodbye.

So the Canon left us together in that small flat,

with the atmosphere changed from oppression to light.

Easter,

the Year of Our Lord, 1991.

The Easter the brainwashing stopped working. I was thirty-nine years old the night of my death. Thirty-nine years old when I really began to live.

And that is how I will stay. Thirty-nine, in a way, perhaps forever. For all eternity.

39 I will stay.

"The battle for which you were born."

Canon John speaking: 1991/92

People forever gone. Lost even in the landscape of this life. People who become shadows of the babes they were in the cradle; shades of the golem, of the zombie. Not in any fictional trash that makes millions for its author, with a bit of ghoul and blood and depraved sexuality. On the film screen or made up.

What happens to people?

"Where have they gone?"

Perhaps they have switched off, or been switched off.

Then they can no longer care, it doesn't matter anymore.

And the music of the mindscape changed. Now I would wake to hear, within my soul, the voice of the Holy Spirit singing the songs of the Holy Spirit. Moving me out of darkness into a new light. The voices of Christian saints and mystics spinning songs of starlight. Even as I had negative visions those voices would sing out; in my sleep, in my dreams, at times of spiritual warfare. Out across the landscape of infinity. Singing the songs of love in the end-time. "Sweet Sacrament divine", "Be Thou My Vision", "My Song Is Love Unknown", the songs of Christians, of angel voices singing within, reassuring me not to fear, the darkness would dim

to become light.

The Christian Church in England, in legend at least, traces its origin to the arrival of Joseph of Arimathea not long after the resurrection of Jesus. So some conclude the English Church predates the Church of Rome. William Blake's lyrics to *Jerusalem* remind us of the legend that Jesus accompanied Joseph of Arimathea on journeys to England. Whether this is true or not, Christianity reached England before or around the second century A.D. However, the English Church always existed in slight tension with its Roman sister. Intimations of the Reformation came in England when the Bible was translated into English in the fourteenth century, so that ordinary people could read it. With the Reformation, the Church in England took a stance broadly between Protestantism and Catholicism. The Thirty-Nine Articles accepted the Apostolic succession and creeds, and proclaimed the presence of the Risen Christ in the Eucharist. The Articles of Faith insisted the chalice be administered to both priests and laity (in the Roman tradition laity did not receive the blood of Christ, something I found deeply disturbing following my experience, because this is a direct ordinance from Christ). Priests could be celibate or married men with stable families, in line with Biblical teaching. With nuances, the Church of England has established a certain unity and diversity within the parameters of the Apostolic Tradition as set down in the 39 Articles.

Of course, I radically reoriented my life and my spirituality. Out went the farce about hell not existing. Out went the Buddhist concept of existential evil as something within the ability of the human being to overcome by the power of their own 'innate goodness'. I, in a feeble way, could now understand when reading some of the passages of the New Testament, why Christ appeared almost distraught at times; he was simply trying to wake people up!

Right back mainstream came the Judeo-Christian view of spiritual purity and the Christian vision of Christ. It was a 360-degree turn round. Years and years of research and reading, and listening to all sorts of thinkers and ideologies and religious beliefs went out the window, *where I felt at points was exactly where I was supposed to have ended up.* It is impossible to describe how mind-blowing it was to confront the reality of hell, and the far more mysterious

– and incredible – power of God. Now, realizing what their fate could be, I found it easy to pray for the most terrible of criminals, the most evil people; because the end of anyone headed for hell is way beyond human comprehension. I also realized that you can't ultimately judge anybody, because in the end you don't want to be judged. Hell as a horror movie was one thing, hell in reality was far, far worse. It was more real and with no exit. The experience was intensely more desperately awful than anything you could project in images, and impacted at every level of the psyche,

physical, mental and spiritual.

At times, I wondered how I would ever recover from the impact of these experiences. So, whereas I'd previously discounted visions and dreams and the odd, rare voice or intimation, I learned now to take note of them and not to split consciousness into an arbitrary divide of conscious/unconscious. I also learned that you cannot easily discern where these experiences are coming from; from God, from your own imagination, or from the Realm of Evil in all its dimensions. So you have to be careful – which is very important for you, my reader, in making up your own mind about some of the visions later in the book, which I included for a purpose – and only after and with much prayer.

But the truth of the Resurrection cannot be denied:

Christ is risen.

More telling, ultimately, than visions and voices is their effect on the life of the individual; the development in the soul of a gentle, loving nature, together with a lack of attachment in a negative sense to the things of this world, the "Nada" of John of the Cross; nothing, nothing, nothing:

you want nothing in the way of wealth or fame or power or any other worldly trappings.

Still, it was the premonitions that proved particularly problematic. Moreover, I've never felt comfortable using the word 'premonition' because it can have connotations of the New Age and the occult, something I feel to be grossly misleading. I couldn't burden the Canon with all of these spiritual insights, because they were too numerous. The problem with the prophetic element was that I felt I couldn't use the word 'prophetic' because I sensed it would make me appear spiritually proud. And I well recalled the vision of my father warning me about pride …

I realized, early on, how peculiar this all was; Judeo-Christian spirituality has been undermined to such a degree that for a Christian to employ the word prophecy – in the sense of the discernment of future events – could well render them to be seen as being on an ego trip, except in charismatic and Pentecostal churches. Yet prophecy in Biblical teaching is a recognized gift of the Holy Spirit, as are other more widely-accepted charismatic gifts such as teaching, various forms of ministry, and healing. As such, prophecy and other gifts are meant to be shared, with discernment, by the Christian community as a manifestation of the life of the Spirit in the Church as the Body of Christ. Christianity, in this sense, seems to me to have become a muffled voice, a low flame. But perhaps, hopefully, a low flame about to blaze.

John profoundly appreciated that the nightmare visions of hell had taken their toll, his explanation being I had "opened up" on a "low level" of reality. His role became that of helping me maintain a steadier spiritual course, primarily by encouraging me to attune my focus at all times to God; the essential and core emphasis of what has come to be termed 'Christian spiritual direction'. Negative, even catastrophic, spiritual experiences in the vein of prophecy I would pray about, because it seems future visions of a negative nature can be prevented by repentance, prayer and turning to God for help at an individual or collective level.

I remember one seemingly minor vision at the time involved me walking into a glass window. The glass smashed all over me.

I was asleep at the time.

I woke, *again feeling the sense of a curse.*

And I actually did walk into a floor to ceiling window which I didn't see, and which nearly smashed over me a while later. The glass shimmied at the force of my impact, and the remembrance of the vision flashed through my mind; with a concomitant sense of deliverance by God. This particular vision recurred a short time later, and a similar thing happened in real life. Other things like this occurred, but description of them would cause me to digress. Some visions of this type happened, others seemed more problematic, and some did not happen.

And so I would pray for extended periods, moving away from my previous life of meditation to a life of prayer and study; particularly study of the Bible, which now became a template for judging experiences. I developed an overwhelming devotion to the Mass. In this way, today, I am always waiting on God, together with many other Christians the world over,

waiting on the Mass,

living in the Presence.

Listening to the silence beyond the words of the ritual.

Listening to God.

If you want to change yourself, and to change the world, who better to turn to than the God who made the world?

And now, also, I felt anguish for all the years I had been away. So the words of Saint Augustine of Hippo resounded deeply, constantly,

"Belatedly I loved thee."

After Mass in our flat that Easter Monday, Michael and I did go for a walk as John had suggested. Strolling subdued, Michael was stressed and quiet. This is the twentieth century; people don't have visions of hell! So it was all incredible for us both. Yet I realized how blessed I was to have Michael, our meeting itself yet another of those 'chance or coincidental' events (if you want to put it that way). Christmas Eve all those years ago, my gift from the Lord with the help of the intercession of Our Lady. Still, it was all too much for Mike, so much so that he made the comment,

"I would give my life for you, but I couldn't take on those visions of hell."

That evening passed quietly and I slept better, if fitfully. The following day two white doves fluttered down onto our window sill and walked around. I watched them with a sense of awe at the mysterious nature of reality, of our existence; of the way realities coincide; signs and symbols and dreams and wonders. The doves reappeared each day for a period of time, and then came regularly for at least two or three years. (I don't recall them ever appearing before my traumatic conversion experience.) Two doves, one for each of us; symbols of the Holy Ghost, linked to miraculous events such as the Baptism of Jesus in the Jordan, when the Spirit descended in the form, or like, a dove.

We were free! Mike. And me.

"For wisdom is better than rubies ..."

Still I was under attack. Such miraculous happenings seem for me to come at a cost.

That Tuesday, while wide awake,

I felt enormous waves of energy, like an ocean of energy. I could see the outline of my soul at one point. It was a few feet away from my body, like a protective sheath. I could see imprinted on my soul a sort of seal; an ancient seal. It was the face of Christ himself imprinted in several places on my soul. Again, a few feet away from me, as if my soul extended like a huge protective halo or bubble. At one point when all this was happening, I could hear what sounded like steel upon steel. And I could just see, at the periphery of my vision, angels fighting over my soul.

I found it incredibly difficult to accept what was happening, even as it was happening; it was as if my mind was totally blown away. I became agitated about it all *and an angel fighting for me remarked, quite cheerfully,* (I couldn't see the angel properly)

"Don't worry, there are more of us than them."

This was obviously meant to be reassuring! But the impact of it all, of worlds colliding around me, was staggering. *It was as if I was moving between worlds,* so at times everything seemed topsy-turvy. I also thought afterwards that it was rather curious; I mean,

why swords?

The Canon arrived later, and took me to a local church a few miles away where he was preaching. The next day I slept late. At just past eleven in the morning lying in bed,

I felt this massive bolt of energy hit the centre of my skull, and shoot down through my body, then down the middle of my right leg and out of the sole of my foot. The energy seemed to blast out and down under the earth, as if heading for the source of the psychic link that had connected me to Silviu.

I was mind-blown again. Every time I seemed to get my head right I was knocked back by something incredible; angels fighting over my soul, and now bolts of energy hitting me. Again, it was as if I was at the centre of a spiritual whirlwind; a vortex.

Meeting up later with John, I recounted the episode of 'the bolt of energy', unsure of how he would react; I shouldn't have worried. After all the years of coping with visionary experiences by sublimation, I had discovered someone who was completely at ease dealing with them. Anyway, hearing my description of the bolt, the Canon reacted as if this sort of thing was not to be worried about in the least, while making the point, in an off-hand way, that the congregation had prayed for me at the eleven o'clock Eucharist at St. Aidan's. (Which, of course, was the time the bolt of energy hit.) The power of prayer from authentic individuals became illuminatingly, strikingly apparent; and undeniable. The Canon added, calmly and thoughtfully,

"The 'opposition' has received a justified bolt of fire from heaven."

So that was that, the psychic connection with the professor had been more than cut; he had been blasted.

I enquired, "How does this witchcraft thing start then?"

"Usually it's with a gift," the Canon replied. And we left it there. For me to ponder. Actually, it rather put me off being given gifts, which is sad really.

I went to Mass as often as I could. The visionary experiences continued, but were more manageable. For instance, I would still get horrifying glimpses of hell. Just glimpses, but that was enough. And usually while I was sleeping. Understandably, at that point I had an absolute terror of hell, but as my spiritual life calmed the routine of interviews with John on a weekly basis moved to a bi-weekly meeting. This continued for a period of several months before things settled even more, and we would then only catch up occasionally, usually when I was experiencing something difficult. The Canon was a brilliant spiritual tactician, with a grasp of psychology that enabled him to diffuse many of the powerful Satanic illusions demonic forces would manifest in an attempt to destabilize the human spirit and psyche. As armor, he encouraged me to read the Psalms, and taught me to utilize certain techniques of prayer when I felt under spiritual attack. I learned, for instance, simple routines of returning mentally to favorite childhood hymns, allowing the remembrance of the words and the lovely, old melodies to stir up happy and reassuring times. I focused paramountly on uplifting tunes, because I found these particularly stabilizing. One of Canon John's chosen prayers of protection was the "St. Patrick's Breastplate". This is an ancient prayer attributed to St. Patrick, but which I now associate very much with John. He used "The Breastplate" when he was called out to a spiritually disturbed situation, such as a house that was haunted. The Canon gave me a copy of the prayer in a little hymn book which I still possess. Other techniques of prayer, such as the 'Encircling' prayers, were borrowed from the Celtic saints. With this form of prayer you invoke the protection of the Trinity, the Father, the Son or the Holy Spirit; or all three – using your finger to trace a circle around you the span of your soul. In doing this, you reinforce a sense of the holy; you remember who and what you are, a child of God, a son or daughter of light.

Above all, John encouraged me to attend Mass daily, and to make private confession on a weekly or bi-weekly basis as well as encouraging us all to visit the sick and care for the needy. But, ever the pragmatist, he looked at me one day and remarked dryly as I left his study,

"And by the way, now you're living the Christian life, don't expect anyone to like you for it."

(And I had thought studying religion meant I'd be with all the 'nice people', and it would all be gentleness and kindness and love; fluffy, sentimental stuff like that: was I wrong.)

So, it is strange, evocative. I would stand in the tiny Lady Chapel at one of Canon John's two churches, St. Aidan's (which was only a few hundred metres away from its sister church, Holy Trinity) where Mass would be celebrated every day, and I just couldn't believe it! I had travelled the world and sat at the feet of 'wise men' and gurus from many major religions, and known people who had come from far and wide in search of knowledge from these 'renowned teachers'. And yet here, just down the road from where we lived in a little English town, I would come to Mass and time would literally stand still. And there would be maybe four or five of us, mostly elderly women. Often now I find myself at Mass, maybe elated, at other times tired or even sad or slightly distracted. And I watch as the words I now know so well are said,

and I know,

something beyond my comprehension is slowly burning; some sort of wisdom is speaking to me, from beyond forever. From beyond eternity.

The words and the fire and the wind of the Spirit.

Ruah. Shekhinah. The Glory of God.

If only I could really see. Yes, if we were not so blind, we would see Him.

But we can only listen. To the speaking beyond the words.

And one day we will see. Not in a glass darkly, but face to face. Even today I hear stories of the visionaries of the end-time who do see Jesus. Around the world,

as the sleepers stir, and the Spirit blows.

I would also go to the Catholic cathedral at Westminster and marvel at all these 'ordinary' men and women; *these keepers of the flame: the flame of the Spirit.* And I would think, they were doing this! While I was running round all over the place with my mad dreams of being a writer and doing glamorous things, they were there, doing what really mattered, keeping the flame alive. It brought me to my knees. Again and again and again. The little people. While theologians argue over definitions and concepts, and some religious and laity did – and still do – horrifically evil things, the little people kept the flame alive. And the best of them were, and are, true to the Cross.

I remember being surprised at first at these individuals of prayer Canon John had praying for me; I mean, I felt almost let down. They weren't the beautiful people I was used to, the models and actors and high flyers or guru types. These were very ordinary folk in the eyes of the world, individuals who would perform seemingly mundane tasks, like cleaning candlesticks or washing vestments or dusting pews or sewing altar cloths. But perhaps their golden quality was that they treasured the sacraments, and especially the Lord's Table. One person I remember particularly was Allen. He worked full time and so was there mainly on Sundays, when he would welcome people. Allen also took care of the accounts. You wouldn't look twice at Allen, because he is tall and too thin and ordinary and wears thick glasses. He isn't cool, or so you'd think. But as you got to know him, just like the little old ladies, you realized that this was someone who shone, this was someone you could trust. Such people are few and far between, but they do exist. And they are like intimations of the holy,

you just can't see it, I couldn't see it … because the glass is so dusty. But as the mirror clears we begin to see, to see with the heart. To see with the soul and its senses ... these women and men ... these keepers of the flame.

These really are the 'beautiful people' of all time. *Because they have a little of the angel about them. And – when you see with the eyes of the soul and the heart – you begin to intuit; intimations of a glory yet to be revealed,*

in a place between places.

A sounding of a distant splendor beyond our present vision. That inner integrity that will one day be fully revealed; when we no longer see partially. People, sometimes damaged individuals in the eyes of the world; aged, vulnerable, wounded from the battlefield of life: but pure beings. People becoming angels, walking the earth and bringing light and healing and peace; *they are the real heroes, the real stars that glitter and lighten this, the darkest of dark nights.*

I went through a period of profound repentance. I hadn't paid attention to the teaching of the Bible. I'd considered it just one holy book among many. That's what I believed, that's common knowledge; it's all relative, isn't it? Everything's relative;

(the shifting sands of time ... if only we could go back.)

Now I was mourning and weeping in this vale of tears. Wondering about all the lies and deceptions that had me buried alive. But there was still that glimmer of the fire, the morsel of faith I still retained; that spark of who I truly was, all but obfuscated by the phony parameters of our limited perception.

And then the trial by fire.

Faith in the crucible.

The spark igniting.

All the fine books I'd read, and the fashionable, famous writers on the telly, the formidable, respected theologians with their convoluted, interesting arguments. Just a new take on Christianity, just a little tweak here; get rid of the virgin birth or something similar. And it'll fit nicer with our conceptions of what 'ought to be'. And no hell. Just a heaven. Maybe the odd angel. No devil. Or, better still, just a social gospel; that's practical. As for Jesus: well, maybe he did exist. And maybe he didn't. The philosophers all explain things so nicely. Until the theories fall apart. Worse of all, the famous, sometimes infamous, gurus you find jet-setting, sitting in white robes on pillows or with kings and presidents and teaching us;

just

so

much

straw.

Only God is true to his Word; and his Word is that faith will bring you through the fire. This is the Messianic Promise. So search the Scriptures. Keep the Lord's Table, the bread and wine: the Eucharistic elements of the sacrament as laid down by Jesus Christ himself; the Holy One of God. Honor confession. Keep the faith of our Fathers, the Apostolic Faith. Strive for the unity of the Spirit,

for the unity of the Church.

Pray for the Gifts of the Spirit, they will be given to you. If you feel you have no faith, or your faith is faltering, just pray for faith. If you cannot love, or love is dying or has died, just pray for the capacity to love. Ask and you shall receive. No one is outside the sphere of salvation, unless they choose to be damned. I have not found one of God's promises false.

But ...

it had all seemed so innocent in my youth. Now the bottom of the pit I had fallen into turned out to have had such slippery sides. And all the questions I still had. Those poems I'd written many years ago I couldn't explain. The visions, the voices, God reaching out to me over and over ... truth buried;

a human being buried alive. The real me buried.

That suits.

So now I was weeping in the churches. Deservedly, on my knees in St. Aidan's in gasping tears of remorse (when no-one was around). The whole thing was terrible; what had I done! Bowing my head, my face awash. Horrified at what I'd been. Singing those childhood hymns to myself. Wandering and wondering what on earth was going on. Penitent for my many, many wrongs. And even those tears could never cleanse me; of course not! The whole of creation itself fell apart because of one tiny act of disobedience:

the glass shattered,

we all

fell through time.

We fell

into

time.

Talking, in my distress, in the aged sacristy at St. Aidan's with the kindly women who did the work tending the sacred vessels. Looking at the broken crucifix on the wall that was one of the surviving sacred artifacts salvaged from a bombing raid that had reduced the church to near rubble in World War Two. Feeling the holiness, as I reached out my hand and touched the broken form of the cross and the figure of the crucified Messiah. And watching these people themselves as they went about their tasks, these candles of hope in a dark world. Remembering also those who had prayed in many countries through the ages, keeping the flame alive.

And the music of the mindscape had changed;

"And did those feet in ancient time
Walk upon England's mountains green?
And was the holy Lamb of God
On England's pleasant pastures seen?"

The silent sounds of the hymn *Jerusalem*,

in an English church.

"Shall I tell you about it?" I burst out one day, unable to restrain myself. Stopping the women as they worked. I was so traumatized I was thinking – at this point – of opening up and relating to these women the amazing story. But all that happened was that Wendy, the sacristan, paused to reply and gently said,

"No love. We think it's better you don't."

She was correct. I would have regretted it. They were all very kind and understanding; totally trustworthy, thank God. They didn't want to pry or ask too many questions. *I had fallen back to earth and found myself in a place that was itself a window on heaven. Born again. Into a renewed creation, talking to them;*

there was that sense of the Holy Spirit moving between us.

It happens because *there are places between places. It is as if you are moving into an area between worlds. That sacristy was one of them; a window looking into heaven.*

The Kingdom of Heaven is with us; among true believers.

And so the ladies returned to the polishing of the silver. And our conversation moved to the days when St. Aidan's and Holy Trinity was a parish where many people involved there felt the call to the priesthood and religious life. And as we talked, so my eyes traced the aged walls, the cupboards with the priestly robes, the lovely embroidery on the linens neatly folded in the long, narrow drawers. And I felt the tremendous sanctity; the purity – *a mystical whiteness*. While these women wistfully spoke of how things were "different now".

So Wendy and Mary and Phyllis chatted away, each in turn telling their stories. Of how, during the Normandy landings, "people in English churches prayed for a miracle; for the waters to be calm". And of how a man in the parish heard "an interior voice speaking to him at Mass, telling him to become a priest". And this amazed individual had waited until the end of the Eucharist, and then gone to the priest and asked his advice;

"What to do?"

And that man did become a priest. The voice of God is still heard in the hearts of many a Christian; and, indeed, non-Christian; the call of the Spirit.

These were my days of wonder, days when the Kingdom of Heaven was near.

Wendy wanted me to take over as sacristan eventually. "Just imagine me," I thought, "cleaning and touching these holy things". I loved Wendy because she saw something in me, something beyond my own iniquity. Like those African theologians from years past, like my Jewish Claire. They looked beyond, to what you could be. While accepting what you were. They intuited,

the tremendous potential of every human being;

that each one of us really is born to change the world.

And sometimes all it takes is a smile, or a prayer: a moment can change everything.

At Mass, and the Baptism of a baby, Norbert the curate would carry the child through the church in a kind of triumphant acclamation, one of Christ's own. Norbert, carrying the baby up high in his hands above the congregation so that parishioners would reach out and touch and bless the newborn. And the whole congregation would sing in triumph that most jubilant of modern hymns, *Shine Jesus Shine*.

On one notable occasion when I was under spiritual attack and this was happening, I reached out to touch the delicate, satin skin of the tiny hand. And something like the sound of metal on glass, a teaspoon on glass; a *pinging sound*. And light from the babe's purity, like a candle, broke through my own gloom and dispelled the darkness in my psyche. *A gentle cleansing of the landscape of my soul; like a spell being broken.*

As always, Canon John was ready to help me handle events like these; and any similar spiritual impasse. If I got stuck we would talk prayerfully, and I would explain what I was sensing or feeling, and he would give me advice:

"Against all Satan's spells and wiles",

runs the "St Patrick's Breastplate". I was learning in the presence of a truly great spiritual director. And such direction of this sort is all about one Christian speaking to another, and allowing the Spirit of the living God to move. It's a powerful and life-changing experience.

Notes on things you might find useful in spiritual direction. (Not a list; just pointers – within a Christian mentoring situation.)

One

It's not ultimately the director or mentor in any way. You always turn to God. The whole enterprise is about you and God and your relationship with God. You start to employ every capacity you have been given; mental, physical and spiritual. You are becoming a fully functioning human being, a dynamic creation in touch with your Creator. You switch on to who you really are. As the mirror of your soul is cleansed you start to see. And you begin to realize the enormous value each human being has in the sight of God. So life itself starts to take on unfathomed meaning. You realize you are constantly in the presence of God, so your sense of sacredness and dignity as a human being is affirmed. This means you also respect the sacredness of others, and of the world in which you live. You may find times of despair, but it will be unlike the despair of the unbeliever, because you come to realize you are upheld by God's arms and that He will never let you go. You will cry "Abba" and know that even if everyone else has deserted you; your father and mother, your family and friends, God will never let you go if you cling to the Cross. And even if you momentarily let go of the Cross, but repent, there is still redemption in God's mercy. For to turn away from the mercy of God, to refuse to repent and ask for forgiveness, is to choose to be damned.

Two

No spiritual director or mentor is better than a shonky spiritual director; and they're out there. When anything starts up in the sense of issues of sex or power or purely human control, get out. This means also any type of subtle undermining or the opposite, get out. You're better off on your own (for only a while, hopefully) with the Bible and the sacraments.

Perhaps the most excellent fall-back is a good confessor. The Roman and Orthodox traditions are particularly strong here. The Anglicans also can have the odd priest with a charismatic gift for this sacrament. A confessor provides someone you can open up to under the Seal of the Confessional, and provides a person to turn to for guidance and even solace. Beware of the confessor who is too severe, as this can leave one depressed and doubting, or, alternatively, who treats sin so lightly that it becomes almost a laughing matter. The attributes to look for in a confessor or spiritual director are humility, piety, purity and gentleness. (These traits are also the hallmark of a trustworthy exorcist.)

Three

Avoid extremes, especially extreme asceticism. Your body is holy. You treat it with respect. Look after your health. The more vulnerable you are the more careful you have to be in every respect. Fasting is for the healthy individual at appropriate times and in judicious ardor and moderation. But it is an important facet of the spiritual life; for the health of soul and body in a robust, balanced individual.

Four

Trust your intuitions. If something, anything, makes you feel uneasy immediately or for any length of time (for example repetitive prayer or singing or chanting going round and round in your mind that doesn't uplift you or links you to a certain person or group) pray about it and avoid the situation, get out. Change course. God will use your gifts and perfect them. But it can be slow. The battle is yours and Christ's, and Christ has won the victory. You will find help on the way from fellow souls traveling the path of authentic love, agape; love that does not entrap.

Five

Avoid talking about your spiritual experiences with people you feel unsure about, and here I include dream events. Little things you say can reveal your level of spiritual development to someone who might appear genuine, but might have less than authentic intentions. If you are extremely sensitive, or doubtful, request the laying on of hands for healing be given with the priest holding his hands a little way from your body. But always remember that you are really before Christ himself in these situations, and he will never let you go; unless you choose to turn away. This is freedom –

the freedom to choose.

Six

Even in churches, be cautious of anyone who prays silently with you rather than praying openly. I am always wary of any sort of situation where people are not totally transparent. If people are genuine they have nothing to hide.

Seven

Priests have to answer for their own purity; it is a tremendously difficult calling. So pray for priests and pastors and those called to the religious life, and try to find a confessor or spiritual friend you feel comfortable with because times of trial will come. We've all heard the horrendous stories of abuse in various parts of the Church. Remember, for those with evil intent, the best place to undermine the Church is from within. We need to pray for purity in the Church. At the Communion table place yourself as if you are standing before the throne of God and as if you are yourself a priest; what matters is authenticity, true prayer. This is the priesthood of all true believers; this is what it is to be a flame of fire – a living Temple of the Holy Spirit.

Eight

If you are in a really disturbing situation and cannot extricate yourself, pray for God to give you a way out; an exit. This includes circumstances like possible telepathy: turn to God,

never engage,

remove yourself from the situation. Whatever happens, however, always envision yourself as standing before the throne of God and praising God. You are a child of the Most High. You have been saved by faith, and so it doesn't matter if ten billion of these pathetic individuals are attacking you or surrounding you. What they're doing is digging themselves deeper and deeper into a pit. They are the sorcerers of the Apocalypse. Although at times like these everything can be employed by the enemy (strange thoughts might arise, your own physical and psychic energy might be used against you, you might feel negative and menacing sensations or emotions beyond description; you may feel you've lost your faith or committed the unforgivable sin). Remember this is spiritual warfare. However bad it is, by placing yourself before God and not engaging, the turned mystic is placed in direct confrontation with God himself; about the worst position any living being can be in. Their power is limited, and it comes from the demons who ultimately control them. I don't recommend praying for these shamanic sorcerers or psychics (or whatever people wish to call them) at such times. Just keep your focus on God, He won't let you go.

Nine

A word of caution; spiritual experiences can be counterfeited by Satan. Look for results; for the fruits of the Spirit and a gentle, caring and compassionate nature. No-one from God can sin. Don't go crazy and think this is impossible. Be realistic, and realize this is a call to be careful about spiritual purity. As human beings we live in the tension between acknowledging our weaknesses and doing our utmost to overcome them. That's why confession is so important. If you do fall you have an advocate, Jesus Christ; we are all penitents in the end. Perhaps a wonderful prayer is to ask God to help us never to sin.

And when you are really down and aware of your own weaknesses, think of Paul; it is all grace. In the end, it is faith alone that saves. While faith without works is useless, ultimately, all is the gift of the grace of God.

Ten

Beware 'the actors'. They're everywhere. And they're the most dangerous people on earth at the moment. Especially when they're in the Church. They do charity to order, and cry to order, and do piety really well. And it all means absolutely nothing, outside of worldly plaudits and gongs. They'd rip you to pieces if they could. That's the reality in all areas of life and in the Church today. We are seeing spiritual fall-out; it's always been there. Really good people can be taken in particularly, because they don't believe how bloody nasty some individuals are. Evaluate situations. Watch out for situations getting worse and worse; dodgy liturgy creeping in, dodgy theology, dodgy symbolism. Always go back to the Bible and sound teaching, the teaching of the Apostolic Faith of the Church. Remember, also, that terrible things have been done in the name of Christ.

Eleven

Nobody should ever intentionally take human life or torture or abuse in any way whatsoever in the name of God. So check passages of scripture against one another, and don't take Biblical statements out of context. Watch what people do, not just what they say. Watch for the results of their actions, and where those actions are taking you and the Church.

Twelve

When the spiritual situation is really bad, hang on to the Bible and the Cross. This may be lonely, because Christianity is about community and people, but remember God is in control. This is most important during times of testing and tribulation. No matter how bad it is or looks, keep your focus returning to God.

Perhaps that early ray of light, those words of spiritual direction that came, I believe, from the Madonna herself, have proved to be the most incisive of all;

"Offer everything you do up to God."

And that includes everything you feel, hear, observe or think; all phenomena you encounter within or without your soul: genius! Just that sentence, heard a long time ago by a little girl; sheer spiritual genius. And you doubt that the voice of God and his messengers speaks to humanity today?

"Set me as a seal upon thine heart ... for love is as strong as death ..." (Solomon's Song; kjv)

As the Canon would remind me, "God will not let you be tested beyond your endurance".

(Although at times it really can seem as if you are.)

Climbing Mt. Sinai
[and continuing the theme of]
From Chanel ... to hell.

Anyway, while this was going on I thought I'd better set myself right; really, properly, finally, right with the Catholic Church. So I duly set out one day determined to make a second general confession. Task completed, a short time later I went to a local Catholic church which was a pretty little building from the outside but possessed a rather gloomy interior. In fact, *the atmosphere was uneasy,* which was funny for a church,

that spiritual dissonance.

Trying to rationalize this, I told myself I was crazy. At Mass the sense of spiritual unease dissipated, so I was reassured. I popped in again, and then came a morning Mass when the presiding assistant priest gave a sermon on how people were,

"Stealing the consecrated hosts and selling them for fifty pounds each for Satanic purposes."

I was taken aback to put it mildly. I couldn't remember ever hearing anything like this in church ever before – as a child I would have been horrified. The Mass just didn't seem the right setting for a discussion of Satanism, so it was jarring, spiritually speaking, all the more so after what I'd been through. As the sermon progressed, with the priest dwelling on this dark topic, I became more perturbed. I was in disbelief! This was the twentieth century, not the Dark

Ages. I mean, what the hell was going on? Had everybody gone mad?

I was unnerved, confused; so perhaps that was it! I'd gone barking mad thinking Satanists were attacking me; and the whole world had gone barking mad with me. Because these people were out there – somewhere. These sons of bitches. Anyway, I thanked God I hadn't contacted the Catholic Church that Easter Monday, because this particular priest might well have turned up. And if this performance was anything to go by, he'd have scared me to death, I'd have been in really deep water. Because, most importantly and fundamentally, the fear element is a major problem in Satanic or spiritual attack; absolutely incomprehensible fear. Fear from another dimension, a spiritual fear that resonates at all levels. The last thing you want is someone who makes the whole thing even worse by talking about really evil stuff like Satanism. Or, maybe not as bad, as in my earlier experience in late adolescence; a priest who doesn't take you seriously. Still, I didn't completely give up on this local Catholic church. I'm a bit of a bulldog, and I thought the sermon might well have been a weirdo's one-off. But a little while later I was in this same church when, at the end of the Mass, a woman came up to me and started talking. It was dreadfully negative and undermining stuff about the state of the Catholic Church (and this from, supposedly, a Catholic). But as if to round off the discussion she ended by declaring,

"The smoke of Satan has reached the Vatican."

That was it. I thought, "I'm out of here!"

And I was – because I'd been there; I'd experienced

that smoke.

And beneath it all was the faint suspicion, just faint, the horrific thought;

"What happens when the exorcists are running the covens;

or vice-versa?"

Where have all the mystics gone?

Perhaps they were drowned ... in the unconscious. To become the witches and wizards of the mindspace. The ones who help spin the spells of control. Perhaps they were afraid, got waylaid. And the ones who survived?

Did they stay quiet? Or just hold the line, become "keepers of the flame?"

Or were burnt alive? By rulers or phony church leaders? On the pyres of wars and Inquisitions;

where have all the mystics gone?

Gone? But not drowned out. They are raising the standard of the Holy Ghost across the Houses of Eternity.

They are rising now. And they will not stay quiet some time longer. So be careful, you manipulators. For many a silent/silenced nun or little child or clever soul, a good husband or wife, or writer of hymns or stirring sermons,

may have a finger to point at you,

the Inquisitorial eye.

To save a soul, or your own soul, you may have to break the rules. Especially the phoney rules.

And you never, ever, let go of the Bible, the Cross ... and the Eucharist.

Agape

Jacob's Ladder.

> And Jacob had a dream:
> "a ladder set up on the earth,
> and the top of it reached to heaven:
> and behold the angels of God ascending
> and descending on it."
>
> The Book of Genesis; kjv

At a major cathedral, I was now also in the throes of attempting to discuss the whole spiritual experience with a Catholic priest. Absolutely petrified of doing the wrong thing, I was desperately trying to do the right thing – and so keep the Catholic tradition. Well, here I fared a tad better. One priest seemed compassionate and agreed I needed to "talk the whole thing through". He offered to see me, which was kind as Catholic priests are under tremendous pressure from a lack of numbers. But by the time I had contacted him five times, and he failed to respond, I simply gave up. (For some reason I noticed he had very beautifully manicured nails. But then they would be; these were hands that consecrated the body of Christ.)

Attending St. Aidan's I made a good friend of Margo, an elderly lady who'd been a Catholic nun, and had never really got over giving up her vocation. Our Margo had also had a negative experience at the same local Catholic church I'd attended, although hers was different. Having been misdiagnosed, Margo hadn't received treatment for stomach cancer until it was too late, and she was now terminally ill. Margo said she had gone to the local church, but no-one seemed to want to know her;

her mantra ran, "You won't get any help from the Catholics, love."

She really sounded down about it, and I don't blame her. I don't know what was going on at that church. I went to another Catholic church, St. Mary's, where the laity and priests were really very good, caring people. I still write to some of the laity. But this Catholic church was too far away to frequent on a daily basis.

And so the twin churches of St. Aidan's and Holy Trinity became my spiritual home. With encouragement from the Canon, I began studying the Bible, reading up on the Desert Fathers and examining the writings of the saints. One of the accounts I unearthed described an early visionary experience – I think it was third century – similar to mine. I discovered the account in a book in a Catholic library near Westminster cathedral (it may have been one of the Desert Fathers writing, but unfortunately I didn't make a note of the details). Up to that point I was a little confused, and this account reassured me, because all the descriptions I knew of hell were of flames of fire; so mine didn't seem right: those icy wastelands with devils swooping and the lost, abandoned souls. I remember telling my mother a bit of what I had been through, and she said it was "purgatory". It certainly was not! But then I didn't go into it too much with Mum, because she lived alone, and I didn't want to frighten her. But as the experiences were continuing, not so much glimpses of hell – but of Satanic attack – and sometimes also heavenly visions, it was difficult to remain quiet. My mother was empathetic but advised me to,

"Just put it behind you, dear. It's over! Just get on with your life."

I really wished I could do that. And I confessed to John that I found it all way too much. I couldn't handle it, and at times felt unable to cope. Deep down I'd become a broken woman. John was kind and pragmatic and advised me to,

"Pray to God to stop the visions."

Which I did, for a long while. But the visions didn't stop. So eventually I gave up. I reasoned, "This has got to be for a purpose". As the Canon would remind me himself, when we were sitting together in the little office at the front of his house, shelves of books on the Church Fathers, works on mystical literature, Biblical study and theology lining the walls, "Whatever is happening, you just have to remember that God is always in control. He's not going to let you go. Just remember, you can't do it yourself. You have to rely on His power. To seek His will in every situation; no one can fight evil alone. And never, ever directly confront evil at this level; always use the Eucharist".

I looked at him and enquired, "How on earth do people end up mucking around with this occult stuff?"

"Evil can put on an alluring face, otherwise no one would ever touch it. Just remember that. And people can be curious."

So John, Margo and I set up flags in the church grounds for the annual fair. And as John went off for more bunting I asked, pulling my hair back as it got swept into the wind, "Why doesn't John become a bishop, Margo? He'd make a great bishop."

"Because the best priests just want to look after their flock, love. There's too much admin and paperwork with being a bishop. And all that messing around with the great and mighty."

So we looked up at the sky of azure blue over England. And, as the wind blew on a beautiful summer's day of endless light, with flowers raging in all their varied loveliness, so the flags of England also blew. And underneath were those arms holding us; God's arms. And it might have been also the sound of Vidor's *Toccata* ringing out in brilliant triumph at the wonder of the English Church, across time and space.

And a while later, when winter had set in, Margo enquired one day with that special look in her eyes; that blaze of light and ecstasy,

"Did you feel it? That day …"

She felt it. I felt it.

But I didn't reply. I just smiled. And she knew. It was a day upon England's soil with,

the wind,

and the fire,

and the breath

of the Spirit of the living God.

The soul is a landscape: but when you are blind you cannot see ...

"Until the day break, and the shadows flee away, I will get me to the mountain of myrrh, and to the hill of frankincense."

Solomon's Song; kjv

A vision in the night;

A sexually polluted priest leads a witch into a darkened Anglican church;

a power group moving in on the Anglican Church.

This was 1991/1992.

How on earth do you tell a spiritual director this? I couldn't! I made an attempt, but I couldn't. I couldn't formulate it, and decided I'd be labeled 'mad', and so John would wash his hands of me, as had the Catholic Church. But, years later, I knew I should have said more, because this is an end-game of the occult; the Church that prayed through World Wars. Now the European and American nations lie demoralized and impoverished,

so hit the soul of our nations: the Anglican Church has got to fall.

But I couldn't tell him. What I did articulate was a modification that turned out to be an accurate prediction. But I couldn't tell John the rest; I failed. Even these words I've written don't totally reflect this vision because you, my reader, would perhaps baulk in disbelief. But my words do give an approximation.

Oh well! I'd been a model who recoiled at the intrusiveness of the camera, a haphazard writer without a topic or passion, and a once brilliant (?) academic who'd fallen face first in the muck. As I regaled the Canon with my career details one day, he at least saw the positives and concluded,

"We can use that."

Which should have given me solace. But the Canon's encouragement fell on disillusioned and jaded ears.

I decided to throw away the writing, except for compiling a manuscript of my experiences upon which this book is based, and go out to work on a voluntary basis. Michael agreed this was a good idea. So, I found an opening at one of the branches of the Society for the Protection of Unborn Children (SPUC). They allowed me to come in during the afternoons and do general clerical work. It was mundane work, but they were a genuine bunch of people and fun. The conversation didn't revolve around purely ethical issues, and we'd talk films and art and politics, as well as discussing personal matters, although I didn't discuss my conversion experiences.

After work, I would often drop into a local church where the rosary would be said at the conclusion of Mass. John encouraged this, and at this point the rosary was, again, an especially strategic form of prayer, because the repetition works to block out intrusive phenomenon, as well as being spiritually uplifting. The Canon's method of praying the rosary included meditation on the different decades of the rosary, so it became dynamic and engaging by incorporating active contemplation; which appealed as it brought the use of the rosary in line with strict Biblical principles.

Around this time my mother telephoned to tell me Elizabeth was dying of stomach cancer,

"I can't bear to look at her! My beautiful, beautiful sister ..."

Mum's voice trailed off at the impact of the ravages of cancer. Unsure of what to say, I prayed before advising,

"Mum, though she can't hear you, just sit beside Elizabeth's bed with a rosary and recite the prayers. Elizabeth will hear in her soul; and God will hear. Just sit with her, be with her, Mum."

My mother did this. And it was one night later on, following Elizabeth's death, when I had;

a vision of that dark sea. And felt the terror of that awful soul's death. I was asleep. But I heard a voice, a definite voice, reciting the rosary.

And, as I woke, I knew. It was the voice perhaps *of angels*. As Elizabeth died, she too had heard the prayers of the rosary; and on hearing knew the love of God in Christ Jesus. So it is, that ripples of love flow out into the Universe from one human being to another. The Spirit of God links us into a world of healing: nothing of love is lost. And I don't even know to this day if Elizabeth was baptized. The incredible power of authentic prayer, the gift of the love of God for us.

At church each morning the Canon used to dress most days in long black robes with a red sash, rather like the garb a cardinal in the Catholic Church would wear. Canon John also wore the most beautiful rosary I've ever seen. Huge and fashioned from some sort of wood of a reddish hue, the rosary fell below his waist. He wore it with a large, silver cross. John loaned me that rosary once. It was such an amazing religious object. Really an icon, and he was a little reluctant to give it to me (I think he was concerned about not getting it back).

In the very early days, I was paranoid about transmitting negative energy. Michael said at one point over the preceding years I'd given him an electric shock, which frightened me. I hated the thought of hurting anyone, so at the Anglican church where we would shake hands or give a hug at the greeting of peace in the Eucharist, I took to wearing gloves, which I realized looked most peculiar. Until Margo suggested,

"Don't do that, love."

Quite gently, but firmly. I looked a complete idiot, basically.

But it really was harrowing at times. One positive experience occurred at Westminster cathedral when a lady I regularly saw there came up and touched me, saying I looked "sparkly". She appeared to be quite taken with me, and repeated the remark on several occasions while touching my clothes. This made me feel good, because having a compliment like that suggested something a hell of a lot better than being a pillar of filth.

The anti-abortion society was staffed mainly by Catholics, although a few Anglicans and other branches of the Church were represented. People working there were aware that you could come under spiritual attack; which surprised me, actually. I don't know how the topic came up, but I recall an animated Catholic girl remarking after broaching the subject one day in an off-hand way,

"You just shouldn't get afraid when it happens."

"Heck!" I thought, "She's braver than me". But I guess she'd never been there, she was a better person. She'd never been there, to that most terrifying of all places.

When I refer to being under spiritual attack at this point I should elaborate. Common now was an awareness of evil thoughts and words, sometimes almost bombarding me – which in the latter case was terrifying; I'd never experienced anything like it before. *It was as if words came from somewhere else, as well as my own mind.* These words were thoughts, not voices or anything like that. But it was awful, they almost showered my psyche, and were accompanied by an overwhelming emotional negativity. When this happened there was a weird sense of fear, so it was destabilizing. I mean, I'd experienced negative and nasty thoughts before – but nothing like this. Trying to make sense of it, in my reading I learned that the early Christians believed that each person has a good angel and a demonic angel. I presumed my demonic angel was a real bastard of a thing. It was horrible.

Again, the sense of negative energy being directed against me was a fairly frequent manifestation of attack. Focusing intensely on the area between my eyebrows. At Mass with Michael in Covent Garden at a beautiful Catholic church one day, I almost saw a little black devil directing energy waves at me. The thing the devil held was like a tiny electricity rod. It was the usual experience,

as if reality was opening up.

Other forms of attack took similarly strange forms. Once, I was wide awake when I experienced what felt like my *entire inner being frozen; it felt like a huge block of incredibly cold ice inside me.* As this went on for some while and felt *terribly evil* I was most distressed. I did mention this experience to the Canon. His response was to raise his eyebrows, as if slightly perplexed, and express the sentiment,

"I suggest you put on something warmer if it happens again."

That's spiritual direction 20th century Church of England style for you. But at other times the Canon was very compassionate; indeed while I was under severe Satanic attack at one point he looked deeply distressed, and asked God to "Let me take the blows". And he would always steer the situation away from any negativity; "Remember everything is gift," he would say. Or, "You're trying too hard". Indeed, one of his frequent uplifting comments that stays with me is,

"You're doing good."

Because, at the end of the day, that's all God wants. And that's all the Canon and anyone on a true spiritual path would want. No fanfares on this earth. No gongs or sainthood or fancy picture in the church even. Hopefully, keep your head down. Just to stand before the face of God and for God to say of you, "You've done good". You may have fallen over a few times, initially maybe got it terribly wrong, but at the end of the day,

"The sweet 'Well done' in judgment hour." As the "St. Patrick Breastplate" runs.

And I would sometimes complain to Michael about what I was going through. My pragmatic husband would respond by shaking his head and saying,

"I knew all that chanting was a bad idea. I did try to tell you."

"It's perfectly normal practice." I would retort, vigorously defending myself. But although some things in Buddhism did seem okay, I recalled the traditional story of the Buddha being guarded by the serpent king, which didn't inspire me. And although I really admire the Dalai Lama on some points, the idea that he is "The Great Sea" now entirely lacked appeal.

I added defiantly, "I really thought that if you were determined to discover the truth, you had to put your heart into it, give it a go. Really give the great traditions and philosophies of the world a go."

And all I would get was, "Haven't you ever heard of faith?"

So I would sit in St. Martin in the Fields at Communion and their healing services. And outside the people on the streets would hang out and come in and find someone to talk to, a shelter from the storms of life. And I'd wander to St. Paul's to cast my eyes on Holman Hunt's painting of Christ as "The Light of the World". Recalling Revelation,

"Behold, I stand at the door and knock."

And the music of the mindscape again would be,

Jerusalem.

"I will not cease from mental fight,
Nor shall my sword sleep in my hand,
Till we have built Jerusalem
In England's green and pleasant land."

The spirituality of my ancestors, the Christianity that brought England freedom.

"I will not cease from mental fight."

(Just listen to the music and the words to evoke the atmosphere.)

So the terror would wash over from the sleeping into the waking state, and then I would be wide awake,

I would sense what was like an electrical grid around me. Often it would feel almost square or rectangular; as if an enormous amount of energy was being directed at my body and the surrounding area. It was so vivid an experience, I could almost hear the buzzing of energy.

This could be extremely disquieting and uncomfortable. I'd had similar experiences in connection with UFO incidents over the years, but consciously took the decision not to discuss this with John, feeling the poor bloke had enough to deal with. In retrospect, I rather regret not bringing up UFO manifestations; it would have been interesting to have had his reaction. But, again, I was understandably wary of opening up on such topics, and being dismissed as crazy, even though there had been discussion with two psychiatrists to determine whether my experiences were of a spiritual nature (the normal practice in Anglicanism in cases such as mine). Genuinely spiritual these experiences might be, I certainly wasn't too happy with them continuing. When I complained about this yet again, John just declared matter of factly,

"It's a battle; it's a war! A glorious war. This is the war you were born for. Anyway, the real war's over, we're just left fighting the skirmishes."

"Nor shall my sword sleep in my hand."

Again, the landscape was that of the hymn, *Jerusalem*.

And always, always; the beautiful

"Song of Songs."

But I must say, I didn't get much comfort from this comment either; the idea of being at war in a war-zone, I mean. I remember going on about this to the Canon, and he seemed about to throw up his arms in despair, because at one point he exclaimed,

"Just listen to yourself."

I don't think even he realized how terrible it was. I rather slunk away that day. A glorious battle it might be. But out there, on my own, in the whirlwind, I would recall Bob Dylan singing *Like a Rolling Stone*;

how did it feel?

It felt bloody awful. It wasn't funny when it was you. And you were grovelling, being ground into pulp. Burnt into ashes and dust,

and nothingness.

What you really were.

What we really are.

Until the day breaks and the shadows flee.

The Song of Songs

I decided to give a call to the Buddhist monk I'd been editing translations for back in the Far East, as I'd got on well with him. He'd even been good enough to send me a few of his latest publications over the years. I wasn't thinking of returning to Buddhism, but I was interested to discover how Buddhists would handle the problem. As I described to him on the telephone what was occurring, he sounded impassive, which Buddhist monks often do. But I felt there were times for being impassive, and this wasn't one of them. Anyway, he suggested,

"Try moving your bed."

I didn't think this sounded too promising, but as suggested I went ahead and moved the bed. Mike, of course, wondered what on earth was going on when he came home and saw the new position our bed was in in our tiny bedroom. I can't remember what I told him by way of explanation, but Mike was too busy to worry. Of course, it was a wasted effort. And the bed was damned heavy to heave back into position by myself.

With all this happening, one of the things that concerned me was the disturbing – and strange – vision of Alice. For all my faults, I loved my sisters dearly. I discussed the vision with Canon John. He was also concerned, and it was a mutual decision that "We should pray about the vision". Practically, there didn't seem much else to do. Again, I didn't stress to him that I had been receiving premonitions all my life; I was far too cowed by these experiences for that. But as time passed, just praying didn't seem to be enough in relation to this particular vision. The whole thing was made worse by what I was hearing from my relatives concerning Alice's glamorous new life. For one thing, my mother visited Alice and was at pains to declare that Mark was, "Deliberately isolating the girl!" Stuck, as Alice was, in a mansion in the middle of nowhere. Mum would remonstrate,

"He's using the dogs to keep her pinned down. He's isolating her from us."

Thus she complained regularly and bitterly, sometimes sounding slightly hysterical. Being Mum she wouldn't shut up about Alice's predicament, and kept on. It rattled me because I was finding, just like everyone else, that when you rang Alice there was always just this answering machine. Not knowing what else I could do, I rang Laura. She was busy with work and the twins, but I was insistent, and, most considerately, she agreed to come and see me. Laura arrived at our flat, beautifully dressed and looking wonderful as always, and I made her some tea, and we sat down and looked at each other. I began, in a hesitant way, to attempt to explain I felt something might be,

"Very wrong in regard to Alice, all this not being able to contact her. Mum's a bit concerned too, Laura."

I had thought of going further, but opening up to my rational, always in control, but terrifically stressed-out sister, informing her of a major and destabilizing conversion experience was impossible. I kept thinking, "This is the twentieth century, and she'll think I'm barmy if I say the wrong thing". So I just touched on the conversion experience, and asked discreet, thoughtful questions, fishing to find out how Alice was. I also mumbled (rather pathetically, I thought),

"I'm not too good myself, healthwise, Laura."

Which was the only way I could formulate it. I certainly did feel stressed out and didn't look my usual glamorous self, even though I'd made an effort and was nicely, but casually, dressed in jeans and had my make up on. Laura sounded dismissive and reassured me,

"There's nothing wrong with Alice."

But I must have let enough slip about the religious stuff because she added,

"Alice prays a lot, and she always carries a little prayer book with her wherever she goes."

So that was that. But as Laura rose to leave she complained again,

"No-one can ever get through to Alice on the telephone."

Which didn't assuage my concern much.

Still, as I let Laura out, I tried to assume everything was okay. I mean, Alice was Alice! We all knew that. Beautiful, besotted Alice. Physically fragile. But she was alright! I mean, Laura said so, and she should know; they were twins and had always been so close. Sitting down alone in the apartment following the meeting, I couldn't help feeling that Laura seemed just a bit cross about the whole thing; short of time and on a very short fuse. To this day I wonder what Laura made of that conversation.

Anyway, as things turned out, I must have imparted something of the message, because Alice and Mark descended on Canon John and went to confession, which was something of a surprise. I spoke to Alice briefly after this. I can't remember much of what was said. Except that, rather plaintively, Alice asked if – as Father had heard her confession and absolved her – was she "okay?" I took it she meant spiritually,

"okay?"

"Forgiven?"

It all seemed skewed, and I don't know why she asked me, because being forgiven means forgiven; that was that. But for her, of course, the problem was that Mark was a divorcee, and couldn't marry Alice because the Catholic Church wouldn't annul his marriage. Or, at least, that was all I could understand from what Alice told me. Which meant Alice couldn't receive communion in the Catholic Church because she was considered to be living 'in sin', and she wouldn't receive communion in the Anglican Church because, from the Catholic point of view, that wasn't right either; presumably also a 'sin'. I felt really sorry for Alice, but couldn't understand why she didn't just move over to Anglicanism as otherwise, as this strange set of circumstances might pan out, Alice would presumably die in sin if she didn't receive the Last Rites in the Catholic Church. This being so, to me at least, Anglicanism was a supremely preferable fate. I pondered also when Alice informed me, somewhat sadly, that Mark had bought a new organ for their local Catholic church in the hope the priest would marry them. I got the impression it was part bravado, part generosity, and part bribe in Mark's way of doing things; a huge organ for heaven's sake. But the priest wouldn't marry our Alice, who would have made such a beautiful bride.

Rules are rules. (But can you get an organ back?)

It didn't sound right to me. Again, I found the scenario of all these rules confusing; rather like a religion of the absurd. I couldn't see it from any way I read the Bible, no matter how hard I tried. But lo and behold! I encountered a man at SPUC who confided he had a similar problem. He told me he'd converted to Anglicanism. I think he concluded if he stayed with the Catholic Church he was damned to hell anyway, so he might as well risk it with the Church of England.

Still, I felt relieved Alice had received confession and absolution, though the problem didn't feel resolved; to me, that is. I think it was the premonitions. To see visions of the future can sound exciting, if you don't have them or if they're all nice. But that's not true when they're of the negative variety. I reassured myself that I didn't know where this vision of Alice had come from: if it was of God, or the demonic realm, or just my own imagination. However, the last option did seem a bit of a stretch, given the nature and substance of the vision. What I also felt at the time was that there was another possibility, and that was that it just might be possible to transmit images telepathically into someone's mind when the person is in a dream state. Interestingly, and I've end-noted this, recent research has shown that this is possible: that images can be introduced into the mind by human intervention during sleep. Of course, with no scientific evidence then, I was unsure about the explanation of human intervention. So my notion and feeling that some of these visionary episodes might stem from human beings tapping into negative – and I mean demonic – energy was purely a spiritual intuition or insight. *It is as if God allows you at times with prayer and discernment, and even sometimes immediately, to realize the source of a vision.* But you would never interfere with the workings of someone's mind in this evil way if you were a person of the Holy Spirit; a sanctified person. I can't go into it here, but I did bring up the point of a human being or group telepathically targeting someone with the Canon, and he wasn't dismissive. So, I repeat, you have to be very careful with visions or any kind of supernatural phenomenon: you don't always know where they are coming from; this sometimes takes a great deal of prayer and spiritual discernment.

Although reticent about discussing premonitions with the Canon, I did lay bare one vision, but this resulted in my feeling deeply embarrassed. The vision concerned a person in authority in a prominent local church. I didn't like mentioning it, because I didn't want to cause any sort of bad feeling – with no real substantial grounds save a vision. But this particular vision was so startling I did hesitantly inform the Canon about it at one of our meetings. John dismissed the idea out of hand, exclaiming,

"Rubbish! The man's totally trustworthy". And I felt disgusted with myself for even having raised the matter. And never again referred to it, except with Michael.

And yet,

the church officer in question buggered the archdeacon, messed up a marriage, and the archdeacon's wife wouldn't go back to the church.

The ordination of women to the priesthood was being considered, so the Canon requested the entire congregation "pray about the matter". I took a day out, praying in the Lady Chapel, trying to discern God's will for the priesthood. John now had Mark, another curate, under his wing. Mark had trained to be an actor before his call to the priesthood, and was a brilliant gymnast. But he was also apprehensive about the ordination of women because he was concerned the issue would involve a breach with the Church of Rome. John brought up the reassurances given; that the wishes and requirements of priests who didn't want women in the priestly ministry would be recognized and honored. When Mark left the table following a heated discussion at one of our regular breakfast meetings on Wednesday morning, I took the opportunity to interrogate the Canon,

"What do you think?" I asked.

I was enough of a Biblical scholar to realize the arguments from scripture for women in the priesthood were tenuous, and I was also aware that you read a passage of the Bible in the light of other passages, and refrain from interpreting passages in isolation. Indeed, later on I would examine different translations to determine even more carefully nuances of meaning and context. But at this point I was a theological novice. The Canon's expression and reply didn't reassure me when he stated bluntly,

"Better a good woman than a bad man."

As if to round off, John evaluated the situation with his usual pragmatism concluding,

"Rome will probably stand back and watch as we make all the mistakes. And then, when the time is right, decide for themselves."

It was a difficult decision. I could see the need for women, particularly in the area of confession, where a woman might want to open up about very personal, intimate details; or in extreme situations such as where there was no male priesthood. But was the ordination of women in this form God's will? Or was it just the spirit of the age;

Human Power ... or God's will?

And if it isn't God's will, then whose will is it ultimately?

> Here comes Solomon's litter.
> Around it are sixty champions,
> the flower of the warriors of Israel;
> all of them skilled swordsmen,
> expert in war. Each man has
> his sword at his side,
> against alarms at night.
>
> The Song of Songs; njb

You know, the Canon wasn't perfect. Even saints make mistakes; they can get it wrong. That's why we need our human angels, our swordsmen, our prayer-warriors; those flames of fire. Because only God is perfect.

Around this time one experience occurred that stays with me. It happened when Theresa, a very troubled young woman, turned up just before Morning Prayer. She related a dream in which she had "to come to a church on a hill" where she could be "healed". Theresa announced that St. Aidan's was the church in her dream. (Well St. Aidan's is situated on a hill.) What Theresa probably didn't know, was that our twin churches had a strong ministry of Christian healing. Anyway, she joined us for Morning Prayer and came regularly to the Eucharist. Then, one day, she asked if she could "receive Holy Communion?" The Canon gave her the sacrament. This would not have been surprising, but I'm pretty sure from my recollection, Theresa had not been baptized – so it was against the rules; you have to be a baptized and confirmed member of the Apostolic Church to receive Communion in the Church of England. I was shocked and expressed concern. Canon John looked at me and asked,

"What would Jesus have done?"

I stood there, and didn't quite know what to say, I was still rather shocked. John added gently,

"Jesus would have seen her real need. If someone is in real need, you break the rules."

The Canon really should have baptized Theresa first before giving her communion; I guess he was thinking on the spot. The man was not synthetically perfect, not constantly smiling, not some laughing guru. Indeed, John had his own trials and was not idealized by many or any. He was not beyond the shadows of persecution. Indeed, I once had a vision of *people trying to dig up dirt on him,* a vision he shrugged off when I told him, conceding with resignation,

"I suppose they are."

And even on an ordinary, everyday level you could see individuals around him inspired to undermine his ministry. John's small band of prayer warriors; those flames of fire, were not unopposed. Because no-one who follows Christ lives without trial and opposition. Yet that day, seeing the flaw, I retained the essence of the message. I went away and never forgot; you break rules to save lives, and souls. Were he talking today he would probably admit,

"I got it wrong."

He really loved, that man. Agape. Not phileo,

"Do you love me, Simon Peter?"

"Do you love me, Canon John?"

Words, tumbling down the centuries to where we are and what we are all meant to be,

Flames of fire.

The Fire of Love …

A divine emanation of the Most High God
The blazing afire of the heart and more
Of a love nothing can ever extinguish
An elevation of spirituality
In a subtle way you become fire.
A divine call
A reorientation
To come home.
The divine love
Infusing,
Inflaming
The spirit of man.
God meets Man

The veil is falling, falling ...
Through the Night
We are all of us falling ...
Falling
Falling

Falling ... back to God.

And ...

"It is a dreadful thing to fall into the hands of the Living God."
(The letter to the Hebrews.)

I continued having visionary experiences.

One I received before a big attack was of me climbing a rock. This was really artistic. *I thought it was as if someone had painted it.* It was like something Caspar David Friedrich would paint. And it was quite amazing,

the figure was me in the vision, but I was dressed like a man in dark, men's clothing; rather the type of clothing that might be worn in medieval Germany. The visionary painting was very dark; a dark sea and an overcast sky. And below the rock was the dark sea churning.

I discovered a painting, *The Wanderer above the Mists*, a work by Caspar David Friedrich painted between 1817–1818, which was stylistically similar to my visionary image, except the vision was more dynamic. It is, perhaps, because of the intense visionary quality of his work that Caspar David Friedrich has become my favorite artist. For a spiritual interpretation of the meaning of the vision, if you look in the Psalms you will find that the rock represents God. However, I didn't put any interpretation on that vision the first time I saw it. Only later did I realize it also functioned as something of a warning; a warning I was about to be attacked ferociously in a spiritual manner. That is, after a relatively quiet period the spiritual assault was about to intensify. When I mentioned these attacks from the devil, the Canon would say,

"Devil? Just a minor devil. Only big saints get *the* devil."

(This didn't reassure me, although I attempted not to show it.)

Another of these rock visions came later, and the imagery was different. This time I was climbing the dark, jagged rock and a boulder from out of the depths of the sea was thrown up.

Again, the imagery was dark, overcast. Spiritually, for some while following, it again became traumatic.

All the time I was out and about. Wednesdays after Mass, Daisy, the Canon's wife, would leave out the makings of breakfast for us at the rectory before leaving for work. There would usually be the Canon and the Assistant Priest, Norbert the curate, and several lay people in attendance. The breakfast would last until about eight-thirty or so. After that any laity who could stay would wash up while the clergy went about their various tasks. At breakfast the discussion ranged widely, from religion and theology to church affairs and other topics of interest in people's day-to-day worlds. I recall one problematic area of ministry discussed was the difficultly of looking after psychiatric patients housed locally in a block of flats. The residents often needed to be in full-time care, and might become mentally unstable. These poor people certainly couldn't always look after themselves, and frequently ended up not washing or eating properly. Occasionally, they forgot or missed their medication; which could be disastrous. Just recently I read one British newspaper report which described the priesthood as now being the most dangerous occupation in the UK. Listening to the clergy talk back then, I'm not surprised.

Our most popular ever curate, Norbert, was slightly off-the-wall; not what you'd expect of a priest in training at all. Norbert was twenty-five, clever, talkative, sometimes slightly irreverent and generally great fun. His ministry centered on the elderly, and he'd be a regular at a local day centre and talk and joke and join the old folk for lunch, usually helping with the washing-up after the meal. The old folk found Norbert wonderful. But John got cross with Norbert at times because Norbert found it difficult to get up for Mass. So we would be kept sitting and waiting, with the Canon reading to himself from the Bible in Greek. John got fed up with this, and one morning broke from his reading. His voice unexpectedly stormed out across the mystical chapel as he demanded to know,

"Where's the curate?"

We all woke up, sitting bolt upright. Shocked out of the prayerful and sleepy silence, I thought the phrasing of this question curiously over the top, superannuated. And I felt a chugging despair, a sort of, "Oh my, this is the twentieth century; no wonder people don't come to church".

Anglicanism could, and can, be like this; you warp back to the eighteen hundreds. To me this was the pits. Yet conversely, and strangely, grounding because of the accompanying sense of stability and continuity, linking us to the worship of our fathers and mothers, and so back to our Christian roots. I guess I also found this in a different way in Catholicism in the Latin rite, with the mysterious and beautiful, but slightly impenetrable, scene of the priest with his back to you, and his gaze heavenward facing the altar. The lucid, lovely, language; rather atmospherically, spiritually, Pauline; seeing in a glass darkly. The great mystery of revelation unfolding before your unseeing eyes. Reflecting on these two branches of the Church, I would often feel that Anglicanism brought a sense of the pragmatic and practical, even pedestrian, to my Catholic-informed spirituality, which otherwise tended to a slight fanaticism. In Anglicanism visionary mystics have their place, but with the caveat "nothing special" etched invisibly above their heads. And, perhaps, also a disclaimer beneath proclaiming in a similar way, "Keep a watch on this!" Yes, visionary mystics do exist in Anglicanism and they are important; everyone is. But ditch the histrionics. If headed that way, you might make the poor soul a cup of tea and feed them home-made biscuits, discuss the garage sale or the weather. Indeed, if things got rocky a shot of sherry or whisky might be the remedy called for. I would often find this a wonderful balance to juxtapose with the Roman tradition, my birth gift and great blessing. Now it was married to a grounding of the solid and practical, the Bible and patristics. Perhaps most enduring, the incredible intimation, the sense of the Holy Ghost; of the holy. In the Mass and beyond, between laity. And, most notably, in the opening of the Communion tables. If the Second Vatican Council had been like *a mystical breath of the Holy Ghost* to me even as a child, then this had to be the answer to the Unity of the Church manifesting on earth; the keeping of the Eucharistic sanctity, of the sacraments and the Apostolic tradition, and that sense of *the fire of the Mystical Shabbat of the Lord*. I was no longer an outsider in my own family, unwanted at the table: I had come home. For me, the essence of love and the Holy Spirit is to be at one with your family. And my family had become the Church. So the Spirit of the living God breathes through the words of the Song of Songs,

"for love is strong as death."

That is the essence, love really is the key. And love is unity with spiritually authentic diversity. The Church is a living body made up of living stones, and each is slightly – but uniquely and importantly – different. Just as each person is born into the world as a totally unique being, never before seen and never to be seen again. With unique talents and gifts. Please God may those gifts, all our gifts, be released by the coming of the Spirit in a powerful way, because when the Kingdom breaks through in your life you realize that, to God, you are the most wonderful being ever made; each and every one of us.

Don't expect God to be like Man. God is Kadosh; God is holy: whole. That is why unity is so important;

love is the key,

Love is the key

For now we see through a glass, darkly; but then face to face.

1 Cor; kjv

When you walk worlds, you have to take care.

So it was that one day I just walked *into heaven.*

It was a wonderful, and lasting, vision of the Kingdom of Heaven. I was, of course, fully awake. It happened in this way. Canon John had two Masses a week where it was possible for the sick to have the laying on of hands and anointing for healing. At one of these Masses quite early on after the Easter experience, I received the sacrament from Canon John. When I left the church I had to travel to London;

again, it was reality transformed. Everything shone from within. Every moment had freshness, newness and vibrancy. It was sheer joy! The experience lasted the whole length of the train journey to London.

A new world, everything forever made new.

Just as Jesus in Revelation proclaims,

"Behold, I make all things new." (kjv)

Such moments, alas, do not last in this life. So I slipped gently back into time. Reality collapsed, folded, and closed back down. Walking worlds, now into the past, then into the present,

then into the future.

The timescape opens out,

and darkness descends.

And how great that darkness can be!

My brother; my dear brother. He was ten or so years older than I. And age had caused a distance, but that did not stop the shadow that fell that day, the day the vision came;

that my brother would go "to sleep in the House of his Fathers".

The words were part of the unspoken message of the vision; my brother *would go "to sleep in the House of his Fathers"*. The imagery of the vision was strange, and for personal reasons I do not wish to recount it all. In the vision, *my brother arrived outside our family home in Newport, being driven in a priest's car. The car was the same make as Canon John's.* But *the car was green* and Canon John's car was black.

My brother got out of the car; which represented life (again this was the message of the vision) *and walked quickly into the house.*

Many of my visions had this resonance of the Bible. For example, it is said in the Book of Kings of King David that "David slept with his ancestors". But other visions were also problematic. There were three that seemed particularly important, so I will write them first;

one was of a place somewhere in south west "X" (I will not reveal the name of the country, just call it "X"). The Serpent was being raised from a pit. The message of the vision was that country X was allying itself with the Evil One, drawing on that Satanic energy.

In another vision related to the vision of the raising of the Serpent, this Serpent was being taken by train out of country X and into a country I will name "Y". There was a train crash and the train was derailed. People were standing around in horror.

There was also a really terrifying vision about a huge underground fortress in country X. The message of the vision was that country X was preparing for war.

I remember seeing a soldier in a small room;

it had something to do with that country using telepathy as a weapon of war. The soldier was lying down: he was a telepath.

As I remember, the room seemed to be made of stone. And the fortress was of stone.

Underground stone fortresses filled with secret armies, and telepathy being used as a weapon of war!

This made me worried, and caused me to recall my own experiences; that the area of reality we have demarcated and designated the 'collective unconscious' is under attack: human consciousness itself is being undermined. As Terry had said, people were being "undermined".

At other times I had glimpses of Terry himself on railway lines, on a railway track.

This was so odd that the image of Terry remained with me. I read a newspaper article sometime later which reported something about Satanists carrying out initiation ceremonies on train lines. I thought it was a peculiar place for an initiation ceremony. (But the concept of Satanism itself seems bizarre; given where it's taking you: to hell.) At other times I would see the most ghastly scenes. These may well have been a call to prayer, perhaps for people or situations. A particularly curious one was where I was taken in my vision to South America,

it seemed to be somewhere on the Amazon. I'm not sure, a huge river was involved. It was as if I was flying over land and sea to get there, carried by an eagle. And there were these huge metal drums with people inside. The drums were elliptical – and hanging from trees – so that the drums did not quite reach the ground. The people inside were roasting alive as a method of torture. It was indescribable at the time; horrible. It had something to do with the drug trade, and these people were being tortured.

Again, one aspect of the vision that disturbed me initially was the sense of being carried by an eagle. Over land and sea and then along a winding river. Yet I would later read of the eagle in the Apocalypse, and also in the Book of Ezekiel, where the eagle is described as one of the four winged creatures around the throne of God. And, of course, the eagle is the symbol of St. John the Divine, the author of the Apocalypse. A writer on the Dark Night of the Soul, whose work I would read much later, describes events of this nature occurring in intense mystical experience where the mystic is drawn to pray for people in the most terrible and terrifying situations. Obviously, I don't know if some of these situations ever occur – or occurred – in reality. But certainly, and again, after experiencing those terrible visions of hell I felt I could pray for anybody. And I certainly would pray for anyone suffering.

Other types of visions I put aside, because I know well enough from reading the Bible that only God knows when the end will come. These were Apocalyptic visions. Visions of a time when terrifying things would happen, and this time seemed to be approaching.

I recall one particularly,

of people crowding into a church and praying, and the sound of a bell clanging out across eternity.

In another vision,

I saw a sea of glass or crystal, with people walking out of the water that was a crystal sea. I think they were people who had died at sea. I was walking into this scene as the vision began. And then I just stood there, looking at the sea of crystal. There were two people sitting on the bank of the sea, or just a bit away, watching this person walking out of the water;

rising from the dead! Fully clothed!

The artist that came to mind was Stanley Spencer. Now presumably I would have seen some of his paintings in the Tate Gallery in London. Again, it was as if the picture was painted just for me. Interestingly, just writing this today, I looked up details about Stanley Spencer on the Internet. (Previously I hadn't got round to doing this, and I don't believe I ever made a study of this artist.) Apparently, a lot of his work involves modern interpretations of the Resurrection. Hopefully in heaven I will get to chat about it with him. It gives the impression these artists are still painting, which is a lovely thought.

I knew, at the time, that this vision was related to the Book of Revelation (4:6 and 15:2). But of course, it was problematic to handle, both intellectually and psychologically. Which was why I would frequently receive the sacrament of anointing; I desperately needed God to help me through this. The visions of hell, in particular, left what I can only describe as a permanent 'wound of warning'; of horror and sorrow in my soul, (a wound I feel I will have to carry with me until the end of my life).

But probably one of the most wonderful visions I had was just a tiny one;

it was of Christ.

I remember telling a nun about it. I think I told several other people,

Jesus was sitting with his back to a wall. I think it was the wall of the Temple in Jerusalem. The Lord was dressed in a simple white robe that was down to the ground, and he was looking down at his hands which were resting palms down on his legs. I think I could just see his feet.

At times I also feel the resonance of this vision was that

Jesus was with his people, with their backs to the wall.

I remember the nun asking me what Jesus looked like. And I said he looked like

a little tramp.

I feel the vision was meant particularly to depict Christ's utter humility. I sometimes pray now, visualizing that image because it resonates. And I recall the vision of my father as a priest-angel telling me not to be so "proud".

"Where do thoughts come from?"

Canon John once asked, with a curious look. Almost as if he was encouraging me to think a little more. Of course, I realized Ignatius of Loyola, the Jesuit saint, attempted to explain this, but I didn't know much about Ignatian discernment at the time, although Canon John did touch on it in our discussions. As far as I can understand, and from my own experience as well, we have our own thinking capability which is independent, we have free will, then we have influences either angelic or demonic. Everything we do and read and see and eat and breathe influences us. So, in a way, we are all between God and the devil: you choose who you 'tune into' (although you might not be totally aware of it). Maybe there are holy people, like Moses and Elijah and saints, who only experience visions of the holy; I admit I really wish I was like this. Anyway, John also described what had happened to me in another way to help me understand. He said the meditation I'd done had "opened me up psychically" but that I was "tuning in" at too low a level. I'd opened up the landscape of my soul and I was in a terrible state. I'd opened up to my own negativity, my own sinfulness:

my position in relation to God.

I was fit for hell. (Although John would never, never, say this to me or anyone else; this was my conviction.)

In Newport, I talked to Aunty Karen a little about my conversion experience, adding that life had now become "difficult". In response Karen described a Baptism in the Spirit she had received, also after a spiritual journey. Karen then related one type of Satanic attack that quite startled me, because I'd been there. In describing the attack Karen motioned with her hands and talked about, *"the airways moving".*

I knew she was talking about negative energy. I admitted I was still having problems and she responded,

"Satan sometimes gets angry when he loses someone."

Talk about a shudder running down your spine! I remember thinking in absolute horror, while attempting not to show it at all, "Oh my God! Why had I taken so many false trails?" At times it seemed to me that we experience,

a million false trails across the landscapes of time ... interweaving, criss-crossing. Deluding, beguiling; often psychologically, emotionally or intellectually engrossing ... but false trails. Rather like being in an enchanted forest. Or a maze. Unable to find the way out. Bewitched by our surroundings, or looking for an exit and unable to discover one.

Religions, philosophies, theories. Histories, songs and dreams. Webs of illusion called 'culture'. In a web you continually rage, because you are trapped,

and the cleverest web of them all, is the web of phenomenal time.

Stuck in a web, or in the amber of phenomenon, there is only one way out; and that is to turn to Christ.

And there I was in Mass,

when I saw an angel standing on the left side of the priest as I was looking toward the altar. The angel was a pillar of fire, about six foot tall, and began to move toward me. When the angel touched me I began to burn; it was so incredible I drew back, I became afraid.

I felt I was being purified in some way, *but something felt wrong* (which I will not disclose). So I drew back.

The angel withdrew.

... for freedom Christ has set us free!

Stand firm, then, and do not let yourselves be burdened again by a yoke of slavery.

The letter to the Galatians

Paris.

Champs-Elysees.

Le Coupole, my favorite brasserie. The artists, the writers, the models. The whole world seemed to be there; eating at the long tables, chatting and laughing. That was, probably still is, Coupole. And Paris, a city of romance, sometimes like a Chagall or Renoir painting in continuous motion. My mother was lonely, so we decided to take her with us on holiday to France. It was a lovely idea, except Mum still disliked Michael and would be exhilarated to see us argue, which we do from time to time like all couples. This annoyed the hell out of Michael, and things became difficult. So Mike was quite happy to be going home. As we drove back Mum became really irritating, and Michael fumed privately he felt like,

"Leaving her at Calais to swim the Channel and make her own way home."

John raised his eyebrows when I told him the trip was something of a failure, but at least he didn't make a mother-in-law joke.

At SPUC I mentioned meditation to Dave, a guy who worked there. He remarked that meditation "opens you up to the ether".

I recalled my own experience of negative energy and wondered; and also wondered precisely how he'd reached this conclusion. Towards the end of my time at SPUC, I opened a drawer one day and came across horrifying pictures of aborted fetuses: these were dead children I was looking at. In shock, I asked a senior colleague why the pictures weren't made public; why they weren't published to let people know what was going on? She replied that "they" (not SPUC) didn't want to upset people. I found this covering up difficult, because the pictures made it obvious, people were killing their own children and it was all being sanitized by redefinition.

Dave, who really was a peculiar character (and I couldn't help but wonder where he was coming from) offered his assessment of the situation;

"In the 1930s someone made a pact with the devil so that women would be willing to kill their own children."

I discussed this with Michael before dinner.

"He's barking mad!" Mike replied, adding, "Where do you find them? They're attracted to you like shit to a woolly blanket."

"But the pictures, Michael, my God! I've never seen anything so horrendous! These are babies, they're not 'fetuses'. Why aren't they letting people see what's going on?"

"Who's 'they'?"

"Well, you know, 'them'!"

"Oh yeah! 'Them'! Don't ask me."

It was like:

a Hiroshima of the soul. A Hiroshima in all our souls, blowing out red dust; the blood of the Innocents. Out across the landscape:

because "we".

Are "them". And yet,

"Before I formed you in the womb I knew you, before you were born I set you apart."

Long ago, those profound words echoing God's love for humanity were entrusted to that most melancholy of prophets, Jeremiah. But we will have nothing of that. We have placed our trust not in God, but in Man. And so Man has become God. We now define what does – and what does not – constitute human life,

who is fit to live, and who is chosen

to die.

The whole experience at SPUC had a tremendous impact on me. I certainly didn't, and don't feel, you can blindly condemn anyone, because you never know people's circumstances in life. But taking life is killing. And I wouldn't like to be killed just because I didn't have a voice. The problem for me was that I was part of a society that was doing this; I was part of it. What could I do? I got passionate. I got annoyed. Mike told me off. I felt crazed and I felt impotent. All I could do was work. And pray.

Meanwhile, the situation with Mike's colleague, Andrew, was deteriorating. At times during this period I frequently questioned my own sanity, but when Andrew's wife, Amanda, informed me she was a "witch" I had another moment when I questioned other people's sanity. I mean, we'd lived in Africa and other places where witches were really, really bad news; grotesquely evil people. In England, they seemed to have deconstructed the whole thing, redefined it so that we could accept this morphing. More and more the cultural mind-set seemed to be to redefine something and so render it socially acceptable, to gloss over negativity and dress up death in a ball-gown. We went out with Andrew and Amanda infrequently, but she made the comment that she was "a witch" several times. When she did I just changed the subject; I mean, I didn't want to go there. But it was kind of odd. Amanda appeared okay on the surface, rather Fortnum and Mason English, conservatively dressed but well-groomed; an attractive woman.

Yet there was this edge, unlike Andrew who could be in your face, out-and-out malevolent.

By now things had settled spiritually, so Canon John gently suggested,

"Why don't you and Michael think of having a child?"

I was willing, but Mike felt he couldn't cope. The strain of the last few years had taken their toll. And a concrete problem was space. We couldn't afford to move, and our flat was only big enough for one person. So I reluctantly conceded,

"Maybe it's not a good idea."

In a way this transition time of a couple of months formed a hiatus of calm, because shortly later Mum began to act strangely. She telephoned, and said she wanted me to come to Newport and,

"Take anything! Anything you want from the apartment; I want you to have something."

Mother sounded distressed when I spoke to her on the telephone, and I really couldn't understand what was wrong. During the course of our conversations she would make strange, terribly soulful and sorrowful remarks such as,

"I've lived too long."

I felt so sad that she was far away. A while later the truth surfaced when Patrick contacted me by telephone. Patrick sounded upset and agitated, and said Mum was "no longer able to take care of herself". Among other things, Patrick had discovered Mum's fridge in a terrible state, and he was worried about her leaving the stove unattended. He also said she was frequently getting lost and had become an erratic – and potentially dangerous – driver. At this point we suspected Alzheimer's disease, it runs in the family. My brother wanted us to put Mum into care near him, but I got it into my head that this wouldn't be a good idea; I knew Mum would hate the loss of freedom. So we discussed it with my sisters. I felt strongly we should bring Mum to live nearby. It was possibly the right decision for my mother's well-being, but it turned out to be disastrous for us; we had no idea how serious and pernicious my mother's form of Alzheimer's was.

Really, Laura did all the hard work. As I said, she has amazing energy and was just incredibly brilliant to do it, because Mother was fast losing her marbles. So it was an immense achievement on Laura's part. But it was the start of a difficult time for everyone. We didn't tell Mother she had Alzheimer's because no definite diagnosis was made, and we shared her care. Laura and Robert were wonderful getting Mum's place ready. This was an up-market and immaculate retirement apartment in a sheltered complex close to me. Alice lived a bit further away. Unfortunately, she and Mark had lost their house and fortune funding a production that flopped, and had moved into council accommodation. So they were experiencing difficult times. It was quite dreadful, with bailiffs called in and related problems. On top of that, Alice's health was very poor.

At first it wasn't too bad. But Mum was erratic. Sometimes so normal that Mike would evaluate the situation declaring,

"There's nothing wrong with her."

And then the symptoms would reveal themselves, like a phantom. So it was that we took Mum to the Dorchester for a celebration. She was quite okay, but then for some reason the pianist, who was on a bit of an off-day, jarred and she threw a wobbly complaining more and more loudly,

"He's too noisy, he's dreadful. Get the fellow out of here. Michael, get him to stop playing that bloody piano. Michael; do something!"

We had to exit without finishing our canapés because she was eyeing her bag with the intention of attacking the poor man. It didn't entirely gel with that wonderful song, one of my favorites, which the pianist would tinkle,

"These foolish things (Remind Me Of You)."

Again at St. Aidan's it was Maundy Thursday where at Mass they have a tradition in the Anglican Church of dramatically portraying events following the Last Supper. So, at the end of the Mass the priest, in a loud, declamatory voice, pointedly emotes the scene-stopping words; "And they all fled!", to depict the way in which the disciples abandoned the Lord. As this utterance is made so the lights dim and there is silence for a while before the choir starts up with a melancholy psalm. But, as darkness descended, Mother began asking, then almost screaming,

"What's happened to the lights? Switch the lights on somebody, I can't see! Switch the lights on; lights! Lights! I'm frightened!"

As she became hysterical, we hustled her noisily out of the church. At least Michael could see the funny side of the situation, because I don't think the sidesmen were too pleased.

As my mother's condition deteriorated we all became stressed. Someone at St. Aidan's stepped in to help us with her care, so we should have been alright. But not having much stamina, I could only take so much. On the other hand, my mother's illness seemed to give her incredible energy; the woman seemed to be on the go twenty hours a day. Mum's deterioration swiftly became a vertical mental and physical descent of catastrophic intensity. She knew something was wrong, and on many occasions with me, would come to a juddering halt as her whole body went rigid and shook: it was as if she was having minor strokes. She was also tending to violence, and would frequently weep endlessly in agony. To top it off, she developed a fixation on me. Perhaps the most terrible thing was to see this once beautiful, proud and intelligent woman falling to pieces, and often being totally aware of the fact. Losing her speech, her co-ordination and eventually, her dignity.

Oh! And by the way I forgot to say: Arrivederci Mr Darwin.

One day the telephone rang in our flat. Before I answered,

I could hear this voice, like a spoken whirlpool of thoughts, saying,

"It's cancer. It's cancer. It's cancer."

A voice that was *in between a thought and a spoken word.*

I picked up the telephone and it was Patrick on the line. Gently, caringly, he broke the news,

"I've been diagnosed with cancer. But don't worry! It's going to be fine."

The shock of hearing the voice in my mind, and then having the information confirmed in reality, meant I didn't handle the news well, and in the course of our conversation found myself repeating several times,

"I'm sorry, I'm sorry ..."

Until Patrick gently rebuked me by requesting, "Please stop saying you're sorry. It's going to be okay!"

He was trying to help me, and sounded confident all would be well. This was Patrick, with his strong faith in God. I will never, never forget his bravery.

It was some time after replacing the receiver that I recalled the vision of my brother,

going to sleep in the House of his Fathers.

With Michael under increasing stress and my mother clinging, stability seemed to fall away. Gradually, everyone was pushed beyond their limit. Even John's joy seemed to dim as his health faltered and his heart condition became serious. The Canon talked a little wistfully, even dejectedly, about "retiring" and contacted the Bishop informing him of the need for "a younger man to take my place". As he talked about his decision he sounded positive, yet intermittently and worryingly, rubbed his chest where a pacemaker that had been installed was no longer working efficiently. Those angelic flames of fire at St. Aidan's and Holy Trinity were becoming older, and some were dying. These dear people who had helped me and been so kind and gentle were fading away, like candles being extinguished in a precipitous darkness. Now life became an unexpected autumn with a terrible winter drawing in, as Margo became chronically unwell and her medications failed to control the pain. One evening at High Mass in the Anglo-Catholic tradition in Holy Trinity church with the choir singing gloriously, I saw my dear friend, so in love with God, double up in pain. I remember turning to the Canon, who was sitting close by with Daisy beside him and being horrified at this dear woman's suffering, about which we could do absolutely, totally nothing, and making some inadequate comment about the horrendous suffering in the world. For once, even Canon John was lost for words. And there we were, Daisy turning, reaching out to Margo; the music and the incense rising as this woman of God suffered such torment she did not even want Daisy to touch her. Margo didn't want us to see her suffering, or acknowledge it. But this was where Margo wanted to be; High Mass in Holy Trinity church, with the altar paintings lit by the glowing of candles, so that the paintings resembled some ethereal and medieval mystical tapestry. The service continued, but it was the beginning of the end. That night was one of the last times I saw Margo, the horrible disease that tormented her gripping closer and closer, tearing her away from us.

So we went out. Out into the night.

Night.

Everything began to fall to pieces

like glass shattering in time –

The Shattered Glass.

A still

from the movie called "Time".
No meaning or explanation.

Humanity in freefall now,
splinters of glass impinging, bloodying us;

all of us.

On a collision path
with Armageddon.

Show me your face, let me hear your voice.

Song of Songs

Life continued, but moving inexorably towards fragmentation. Some things I cannot write ...

Another close friend became tragically ill. Her name was Elaine. Elaine was well into her nineties, a New Testament scholar working on a translation of Paul's letters. This inspired woman took her work tremendously seriously, and attended Mass as frequently as she could, given her age and the times of the Mass would allow. Realizing how these translators work, and becoming acquainted with this intensely spiritual woman gave me confidence in authorized versions of the Bible. Elaine would work in the morning, and then – perhaps – go out with friends in the afternoon; she was unstoppable, and still in possession of a scintillating intellect, so much for declining mental abilities with age! In getting to know her, I would have discussions with her about her work. She once remarked how curious it was that people could be so intense about the Mass in Latin; Elaine thought she could understand it more if people wanted the Mass in Aramaic or Hebrew. When I first got to know her, she used to ask me to buy Marks and Spencer's chicken pies for her (I really think she let me buy the pies because she knew I felt a need to make amends for my past). Just being able to do something positive and kind made me feel good about myself. Elaine was a great gift to me, and something of a persona at Holy Trinity, being a countess as well as having been one of the first women to graduate from Cambridge. Her humble apartment did not reveal this status, and I think her family had fallen on difficult times. But, even bent with arthritis, Elaine was always aristocratic. Her manners, especially, were exquisite and she would somehow always find time to write thank you notes and birthday cards. Her face was fine boned, and her hair in its grey bun with wisps around her cheeks echoed a younger beauty when her eyes must have shone. Now those eyes were dim, but with a loveliness that could never be erased. Elaine had told me several months before her death she felt her life was overly-long, and that she wanted to leave something by way of an inheritance to her children who were struggling financially. Her exact words at one point I don't recall, but I felt from them Elaine had received some sort of premonition of her impending death. I recall one day just before her death, when the Canon was walking the hospital wards with his tiny box of holy oils for anointing Christians he knew were sick or dying. Praying over people, even though they were sometimes only flickering consciousnesses, fading lights. I knelt and wept, about Elaine's suffering in the hospital chapel where the Canon discovered me, and we talked. So, there was a sense of despair. And after the funeral her son seemed beyond comforting; but that woman was holy.

Joyously, Alice was pregnant! Yet back in Newport Patrick and Genevieve were in the fight of their lives, so we all knew better than to impose on them. My desperate sisters began putting pressure on me to put more effort into caring for my mother, as this was more time consuming than anticipated, not to say emotionally and psychologically draining. I went to visit Laura, my object being to discuss the situation, and found her sitting looking forlorn in the large and elegant kitchen of her house, nursing those beautiful twins. She appeared stretched to the limit; her normally perfect and glistening auburn bob tousled, her face tired, worn. The air was so tense you could feel it: she didn't want me there. Laura's Bette Davis eyes seemed to accuse, her lovely face displaying irritation, exhaustion; perhaps even anger. I tried to find some way of addressing the issues, but the pressure and unfolding tragedy of it all meant there were few words between us; I felt a waste of space. After visiting Laura, I went to Mum's doctor in a vain attempt to get additional support for her care. I had thought, initially, more nursing help would be available for us: how wrong I was! The doctor was a terse individual, an Indian, with a ten minute slot for me and dozens of other patients lined up in an overstretched health system. He obviously knew of the distressing conditions in hospitals in our area for the elderly with Alzheimer's. The doctor had been unhelpful before, his attitude being we three daughters should be able to cope. Plus we shared the blessing, and at points like these the disadvantage, of looking put-together even in disastrous situations. Mike would describe it by saying,

"You all seem to look as if you've walked off a film set."

This was our upbringing, it was imbued in us to keep up appearances. But while we looked okay on the outside, we were all in a hell of a state on the inside. My parent's bones and skin I guess; my mother's prayers answered.

So there it was, from Chanel to hell. Literally, for me.

Upon my bed at night
I sought him whom my soul loves;
I sought him but found him not.

The Song of Solomon; nrsv

Mum now only seemed to sleep a few hours. When I or my sisters weren't with her she would telephone, so it was difficult to get any peace. I was receiving over forty phone calls a day from her, with Alice and Laura receiving a similar number. The coin began to drop that one severely mentally disturbed person removed from a hospital situation needs a dedicated team, with at least two individuals taking turns in the role of main carer, for it to really work. As part of her routine, Mother went regularly to our church. She got around extraordinarily well at first, and when nobody was there to stop her, could sometimes be seen sprinting the half mile or so to St. Aidan's in her elegant suit with a Hermes scarf, purchased by Laura as an indulgent present, flying from her coiffed hair. Mum's sheer physical strength, and body of a much younger woman, now became a distinct disadvantage. I recall sitting at the train station on one of our regular trips to St. Mary's Catholic Church, feeling I was going mad with fatigue and anguish, but still not being able to do enough; never being able to get away from the situation for a break to recoup strength and sleep. It got so bad on one occasion, that when I saw Mother with her companion I ran away, because I didn't have the inner strength to have her continuously clutching my arm and crying, those now childlike eyes begging me to help in some way; to stop what was happening: this terrible illness,

"Don't let them put me away!"

She would plead. And I would pray and pray and pray that something would eventuate to forestall the inevitable. I was doing all the research into Alzheimer's I could, and so was Laura, and we were feeding Mum vitamins and minerals, and she was eating like there was a famine situation on the horizon, yet still she remained as slim as ever. I even tried to persuade the noxious doctor to put her on HRT, having heard of Japanese research that hinted it might halt the progression of the disease. The doctor looked at me as if I was stark-staring mad! But that's how Alzheimer's can get you, it can drag you all the way to desperation zone. As things deteriorated, the relationship with my sisters and their spouses broke down entirely, to become nothing but a series of terse and sometimes angry accusatory conversations. All the support structures were falling away. To top it off, Mike's business involvement became so precarious and difficult the decision was made to liquidate the firm, which meant we lost our income. The optimum situation would have been to move to a bigger place further away to give us space to recoup strength. This was what I wanted, deep down. But, of course, we couldn't afford it. Our migration approval had come through some time ago, and with life falling to pieces, we decided the only thing to do was to go ahead with our plans to migrate.

It was the most terrible decision I have ever made.

Mike left England first, leaving me to sort things out. It was a time of hurry and duress, during which I put together the materials I'd been writing, including a manuscript of my spiritual experiences upon which this section of "Hannah's Song" is based. Before leaving, I had a short vision of someone, *tampering with my food at the airport*. I dismissed this, and didn't mention it to anyone. With this experience I realized I was in a very difficult period, so I suspected the vision to be an anxiety reaction. Anyway, I trusted God would take care of me. And left it at that.

And there was the leaving. Memories of an English saint. Memories of the time we put up those flags for the church fete. Margo and John and I. And the wind and the sun spinning. *And the sense of the fire of love* blowing in the wind over England.

All those wonderful moments. I was letting go because I was beyond my limit. Yet across the landscape of my soul, forever ringing out, there would be the stirring sounds of the British people singing their hymn of hope and joy and freedom to God;

William Blake's *Jerusalem*.

I looked from the plane. Far below the White Cliffs were disappearing as if into the past. All those memories! Memories of this country of my birth that I was leaving; possibly for good. The country which, with its allies, had stood out against the whole world and fought off that other, and terrible fire, in battle after battle. The graves of the war dead in the graveyards of the Somme, where times past Michael and I had stopped to pray and give thanks. And now the sense deep in my soul that another, and yet the same war, was being waged; the war for hearts and minds and souls. Stirring the consciousness of my people: and I was leaving them. And still the hymn,

Jerusalem.

"And did those feet in ancient time
Walk upon England's mountains green?"

Echoes in a landscape.
Farewell, adieu, my forever beautiful
Mother.

I sought him, but I found him not.

Solomon's Song; kjv

I thought I wrote so much in that last chapter out of guilt. And yes, I do feel guilt; I had failed in my duty as a daughter because I lacked the resources to do any more. How wretched, how hopeless, an individual I was. But there was something else, something until now I couldn't fathom ... the vision that I didn't speak. Would it have changed anything if I'd said something? Perhaps it would. But no-one wanted to know. So what has become of prophecy? Where are the prophets who only whisper to me in churches because they are afraid of being called crazy? And what of the Catholic priest with his eyes on his nails – and away from me – as he turned to go. And didn't want to talk. What has happened? What has happened to the visionary-mystics? How many are being dragged down, or silenced, or 'edited', in the Houses of Time. What is truth when human beings can become so evil that they can strike at the House of God? What sort of hell are they headed for? You make a rule not justified by the Bible, a rule that's difficult to keep. And if a priest breaks the rule, and doesn't repent and try his utmost to avoid the sin and then says the Mass, you pollute the priesthood; and the priest pollutes himself.

And so it was;

evil seeping through the cracks of eternity, as if something terrible had occurred. And we were all of us, falling. Falling through time ... and into sin. Drifting apart, drifting down. Tainted by the fragments of glass. Splinters impinging as everything fragmented: fragments,

and the darkness of despair upon us all.

Kristallnacht for the Anglican Church! First the priesthood; then the sacraments; then the teachings of the Church have to shatter. By pollution. Kristallnacth; violence! And a hammering at the door of my father's house. The mobs are upon us.

Vatican 11 and the Mercy of God ... the Anglican Church opens its communion tables to all Christians; the release of the Spirit as in the early Church.

One Lord, one table: the Mystical Shabbat.

And so the knocking at the door of the Second Coming of Christ; which has to be stopped. But the webs of illusion are tearing and the Houses of Time are opening,

so the only way out for the Evil One is backward into bondage.

Unity has to be stopped. Western Christian Civilization has to fall. To destroy a nation you have to pollute its entire soul,

and to pollute its soul you need to desecrate its Church.

First they came for the Jews. Now they're coming for us:

Kristallnacht for the Anglican Church.

Kristallnacht for the human race.

God is Night to the soul.

That sense of God's light exposing our darkness in "En una noche oscura", the poem *The Dark Night* composed by John of the Cross (16th century Spanish mystic, poet and spiritual director).

The time was the Inquisition. Spain. The sixteenth century. Spiritual fanaticism was wiping out dissent. People were disappearing in the night. John of the Cross was taken, and incarcerated, by his fellow Catholics. Locked up for nine months in a cupboard barely big enough for him to stand up in. Removed only to be beaten by his monk captors so badly that he would bear the scars for the rest of his life. He survived, escaped, and his work lives on; together with the knowledge that he was not broken by his experience. John felt no hate for his captors, just pity. His legacy is in eternity.

The only caveat I would add when writing about the sublime "Song of Songs", and the imagery of the Dark Night of the Soul itself, is that it's a very bad move to envisage this experience in terms of earthly eroticism when we are talking about the relationship of the soul to God. Whoever wants to approach the Shekhinah must be spiritually pure: there is no other way. So beware of those who depict the imagery uni-dimensionally, in terms of sensual eroticism. I repeat: "this is not a good move", as Canon John might understatedly, but pragmatically, describe it. In fact, it's a very dangerous move.

But back, back to the night. And to an awakening sleeper.

Feeling a sense of relief, I boarded the plane for Australia. I had no idea how physically and emotionally run-down I'd become. I still had a problem with allergies, and the meal on the plane might well have contained sugar. Mid-flight I had a massive reaction and went into anaphylactic shock. I was finding it impossible to breathe, but the cabin crew were brilliant, and a Singaporean doctor on board, an expert in allergic reactions, took charge. The doctor was carrying adrenalin, and monitored my blood pressure. I was given oxygen, and spent most of the flight to Singapore in an oxygen mask. When I was able to talk, I discovered the doctor to be a fellow Christian. I got him to write his name in my Bible, and meant to write to him when I got to Australia and thank him. But being a bit of a mess, I never did;

(so I'm thanking him now).

In Australia I received counseling. Here I discovered our experience of caring for an Alzheimer's victim was not unusual, and the scenario of family breakdown could be a spin off. We'd been unprepared for how bad it could get. For my sisters it was to become worse. What I found strange, was that I had always thought Alzheimer's just sent you happily gaga, something which even today can be a common view of the disease. One plus point was that although my relationship with my sisters had ceased, Patrick and Genevieve were still on speaking terms. My brother and sister-in-law had realized how difficult things were for us all from the beginning, and were more gentle, more accepting.

My spiritual life having calmed, we rented a place near a church and I resumed studying, while maintaining a daily routine of prayer and Mass. Meanwhile, Michael ran someone's business. While waiting to receive a research stipend and commence college, I worked for a time as a volunteer in a local hospital. My duties there involved sitting at the reception desk of the intensive care ward and ensuring the interface between relatives, staff and patient went smoothly. The job was rewarding, both psychologically and spiritually. Showing people around the hospital though, I had a disturbing experience when walking past one of the rooms on the lower floors that froze me in my tracks; a sense of *dry terror* emanating: something difficult to encapsulate in words *knives and steel and clinical death*. The sign on the door when I looked indicated it was the IVF room. Only later did I discover that the treatment of patients receiving IVF involved the destruction of embryos. To me it was a dead zone, and thereafter I tried to avoid this area of the hospital.

During this time my mother's condition deteriorated, and she was hospitalized. Laura and Alice found this a terrible decision. The details of my mother's life thereafter are not pleasant. Anyway, some while later she passed away. Not long after my brother also died. The funerals came and went in something of a blur. In fact, I still find it difficult – looking back at this period – to situate events in chronological order. I had developed asthma, and in an effort to regain my physical health, used medication and would also visit Christian healing services and receive the laying on of hands. Becoming desperate after being taken by ambulance to hospital suffering breathing problems yet again, I expressed my hopelessness of ever being cured to a person involved in the healing service at an Anglican church. The minister replied,

"Just repeat the phrase, 'By His stripes I am healed'."

I thought, "This guy's crazy!" But decided to give it a go anyway. Lo and behold, that was the end of the asthma! I still have terrible allergies from time to time, but I haven't had an asthmatic attack since.

Mike was working with lovely people, and the firm was successful, all of which helped enormously after the stress of constant tension in his UK practice. Also, we could afford to rent a nice house which was much larger than our place in England. Things going well, we decided to start a family. Being a late decision, we prayed and prayed. Nothing happened, and I became desperate one day and went down on my knees. I was crying and begging God to let us have a child. The words I used were,

"If the time is not right now, then a child in heaven."

I was weeping so much, and begging so much, I thought of the prophet Samuel, and the story of how his mother Hannah had wept, and of how Eli, the priest in the Old Testament story, had admonished her because he thought she was drunk. So I decided that if the child was a boy I would call him Samuel.

Shortly following this I did become pregnant.

I didn't have a definite premonition, but I did feel strongly that it was a boy and that he would look like Michael. I was carrying Samuel over the Christmas period, with all the wonderful Biblical readings at services in church about Mary and others, and the joy of the birth of Christ. With January upon us, and so the annual vacation period, Michael admitted he was exhausted, and said he'd like to get away and go on a walking holiday. He was reluctant to go with me pregnant, but I persuaded him I'd "be fine!" While Michael was away I started to miscarry. I remember going for a scan, and a doctor frightening the life out of me, which didn't help. Anyway, I miscarried at home; I wanted this and not some horrible operation as another doctor suggested. The child was a boy, and he looked just like Michael. I couldn't believe how perfectly formed Samuel was, even though he was only nine weeks old. He even had Michael's shoulders and nose and bone structure.

Michael returned early, and in a hurry, and in great distress.

My medico insisted I undergo a surgical procedure afterwards. Because I felt guilty that it was something I'd 'done', I had the operation with no anesthetic because, in the perversity of my grief, I wanted to suffer. A few days later we had a little service at home (without a priest of course) and baptized Samuel. We then went along and took the ashes to a church where there was a grotto dedicated to Our Lady. We prayed, and scattered the ashes (which made me think, afterwards, it would be a good thing if the Church did something formally for those who lose an unborn child, it would help with the healing). Anyway, Samuel's with God now; and, of course, the Virgin.

I was once again in mourning and distraught. I remember being comforted by some Catholic friends including a lady called Tee. Tee is an amazing woman, a Cambodian immigrant, charismatic and imbued with an intense and empathetic spirituality who worked in a challenging – and sometimes dangerous – occupation. Hers was the life of a "contemplative in the world of action", to paraphrase a descriptive book title from a work by Thomas Merton. Because I knew her well I asked her to pray for me, and as we sat together in the light-filled void of the church, I asked Tee in the stillness why women didn't talk much about miscarriage; why it was almost a non-event in women's lives. To which she replied, "It's just too painful".

Pain! The agony of loss ... I often think of Tee, and sometimes still see her in that beautiful church. She is older now, her beauty like that of a full rose: a Cambodian rose, dark haired ...

Anyway, for a while Mike and I kept praying, hoping I would fall pregnant. Then, when it seemed unlikely, we decided to adopt. This was a puzzling experience. The whole process turned out to be fraught with difficulty. As I was just over the age limit by then (Mike is a little younger than me) we were informed we "weren't eligible". This was completely ridiculous, of course, because we would have made good parents. I couldn't help wondering why IVF, which is expensive and entails discarding unborn human beings, was easier to access than adoption. We thought of trying to adopt from abroad, but this turned out to be problematic as well. In the end I just gave up. I really think I would have made a good mother, and Mike would have been a brilliant father, but because of all this bureaucracy it wasn't to be. I also feel it would have helped heal us after our loss. Certainly, what follows might never have occurred; at least in the same way. Michael started his own business, a consultancy, while I moved back into research. I felt it was only right to make use of all those years of study.

They beat me, they bruised me.
The Song of Songs

Where does this take us?

Meditation and contemplation expand consciousness and awareness. Wishing love on all creation is problematic when it develops to a point where you actually open up to evil. One Tibetan method of meditation I encountered shortly before my visions of hell, and even practiced for a while, though seemingly innocuous, is spiritually very, very dangerous. You are a temple of the Holy Spirit: you cannot love all beings because some beings are evil. And as a Christian you break your baptismal vows – you open up to evil. I recently encountered a book inviting readers to practice a similar method of meditation, which was aimed at Christians as well as others. But to meditate in this way is analogous to inviting a murderer armed with an AK-47 into your home, or a terrorist into your country, when he or she has the intention of killing you. Unfortunately, it's much worse; spiritually you open up to attack at the very centre of your soul. Mirroring Silviu's words, spoken years past that I did not then understand; and they are a warning to all people and at every level –

"We will trap you with your love."

It's not funny is it? Because this took me all the way to hell! Neat little trick though. And it can happen at all levels; evil doesn't tell the truth. And avoid making light of Satan. Even so-called 'great writers' have gone down this path, and it's another very bad move. Because you have to be very, very careful. That's why you keep relating to the commandments and the Bible. You cannot ultimately fight evil yourself; you have to turn to God. Interestingly, I even find myself wary of focusing on the breath in meditation, an exception being practices such as the Jesus prayer in Orthodox Christian spirituality. The very activity of this form of meditation, without a focus on God, can have the spin off of making physically automatic processes conscious, which can be problematic.

The visions of hell were so traumatic that twenty years on, even with regular prayer for healing, I find every attempt at writing and editing this manuscript, even just doing minor corrections, excruciatingly difficult. It is a book born of tears. I repeat you would be better off never being born; indeed, you would beg and plead never to have been born, than to go to hell. The experience was beyond description. The saints of the Orthodox Church say that those who see hell in this life will not see it in the next, and I pray to God they are correct. Again, people who say hell doesn't exist are misleading, whatever discipline they come from, even if they claim to be some famous mystic or priest or psychic or teacher or theologian. It's not scriptural, it's a lie; it's evil to even suggest it.

To be honest, I don't think the average person would consider me much of a sinner at the time of that terrible ordeal. In all truth, I was searching for God. And I certainly am no saint, but rather a penitent. Faith in the Judeo-Christian God is being undermined in many ways, not least by some priests and religious in the Church. As a result, terrible things are happening, and ordinary people are doing dreadful things with no regard for the consequences. People are selling their souls for trash; we are and have been systematically brainwashed. God is not to be trifled with. You strive never to sin. You even avoid negative fantasy. Interestingly, one of the spin-offs of a great deal of meditation and contemplation is that you realize the incredible power of the human psycho-physical system. Areas like the fantasy world and cyber-worlds are loci of energy we don't yet understand: real worlds within worlds. Areas of existence that have a reality we can open to and participate in. The possibilities for humanity are enormous, but we have to 'tune in' to God because otherwise we are tuning in to forces that will overpower and destroy us. We become puppets; actors who only feel they are free.

I'm writing this because I passionately don't want anyone to go to hell and, having had these experiences, know it is my duty to write. Hell exists. Christ died and rose so that we don't have to go there. Christ did not lie. I reiterate: writing this book is and has been such a harrowing experience that on many occasions my husband has begged me to stop. I have been near breakdown over and over again. I can't keep making it more eloquent because this involves opening myself up to recounting these experiences. No one who has ever lived can possibly describe the horror that awaits those who flout God's laws.

No one.

No description is humanly possible – or adequate – of what awaits people who do evil things. Who deliberately kill innocent people, who are fornicators, or practise deviant sexuality, or delve into the occult, or who lie and deliberately manipulate and brainwash people into thinking God doesn't exist and that Jesus Christ is not the Messiah. We all have to stand before God at the time of Judgment. That's why I'm writing. Not for money or fame or for any other gain on this earth. Nothing matters to me more than reaching out and trying to save as many people as I can from the terrible fire that awaits.

Hell exists.

The Great South Land of the Holy Spirit.

Episodes from "The Dark Night of the Spirit".

Weaving together the cloth.

The concept of the Dark Night of the Soul is developed in the work of the Christian mystic, John of the Cross, and also in the writings of more recent exponents on the subject. It became the topic of my PhD thesis in its latter stages of development. I've used the title "Night of the Spirit" here to describe these actual occurrences in my search for God and Truth. On the other hand, I don't find a strict demarcation between the two traditional nights, the "Night of the Senses" and the "Night of the Spirit", entirely justifiable here. Saying this also, the Christian journey, for me, has been more like climbing a mountain; an arduous, at times horrifying, but at other times exhilarating adventure: we are climbing the Eiger of the soul. There are times when your foot slips, and you find yourself hanging on for dear life. There are times when someone, Christ perhaps in the form of a fellow mountaineer, throws a rope. Times of desperation and despair when you are about to fall. Times of exhilaration that take your breath away when

you stand and look out from some high peak at a scene of engrossing beauty that is the fabric of reality in its perfection. You look out across the landscape of existence. The valleys and the shadows and the rivers and the glittering, dancing sunlight. Moments of glory and transcendence. These are the times when the glass of reality which has shattered re-aligns: comes together.

The water flows, and the wind rushes out into eternity, and beyond forever. And you and everyone you ever loved; everything that ever gave breath and looked up into the sky and wondered at the miracle of life, of existence, they are all with you.

Nothing of love is lost. All is perfect.

And then the mist descends again, and you find yourself struggling; the faltering step, the gasping breath.

The landscape of the soul – and of all existence – blurs.

The mystics can be the Mountaineers of the Spirit, and we are all mystics. Mankind is a mystical race. Don't you ever wonder why people drown themselves in booze, in drugs, in food, in anything? They have an emptiness within; a longing for something they cannot quite recall, cannot quite pin-point. People caught in webs of strange systems and ideologies, thrashing about and continually turning to violence against themselves or against others because of the rage and pain and torture of being trapped. We are all called by God. But we are all sinners. So, to be an authentic Christian is to be a mystic, although not all will have the same experiences;

we are all unique.

So then; the Dark Night of the Soul is a purgatory experience and may be described in terms of two moments or movements. (Again, to some extent I am using my own interpretation of the work of John of the Cross, with apologies for lacking John's beauty of prose.) The first, the "Night of the Senses", roughly might be seen as an initial purification of the upper levels of the psyche. The second, the "Night of the Spirit", depicts another grueling purification. Also harrowing; a wasteland experience. In both movements, reality is shattered over and over: you are broken. Torn apart by grief and horror at your own darkness and inability to cope. There is no firm ground anymore on which to stand. In a sense you are a figure down and out on the streets. You are the fool, an object of ridicule, down on your luck. Many turn and walk the other way. Even when I was going through these experiences, again and again, lines from that song by Bob Dylan, *Like a Rolling Stone*, would come to mind:

it wasn't nice to be there. You see things you feel no-one should ever see. Bear in mind also this process of purification is God's; it is not Man's. You do not deliberately seek out suffering for yourself; this is masochism. Suffering is part of our fallen world, it is horrible and none of us escape it. And, remember also that the purification of the Dark Night cannot be achieved by the violence of sometimes secret initiation ceremonies that are in any way damaging to the body, psyche and soul; this is paganism. The body is sacrosanct. It is the temple of the Holy Spirit.

We are all in the Dark Night of the Soul.

We are, at this point, in a landscape of imperfection of our own making. The glass of reality has shattered. So we have to face our own darkness, and the darkness of the abyss. And as we look down as we climb we realize we too can fall into the pit; or we might even be in the pit. But there is a way out. So we can also look up and out across the landscape of infinity;

we can all choose to open up to God and become what we are meant to be; healers of the world.

We can wipe away our tears and the tears of others,

and we can also see,

The Stars

Those lights in the dark night:
Those "keepers of the flame"
Are virgin souls
Who have kept their lamps alight
Within the Houses of Time.
And although stars are beautiful to behold
They bear no comparison to what will be revealed
For the morning is breaking, and shafts of light reveal
A dawn more wonderful
Than the world has ever known.
This is the promise of those rays,
the Word of our God;
that He will wipe away all our tears.

The shattered self:
the keepers of the walls took away my veil from me.

Solomon's Song; kjv

They took away my burial shroud.

As part of my work I was enrolled in a course in computing. To me computers are a replay of that sewing machine episode I had earlier in life, although – perhaps – I'm a little more skilful with computers. Anyway, we sat in a room, and they had one of those daft modern 'define yourself in a word' moments when we were asked to reveal how we 'defined' ourselves in a word. Huh! People gave nice, pithy definitions like 'happy', 'gentle' and 'thoughtful'. Then came my turn,

"I'm Hannah," I said, hesitating, because I really didn't want to go there, yet I wanted to be truthful. So, figuratively scraping my brain cells, embarrassed words of description spilled from my lips, "And I'm hopeless."

And everyone just became, like, silent.

Stone silent.

And I wanted to crawl under the computer desk and die. Without a word the lesson continued. As if it had never happened. And that was what it was like,

'I'm Hannah. And I'm hopeless."

It wasn't a good place to be. At all. But for some of us, unless you have touched nothingness yourself you cannot really start to empathize with the lost look in the eyes of the figure on the street; the person who just can't 'pull themselves together', as the commanding phrase runs. With the drug addict, the alcoholic, the war victim, the raped woman or man; the person pushed beyond their limits. The child redefined so that she or he can be exterminated to fit society's plan and viewpoint for humanity. When you fall to your knees, and see who – and where – you are in relation to God and you hear the *screams of silence,* you can feel for the animal in terror on the way to the abattoir. For some of us, to suffer is to open up to the crucifixion that lies at the heart of Man.

And, most of all; the crucifixion that lies at the heart of God.

To suffer yet to reach out for God, is to find salvation in the love of the suffering God. It is to discover the awesome nature of God's love for his creation, and for us. This purgatory experience that is an integral element of the Dark Night of the Soul, allows us – as we reach out for Christ – to become who we really are. Who and what we are meant to be. The layers are stripped away, purged; the distortion is purged by the fire.

This is the crucible of love; this is where we become gold in the crucible.

So, that visionary image of the holy in the fire, becomes the crucible of Divine Fire;

where we discover we are nothingness and dust.

We are glory and we are incandescence.

We are saints and we are

Mystics.

Crux

The symbolism of the cross.

The very sign of a cross displayed opens a doorway, a gateway in your psyche to the Kingdom of Heaven.

The cross is a symbol that breaks reality, and allows the entrance of the sacred.

When people begin to ban the cross, the symbol of freedom; of the right to choose between right and wrong, good and evil, then we are beginning to see the beginning of the end of the freedom of humanity.

Wear the cross as a symbol of human freedom.

Wear the cross with loyalty, humility, and reverence.

For the cross will set you free.

And give thanks to God. Because without the cross you will not survive.

A Great Darkness. A Great Tribulation is with us, and beyond that another tidal wave is coming;

something so terrible, more terrible than the world has ever seen.

Without Christ, the Biblical Christ; (for there are now many false churches and many false Christs).

Without Christ we will not survive.

Crux.

BUT NOW ...

NIGHT:

THE SECOND NIGHT

Sometimes known as

"The Night of the Spirit"

YOU ARE ONCE AGAIN ENTERING

THE NIGHT

In Africa; some while ago.
   A sangoma throws the bones –
for this is the time of

The Psychic Crucifixion

The Web:
The symbolism of the spider.

Another vision from long ago – *the spider.*

Within the psyche ... within the soul.

I began my research confidently with the idea of looking into concepts in Buddhism and Christianity. I was taking up – and developing – a theme tentatively explored by a noted scholar, and I seemed to be spiritually very open at this point because I immediately felt something as I walked into the college grounds which looked so beautiful,

it was like walking into a web: a spiritual spider's web. It was as if, just below the level of normal perception, there were these linkings and weavings of negative energy.

Unwisely, I dismissed the thought and watched the sunlight dancing. To put the whole situation in perspective of where I was; I'd been through a period of intense spiritual suffering, followed almost immediately by emotional suffering. I was away from Canon John. Christian mystics are not mainstream people at present, and because the very word 'mystic' has itself been flattened in the literature to include an array of deviant, evil spiritualities, I now move to another terminology for these experiences; that of the 'Christian-Prophetic'. Because the crystal castle of Teresa of Ávila that is the soul of a charismatic Christian during purification and sanctification contains profound potential (but more about this in a later book). At this point I was in uncharted territory spiritually and psychologically, but I should have paid attention to my spiritual intuition and got out, extricated myself from the situation; I didn't –

and I was to pay a very, very, heavy price.

Anyway, the department had the feel of the *centre of a web*. It felt almost 'sticky' spiritually,

as if bits of web were falling on you and attaching.

I found it so difficult to go in there I would just nip in, grab as many books as possible, and go home to study and research. I tried to work like this, not allowing myself to stand back and say,

"You just can't do this; it's not for you."

I hadn't learned the lessons; I wasn't listening to what the Holy Spirit was telling me.

I spoke to several people who said they had trouble with the way Christianity was taught at this theological college. Postmodernism was still a bit fashionable. I mentioned something about the Resurrection to one of my supervisors who taught Christianity. The reply I got was,

"Nobody believes that stuff any more."

The remark took me aback, I certainly believed! But I didn't say anything, much to my dismay.

"Not much of a disciple of Christ", I mumbled to myself when I got home.

And then, quite early on, came this strange visionary image. A kind of glimpse while I was asleep,

of a doll. And it was to do with the university in England. The doll was in a box. It was wrapped in bandages so that it looked like a doll in the form of an Egyptian mummy. And there was the implication that this doll, this fetish-like effigy, was on its way to Australia.

I thought it was unbelievable, of course. I didn't tell anyone and just dismissed it. It was shortly after that, as I walked out of a meeting with one of my supervisors, I heard the supervisor's voice. Not spoken, but quite clearly articulated in my mind. For which I now introduce the concept of a 'fissionary thought',

"I've seen your doll."

The words had a cruel and menacing edge. Again, I dismissed the whole thing as irrational, (I guessed I had developed some sort of persecution complex and had to get over it). I really, desperately, wanted to put the horrible events of the last few years behind me; I wanted to get on with life and be like everybody else: this was very important to me; I wanted to stabilize and be 'ordinary'. But the web seemed to reach out when I was in the college. It was as if I was beginning to link in with other minds; down, down, down. As if I was caught in some sort of vortex. I remember picking up the fissionary thought,

"in hate."

As if hatred and fear ruled in some way in this place. And then there was the phrase,

"You don't know how evil we are."

This I would pick up from time to time.

Another concept I picked up was,

"transmogrification."

This seemed aimed sometimes at me (I actually didn't know what it meant). More recently I looked the word up; apparently it has the connotation of a change in spiritual state in a negative sense.

And the words,

"moral turpitude."

I decided I was totally paranoid, and I wasn't going to put up with this! I put the fissionary thought aside. Another fissionary concept I seemed to tune into was,

"warlock."

I was unsure what a warlock actually was, but it sounded decidedly unsavory, rather ghastly; I presumed a male witch. I'm still not sure. I really don't even like to look this sort of stuff up on the internet. *"Witch"* was another fissionary thought, but that was less frequent. Aspects of what might be termed the occult were taught at the college, but I disregarded this even though I should have been more wary. Yet another fissionary concept I tuned into was the word,

"imprint".

This seemed to have something to do with the animal world. As if to imply there was some effort to 'imprint' me. Later, I would sometimes 'hear' the fissionary words,

"I hate Michael." And,

"I hope Michael gets cancer."

Another thought stream I would tune into was,

"This is just the tip of the iceberg!"

As if something really massive was going on.

Again, the philosophical and theological ethos prevalent was pretty much the postmodernist idea of the relativism of all belief systems. So Judeo-Christianity is presented as just one belief system among many. And, even though I recalled Canon John's advice, I was determined to be like everybody else. Telepathy does not exist; you can't hear other people's thoughts! Anyway, I was over that; or so I liked to tell myself. Now, I feel it's more accurate to describe phenomena such as telepathy as 'enhanced empathy' at the level of the pagan-shamanic (differentiating this from the Christian-Prophetic which is another order of experience). But at that point I was unsure of what was going on. Basically, I was in denial concerning these events. Anyway, this all happened over time and for most of that time things were pretty much normal, although I couldn't get out of the college fast enough and the atmosphere *felt spiritually bad*. I was at the college for a period of just over twenty-two months before I pulled out and eventually changed course. When these occurrences happened I would just reflect,

"This is all a bit weird."

And get on with it. Yet one, almost amusing experience, looking back, was *hearing* very occasionally a little angel following me, informing me emphatically,

"They're all Satanists! They're all Satanists!"

And then there came the day when I was in an open lecture. I was sitting there, and some women were behind me. I remember one of them got up and walked past and seemed to deliberately tug out a piece of my hair, (I still had very long hair). Most people would have said something, but I'm too easy going for that. Again I thought,

"Well. Bloody odd."

And a person (I'll name the person "Z") walked – marched – out of the lecture theatre. And I *heard the words,*

"*Crucify her!*"

And the woman who'd yanked out my hair followed Z; as if she had heard the command.

I thought, "I'm barking mad! You can't hear other people's thoughts."

I mean, I'd studied the literature; the psychic stage of Christian spiritual experience is only temporary. This appeared to be a common presumption; the psychic stage is merely a stage on the path to spiritual maturity. Yet it occurred to me also – in a kind of deep, spiritual way – that this was a repeat of what happened at the university in England some years back; that it was the same sort of thing: the hair pulling just didn't feel like an accident. To be honest, I can't think of other occasions in my life when I felt that my hair was being deliberately yanked out (nasty really, when I think back). It was shortly after this, I had another vivid visionary image: *"Z" was holding up the strand of hair that had been pulled out. And it was covered with disgusting slime. "Z" was exclaiming,*

"*Look what they've done to her hair!*" *As if in mock horror.*

The strand of hair was coated with filthy stuff.

I woke up; I was rather proud of my hair. A lot of Dad's family had nice hair; even my auntie all those years ago, hidden beneath her nun's veil. And perhaps deep, deep down there came a vague memory; tales of sorcery. Of the use of body parts such as hair and nails and other, really revolting physical excreta employed in witchcraft. Stories I'd heard, but discounted; nobody did that anymore: twenty-first century people weren't into spells! And magic! And the occult – for heaven's sake!

(But, babe, just go into major bookshops in Britain and Australia and elsewhere and it's out there. Books on spells. It's fun ... isn't it? One chain even sold a book of spells for kids a few years back. Still, it's just fun, isn't it? Then why do people kill themselves from fear in societies where this stuff takes hold? Or, as one Christian woman, a highly-intelligent, charismatic individual, exclaimed in spiritual turmoil,

"I'm sick of people mucking with my head!"

Because that's what it can feel like to a spiritually sensitive and receptive or open person, as if someone's messing with your mind. But I didn't know that then, or rather I wouldn't accept it.)

Increasingly perturbed, and torn between experience and accepted psychological and spiritual paradigms, I made an appointment with a priest who was also employed as a psychologist and counselor. I'd known Cyril and Meg (his wife) for several years and considered them trustworthy. Cyril also had a good professional reputation; he was down-to earth and highly intelligent. After an initial discussion of my emotional turmoil during the preceding decade or so, I raised the issue of spiritual experience and the possibility of telepathy. Reverend Cyril was unconvinced, definitively shaking his head while proclaiming,

"No! No! That's impossible!"

Despite Cyril's protests, I timidly suggested it had happened to *me*. Cyril shook his head even more decisively, and (to illustrate the utter absurdity of the notion) drew two heads on his office whiteboard. This done, Cyril pointed to the heads one at a time using a stick to illustrate and describe the location of the heads, and so minds, as totally separate entities in space. As he did so he concluded authoritatively,

"This is one mind; and this is another. There is no connection, there can be no connection!"

Cyril's voice had been raised in exclamation as he awaited my response. I looked at the heads and reasoned,

"I'm going to end up banged up with the key thrown away if I keep this up."

Now on the defensive, I nodded in agreement, and we wound up the consultation. Cyril smiled gently as I departed. On the surface we both appeared reassured. He was a very pleasant chap, and had even arranged to give me a discount as a student. I paid his receptionist the fee, and exited the consulting rooms. Determined to keep my mouth shut and my head down for ever more.

So it was, that even after everything that had transpired, I continued to try to convince myself that all this talk about telepathy wasn't plausible. And yet I was quite aware – at the same time – that material was being disseminated in the area where we were living relating to the practice of witchcraft, or wicca, and that spells and negative manipulation were being re-worked to sound acceptable, or a bit of a lark perhaps.

But if it has no effect – why bother?

Arise, my darling, my beatiful one, and come with me.

The Song of Songs

Anyway,

at another time, *I had a weird visionary image of this professor and what seemed like a number of people in the department, all sitting in a rather nice, middle class sort of garden. The funny thing is, that the main person I'm alluding to was sitting in – it was like a circle of seated people – and he was dressed in women's clothes.*

As I'm writing this I realize it's all quite strange, and I'm not sure why I'm including this vision, because it doesn't seem relevant. So it was kind of a slow thing; a lot of the time there was nothing but this awful feeling.

At other times, the weaving of worlds together was so intense I really believed I was tuning in to what other individuals were thinking. It was almost as if there was a kind of telepathy going on in the department; as if people were, literally, tuning in to one another and sometimes to me. It was quite weird.

I put the idea aside. Again, the whole mood being,

"Get out as fast as you can."

I tried to ignore it all. But divulged something of my experiences to a Catholic priest, a charismatic and exorcist. The priest sounded surprised and responded,

"You are a free human being; a child of God. You are free to go wherever you wish."

This seemed to make sense, I agreed with him. He was sympathetic, even empathetic, and a good man; he was right! I was determined to hang on in there! However, another very kind – and even saintly – priest I spoke to appeared to take fright, and almost ran out of his office when I described just something of my experiences in an effort to come to terms with them. It was deeply humiliating. And I felt scared myself, I mean; he was almost running away from me. He was scared,

I was scared!

At the same time, I would have the laying on of hands for healing. I would confess things that would seem, even to me at the time a bit over-the-top and terribly badly explained, probably giving the wrong impression. But I felt I wanted to confess everything I had ever done, or might possibly have done. I believed I had done terrible things wrong, and I had. Because at this level of experience you are very aware that sin of any sort causes a terrifying fracture of reality (the Garden of Eden story flashes to mind). It was grueling to realize how sinful I had been, and was. I was now also subjected to the most horrendous temptations. In the Lord's Prayer you pray not to be led into temptation. And now I know what Jesus was getting at – to some extent – at least. This was really strange, indeed awful, and I now feel strongly this was why the Holy Spirit was telling me to "get out!" I was too vulnerable, too damaged emotionally and psychologically for this. So at times I didn't quite know if I'd succumbed, and given in and thought and dwelt on doing something nasty; and I had dwelt unhealthily at times of weakness. So it was horrible. Extremely distressing and, at the same time, understandably totally impossible to describe to someone who hasn't been there. Of course, I should have realized the whole situation was out of hand. But I didn't. I really didn't understand the whole idea behind spiritual inspiration within the life of the Christian, (and this is very important) that when the Holy Spirit is guiding you out of a situation it's because this particular situation is *not for you*. Each of us has our individual abilities and calling in the spiritual sense. I was somewhere which might have been perfectly okay for another Christian or person being called by the Spirit of God, but it was not okay for me. However, my gift of discernment was not developed; I was not listening, I was trying to do my own thing.

The Mystic Cloth of Hope.

In my search for the healing of my soul, I attended a Mass presided over by a gifted Catholic priest from America. This priest had a worldwide reputation, but the whole Mass was much longer than usual, with a lot of extra praying and singing. I was annoyed, and terribly disappointed, because I couldn't stay for the actual laying on of hands. I remember saying to myself, and to God, as I left,

"I have to leave. But I really do believe in the Resurrection! And I'm sorry I can't stay. But I know, God, that anything is possible for you."

It was late. And when I got home, still disappointed by the protracted service, as I slept I had this absolutely miraculous vision of the body of Christ rising in my unconscious ...

A white robed figure in the blackness, in the darkness. Out of the Night. And not just my unconscious. As if this was something happening in what we call the 'collective unconscious'.

Christ rising.

I find it difficult to write. It has had a tremendous impact on me, this beautiful, wondrous vision. Not then so much as now; more and more. It was one of the most wonderful and inspiring visions I have had. It was incredible: it was hope! It was the Messianic promise;

Christ rising and everything else fading into insignificance.

Joseph had a coat of many colours.
Joseph, the man of dreams.

"In the last days, God says, I will pour out my Spirit on all people."
(The Acts of the Apostles (see also Joel 2:28).

"I am black, but comely, O ye daughters of Jerusalem, as the tents of Kedar, as the curtains of Solomon." (The Song of Solomon; kjv)

"Go forth, O ye daughters of Zion, and behold king Solomon with the crown wherewith his mother crowned him in the day of his espousals, and in the day of the gladness of his heart." (The Song of Solomon; kjv)

A gift given in a church by a stranger and a visionary dream;

people sitting in a circle outside my home: a curse.

In the library in the spirituality section I noted books on the demonic, and on what I would term very dark areas of spirituality. I would also look for books for my leisure reading in the English literature section. Here, I came across books of a Gothic genre. This literature also felt *dark, nasty stuff; really edgy: you don't go there*. Spiritually, the whole atmosphere was *'sticky'*, as if I was picking up something that was not at all healthy. It jangled with my sense of what is 'good', and it made me uneasy just to be there;

more and more I felt something was wrong.

Not handling my research well, and being thwarted by a disinterested and negative supervisor, it seemed a good time to get away and think things through. So, I persuaded Michael to accompany me on a holiday that would also be a pilgrimage in memory of my mother. I decided on a self-drive holiday to Israel, because this seemed the ultimate pilgrimage spot.

We had a stopover for a day or so in Singapore, a place I loved, before flying on to Heathrow. I had sometimes, in the past, flown alone and would always pick the island as a stopping-off place, finding traveling tiring. Singapore always felt safe; I could wander the streets of Chinatown or the Malay quarter alone with no sense of fear. I loved the mingling of cultures, and despite the political restrictions, felt a tremendous sense of religious freedom spanning Malay Muslim to Buddhist and Hindu. But most of all, I was inspired by the Christianity in Singapore; especially the deep Catholicity of St. Joseph's on Victoria Street with its statues of colorful angels; too pretty to believe – as if they should be on a spiritual wedding cake. And the contrasting dim light of the Anglican cathedral with Mass after Mass on Sunday, and memorials to the fallen in war, revealing so emotively the stalwart spirit of Anglican Christian Singaporeans. In earlier days, Mike and I would go to Raffles and find a seat in the Writers Bar, where the bartender would remember my drink. Hand in hand, we would wander the evocative hotel and stop at the museum which contained, among other memorabilia, a picture of Ava Gardiner that always struck me because of its evocation of Hollywood glamor. The photographer had caught the actress with a surprised look, as though she had been startled by a flash-bulb.

Additionally, we had some very good Chinese friends, which made Singapore a highlight of any trip. Willy Chong and his wife Vivienne had been friendly with Mike and myself during Mike's college days in England, and Mike counted Willy as one of his best and most trustworthy friends. Now Willy was a very successful businessman, while Vivienne had a career in International Relations which took her all over the world. She was charming and elegant with a graceful disposition, impeccable manners, and that beauty which some Oriental women posses; slim with a porcelain-like fragility of bone in the deft etching of her features, eyes dark but gentle in their gaze, clear skin and well-defined black-as-jet eyebrows.

This being so, as always when in Singapore, we invited our friends to Raffles for a late afternoon drink. But now, as the pianist played and Vivienne brushed her shoulder with her hand, her red-lacquered and perfect almond-shaped nails dismissing a hair, Willy looked across at me with genuine concern. He had noticed my loss of weight and enquired,

"You look so pale, Hannah ... are you eating enough? Is Mike feeding you?" Willy made the remark sound like a jest. But his face betrayed him; he couldn't hide his worry. Mike didn't hear, but Vivienne caught her husband's words, and very politely and without casting so much as a glance at my extreme slenderness suggested,

"Willy, why don't we go for something to eat?"

My mind turned, briefly, to Laura. She had once dismissed me as "too womanly to be a model" (as Laura tactfully phrased it. Really she meant I was most definitely not the desired size "4").

I wondered what Laura would have thought now.

Raffles Hotel. Lillian with her butterfly laughter and beautiful clothes and favorite Ferragamo pumps. All the loveliness of the past and still today. And the monsoon rains. The next afternoon I wore a dress of yellow with blue flowers scattered across the silk. And stood in Raffles courtyard with an umbrella in my hand as Mike photographed me. But it was not the same. Nothing would ever be the same anymore. Ever again.

Jerusalem ... Jerusalem.
The centre of the world;

where reality is tearing across tectonic plates of consciousness –

lighting a fever in men's souls.

Preparing to board the El Al flight, we marveled at the impressive security; the questioning and cross questioning. An Indian man in an adjacent aisle waiting to board, was transporting a rice cooker in his luggage. We watched in amazement and concern as this cooker was meticulously dismantled by a diligent Israeli female security guard. The man and his family looked on, with one or more family members occasionally gesticulating. After an uneventful flight, and on arrival at Ben Gurion Airport, we hired a taxi. The cab was so decrepit I was worried the engine might fall out. It would have helped if the driver, who was an Arab, had knowledge of even a little English, or more to the point, if we had spoken some Arabic. Not for the first time Michael enquired of me uncertainly,

"You're quite sure about this?"

I made no response. The driver drove erratically – and extremely fast – along the dark road to Jerusalem. As the morning light broke we reached the city, at which point the driver gave up on trying to find our hotel and, despite Michael's protests, we were disgorged unceremoniously at the end of a narrow street adjacent the Via Dolorosa. Miffed and tired, dragging our bags behind us, we threaded our way though the narrow streets of the Old City. Luckily, the driver wasn't too far out, and we were close to our destination because, by chance, we stumbled upon an obscure doorway that was the entrance to the converted convent that was our hotel.

Although relieved at not having to walk far, the interior of the hotel seemed drab and uninspiring: not quite as anticipated. We rang the bell at the reception desk, staring sleepily at the videoed pictures of the street outside, relayed by security cameras onto a screen behind the desk. A thirty-something male receptionist emerged from a back room, introduced himself as Al, noted our details efficiently, checked our passports and handed us keys; informing us – as we were escorted along the ground floor corridor and up a narrow staircase – that he was a fellow tourist who liked Jerusalem and was taking some time out here. Al opened a door to reveal our room, which reflected the monastic ethos, being small, drab and containing only a double bed, basic shower, functional dressing table and a rather unstable looking oil heater. There was a narrow window at the end of the room near the bedhead, and a dressing table, but the window itself was too high off the ground to give any view. Not having to explain anything about the room's sparse facilities, Al departed leaving us to fumble with the heater. It was still very early, so we decided to shower before searching out the breakfast room. For some reason, as I washed, the water went all over the shower floor, spreading into the room. This irritated Michael, who had showered previously, and had managed to exit the shower leaving everything pristine and dry;

"How come you always get water everywhere?" he enquired with extreme irritation.

To which I retorted defensively, "I don't know. I seem to use more water than most people."

Sullenly, we commenced to mop away the water with two of the small, rough cotton towels provided; a third and last cloth I had wrapped, rather ineffectively, around my head. This towel was nowhere near big enough, and fell off as I mopped, leaving my wet hair falling like seaweed. I was wearing a thin, cotton robe provided by the hotel for our personal use, but it was cold, and even both of us mopping didn't work that well.

The room was now both damp and barely heated in the January chill. After dressing, we made our way downstairs to have breakfast. Tucker was served in a dark, communal dining room. Here we were encouraged to serve ourselves from a long table situated at one end of the room. The food was basic but good, comprising cereals, reasonable toast, yogurt and fruit as well as tea and coffee in large standing flasks. Sitting down at one of the small wooden tables with a cloth of faded gingham laid across, we introduced ourselves to a guy called Daniel who'd arrived recently after backpacking through Egypt. Daniel gave us tips about driving in Israel, and Michael started to cheer up. (This was a relief to me, as, as I have hinted, Michael had not been at all keen on our trip; in fact he considered Israel a war zone.) But Daniel and Mike got on like a house on fire, so the atmosphere improved immensely.

Oh dear, "Jerusalem fever", as the craziness that can overtake a visitor to the city is called, soon hit! That first day, driving to Bethlehem, we were turned back because of a road block; for some reason I'd interpreted the road map incorrectly. Heading for Jericho, we got pelted by snowballs aimed our way by young Palestinians who seemed friendly enough, except that the balls were large and comprised of solid ice. We started to get nervous as the car windows shook to pummeling after pummeling. Michael glared at me, his face betraying worry in case the windscreen shattered, and made the less than casual observation,

"I knew the stupid bastard at the car hire place shouldn't have provided a car with an Israeli registration." Mike became pensive for a short while before enquiring in a worried tone,

"Where are we?"

I studied the map (I find interpreting maps problematic).

"I'm not sure." Actually, it didn't matter, as we came to a stop in a line of traffic; yet another road block. Again, there were Jewish soldiers with guns checking the cars. Mike wound the window down, and before addressing the approaching Israeli army official, turned to me and enquired sarcastically,

"You're sure about this, are you?"

I felt a twinge of guilt, but the repetition of this particular question was beginning to irritate me. Meanwhile, the young soldier poked his head through the window; he seemed amiable enough.

Mike enquired, somewhat pathetically, but genuinely confused,

"Excuse me. Where are we?"

"You're just outside Ramallah. This is a checkpoint. Just wait here."

The soldier ordered us to move towards the kerb, directing the car by waving his gun. As he maneuvered the vehicle, Michael glared at me demanding,

"Where's Ramallah?"

I looked guilty and replied,

"It's on the West Bank."

"You don't self-drive through the West Bank! Where the hell are we?" He paused before adding, "I thought we were headed to Jericho?"

"We are," I replied. I should have added "I think", but didn't. Worriedly, I stared down at the map in front of me, hoping I had us on the right road.

"You've got the ruddy map the right way up, haven't you?"

"Of course I have," I responded, becoming more and more irritated. Michael was unconvinced, and glanced across and down at the map on my lap. (He was, by the way, making a reference to an episode years back when I read a map the wrong way up. We'd ended up going miles out of our way then; I was stigmatized following that.)

I checked the map again. We checked together. We looked at each other. The soldier seemed to be continuously, warily, wandering back and forth along the line of cars. Mike poked his head out of the window to attract the guy's attention,

"Which way's Jericho?"

"You can't go there", the soldier replied, "Jericho's closed."

"Thanks." Mike replied, before turning his attention to me as if he was asking, "How the hell do we get out of here?" And fumed aloud, "Who on earth would want to go on holiday to the West Bank? Even the Palestinians don't want to be on the West Bank. What are you, crazy! There are road blocks everywhere."

With that we gave up on reaching Jericho, returning instead to Jerusalem. There, after walking for some while and finding ourselves near the King David Hotel, we stopped at an art gallery where I became rapturous over a Chagall print. (I adore Chagall! Has anyone else come close to expressing romantic love in so exquisitely mystical a fashion?) The print was of Chagall's painting, *The Lovers*. As this was a $1000.00 US without P & P it was gravitationally out of our range. But I did argue my point, and Mike was hesitant. So we almost got there.

Dinner at the convent that evening was again a communal event, and we started up conversation with a youthful Dutch doctor named Ingrid, and her companion, Bennie. Ingrid was blonde, blue-eyed, slim and attractive but with a deep scar running the length of her left inner forearm that was noticeable with the beige sleeves of the pullover she was wearing ruched back. Bennie, her companion, was shorter with dark skin and hair, and so less Flemish in appearance. He was an accountant, and I guessed them to be in their late twenties. The red wine was rough and Israeli, and not quite brilliant and, curiously, could only be obtained from a locked cabinet in the dining area on request, and with immediate payment. Although the food was average the atmosphere was vibrant – incredible. And, probably because Mass was said every day in the chapel, there was a sense of something supernal about the whole place. Again, Mike was in his element and the evening was immensely enjoyable all round.

Unfortunately, the flooding problem with the leaky shower in our room repeated and repeated. Water always seemed to squidge through the shower door; but only in my case, Mike seemed to manage. Maybe it's his short hair – or aerodynamic body – or maybe he's totally static while he's showering. Whatever, I couldn't handle treading in water all the time, because much of the floor of our room never entirely dried out; I even found I had wet feet in bed. Cold I could tolerate, not cold and damp, especially when combined with the thin bed-linen. Now, snow was falling heavily and consistently, so I came up with the suggestion that we move to a more up-market hotel. Mike was not happy about this, as he was enjoying the camaraderie amongst our fellow travelers and explorers. This was cheering, as initially he also had misgivings about the convent, convinced he would be surrounded by religious fanatics. But I was insistent about the move, and so we left this wonderful place and our friends, Ingrid and Bennie and Daniel. But not before praying after Mass in an underground cavern where Jesus was scourged.

And so Jerusalem: the unbelievable sense of then and now ... touching the Wailing Wall and inserting a prayer; walking through streets where King David would have danced. You could almost hear the music, and experience David's joy, and come to realize why God loved him so much, this man who danced for God. It seemed to me, it was this very intensity of atmosphere and ambience that imparted something more than the supernatural,

the most beautiful city in creation;

realities breaking through.

The tomb of Jesus; the narrow opening you have to pass through to enter,

the narrow door.

The oil lights flickering, as if there was not enough oxygen. A kneeling lady in a scarf and dark clothes intermittently praying, and then wailing, and then praying again. With us inside the tomb. The raised area where the body of Christ would have been placed. I was pressed next to the deeply distressed woman, Mike couldn't move. He was last in, and so was jammed against the opening. Michael appeared perplexed, as if he didn't quite comprehend something in some way. Then, pushing at him, came another head through the narrow entrance. This head was attached to a very large female body. Mike grasped the lady's shoulders, and told her quietly to,

"Back off, lady."

But she kept coming. Panicking, he took her head in his hands, holding her in place as she looked at the floor; she was attempting to crawl her way in, squeezing her large torso through, which was the only way she could get in.

"Go back! There's too many of us! There's not enough air. Get out!"

Mike was truly terrified. With this pilgrim's head in his hands, he pushed her back pleading,

"Lady! Please! There's too many people in here, we'll all suffocate. Go back for heaven's sake!"

This place of grace. Of agony and ecstasy. Of death and resurrection. Of exile and redemption, of coming home to God.

Beside me the other woman, whom I guessed to be of East European origin, continued her loud wailing and praying. And we were all praying, really. For the Jews, for the dispossessed Arabs, for ourselves; for the world. Amidst all this tension of experiences we heard the priest outside calling that our time was up. Anyway, it was for some reason unbearable to stay too long. And, because Mike finally successfully ejected the woman, we ourselves were able to exit this holiest of places. With Mike almost unable to speak, overcome with many emotions, just occasionally muttering,

"It's a fire risk."

His voice echoes, as I write and remember. Michael for once utterly disconcerted, totally out of character, it was all too much. Too much for him, for me. For those women. For us all. And the lamps flickering … the lamps flickering;

the lamps of Israel.

Walking by the Sea of Galilee, my foot touching the rippling water. Imagining Simon Peter, as he rushed from the fishing boat on hearing those amazing words,

"It is the Lord."

What a wonderful, wonderful moment that must have been, with the blue sky turning and the sun dazzling Simon Peter's eyes. I was there, realizing this was the water the Son of God had walked on. Turning, also with the sun in my eyes; being there, being here, imagining hearing, "It is the Lord!"

From long ago. And now; to us today. This was what it felt like. No vision really, save of the soul's illumination (and I think the great Teresa would have something to say about this).

Just this quiet, mystical place. A candle; a light: a flame in the soul of mankind.

Lightning in the Night.

Back in Oz, I concluded my supervisor wasn't interested in what I was doing (this isn't at all unusual). I should have changed supervisor long ago, because you need to have resilience and manoeuvre in the process of academic research if it's not pulling together. Anyway, I began to realize the topic I was focusing on was not going to get off the ground, even though I felt it was viable. Being emotionally and spiritually fragile, I began to question the wisdom of continuing. In a random fashion, as I weighed up the options, my interest moved to Thomas Merton. I can't remember exactly how.

It was at this point the crucible really seemed to begin to burn fiercely.

I pulled out of the college, and enrolled at a different theological college and found a new supervisor. Because I was curious about what I was experiencing, and trying to come to grips with how to handle it, I was looking at the mystics, particularly John of the Cross and Teresa of Ávila. At some point (and this proved insightful) I came across some modern writers on the Dark Night of the Soul. One particularly struck me. Reading this analysis would later help me understand, and so cope better with, what was happening spiritually and psychologically. What I discovered, was that I seemed to have reached a stage on the spiritual ascent where purification was again at work. Once more – at this point – what we describe as the unconscious of the individual surfaces; and so the wider landscape of consciousness. However, I wouldn't so much take this approach, rather I suggest and feel, that this is part of the whole process of starting to wake up, of seeing reality as it is;

of starting to reintegrate consciousness, as one rouses from the slumber of the night.

This, for me, is best expressed and felt, in a mystical and poetic sense as the road from Jerusalem to Gaza, the desert road. Where sometimes you feel totally alone. Yet you are, in fact, walking with a companion; the inscrutable and mysterious presence of the Risen Lord. So, consciousness opens out on the road that for the mystic is the spiritual ascent.

It was at this point that I experienced levels of consciousness I term 'primordial', where I felt instincts and desires rising up from a primitive animal level;

I was again entering the crucible.

But I wasn't aware of this, or at least of this in these terms. And I was also having trouble with John of the Cross, whose descriptive language and profundity, I found difficult. So I was very unsure of what was going on. Anyway, even with the move away from that first college I still seemed to 'tune in',

it was as if a piece of the web had linked on to me, and I couldn't quite detach.

Another concept that comes to mind (a term I dislike but which I include because it gives some sense of what I was experiencing)

an etheric trail.

I began to experience terrible sleep problems, and would be just about to drop off but would come to a juddering, waking state. Or, I would begin to dream and then be shocked into wakefulness;

I would also sometimes hear a particular song in my mind, just as you do sometimes, so that didn't seem strange. But as time went on the song, this same song, seemed to be linking me to a particular person, or more broadly, a group. It was almost like a negative mystical call from some sort of underground world; very, very nasty stuff. A kind of weird,

"Come away, come away with me."

Haunting. Like something from the world of myth, out of a dreamtime,

someone reaching out.

I would hear the music, and get the sense of someone tapping into my consciousness.

It was terrifying, strange; eerie. A compulsive call to a dark fascination; a mood downwards, projecting into a vertiginous negative reality: everything twisted. I wanted to get away, but there was this psychic, spiritual link;

it was like a bird singing its territory, in experience. Or, what I seemed to pick up; a warlock. Reaching out, using music as a kind of entrapment or enticement. A telepathic singing. An energy that linked in to very basic areas of my psyche and emotional being,

negative areas. One of which was the most tentative intuition of a terrifying primal fear. Writing it in this way is as raw as I can formulate it. This was exactly how it felt; an *unearthly thing*. I would pray and block it out, and attend church, of course.

St. Augustine's, the Anglican church I attended on a daily basis, was blessed by the presence of Rev. David, an exemplary priest and his wife Sue. Sue herself was a very gifted woman, both spiritually and linguistically, who taught linguistics at university. David and Sue were really helpful and supportive of Michael and myself during this time, and I mentioned to David something of what I had experienced at the first college I studied at (he'd been a chaplain at the same college some years previously). I suspect David thought I was – perhaps – a little odd in this respect, although he was very kind and not in the least patronizing. David had found nothing untoward, or out of the ordinary, at the college. I respected his opinion, and felt a little embarrassed about having mentioned anything. On the other hand, around this time I did meet one young girl who'd experienced something similar. A beautiful, dark-haired Christian woman, who'd left the college under similar circumstances. This girl gave a brief explanation, and concluded by saying of the college,

"I couldn't go in there."

Her experience resonated, but being damaged myself I felt the best thing I could do was to advise her to speak to a priest. Which I did.

More and more I would hear this haunting music. It was a popular tune, but not that recent.

I would, maybe, just be sitting down to read or something, *and it would be there: in the back of my mind. And then I would hear the words (the song repeating). And, as time went on, I could literally almost see this person – or perhaps, rather – intimate their presence. As if they were calling,*

"Come away. Come away."

When I read the words 'songlines' this is exactly what it was like. (But I don't know enough about the traditional Aboriginal concept, so I can't refer directly to that.) The experience would be such that I would feel intensely emotional, but in a puzzling fashion. It was rather similar to instances when you listen to music, and become involved at an emotional level, but this experience was of greater intensity. Again, it had that sense of the primordial and of being just beyond my total control, as if something or someone had accessed whole areas of my consciousness;

a shamanic singing.

As if areas of my psyche and emotions were being pulled by strings, energy centers of feeling and emotion that resonated to the physical level. There was the distant sense that this was all intended to tear me, and everything around me, to pieces.

But that latter sense was just very quiet; a tiny intimation, the breath of the Spirit,

"Don't go there!"

Don't go to that terrible place!

At another time, I was praying in a Catholic church. It was evening ,and everyone had left the church, the light was dimming and a placid Australian night was drawing in. The world was calm, and everything else appeared totally normal;

I felt, almost saw, this horrible big demon thing:

reality opened up.

(This, again, is what I term a 'fissionary event', because when this happens you literally see into another dimension of being alongside the reality you are part of.)

This horrible thing seemed very tall, over six foot. For some reason it seemed to be a 'lust demon' trying to get hold of me. That's the word that came to mind.

Anyway, there is a receptacle in this church where the Blessed Sacrament is held for Perpetual Adoration; it's out in the open and easily accessible. I was so desperate I went and grabbed onto it and prayed. The priest was about to close the church, and sternly ordered,

"Don't! You might leave marks."

It was that saintly priest again, who had sort of run away from me; dear man. I was in a hell of a state, with this demonic bastard of a thing scaring the living daylights out of me.

The sleeping problems grew worse;

at times it was as if someone had that hideous doll, and was sticking something like matchsticks under its eyelids to prevent me sleeping.

Of course, I told myself – over and over again – this was just my imagination. But, still there, was *the intuition of some sort of sympathetic magic being employed*. I started to take tranquilizers and sleeping pills in an effort to sleep, shoving down four or five at once. Little distorts rationality like sleep deprivation. I have a resistant system, so the pills didn't work, and I went from doctor to doctor to obtain scripts. The mixture of medication, valium and sleeping pills, was dangerous to say the least. One doctor went out of her way to help; I guess she might have thought I was lonely or something. The first time she saw me I was in a very distressed state. We talked for a while, and I explained what I'd been doing at the college, and something about the area of religious experience I was researching. She was concerned, and extremely compassionate and caring. Unfortunately, this particular doctor left to have a baby and I didn't see her any more.

Sleep deprivation is torture. It's unimaginable if you haven't experienced it at this level. You start to lose your ability to function, to co-ordinate and react normally. I was stressed too easily, and would fly off the handle with Michael. At times, I was like fractured glass. My psyche, and particularly my mind, was a vortex of energy; a deluge, a monsoon. My consciousness was stretched to capacity, with every nerve and sinew of my body under psychic duress, every faculty working at intensity. I was existing in a state of heightened awareness that would hit randomly. Consequently, no matter how much I ate I was losing weight;

I was the shattered self.

The psychic stress impacted at every level; I was drained, I was fractious. At times, I was terribly difficult to live with, sometimes bursting into tears or displaying brief outbursts of anger for insufficient reason. I did some crazy things. One time, probably in fear because of some really disturbing experience, I laid out a cloth on the table in the dining area, and placed a crucifix upon it with my holy water bottle, and started to say the Mass. Mike was horrified by my bizarre behavior and exclaimed,

"You're a woman, you can't say the Mass."

He was so dismayed, he went upstairs and slammed the bedroom door. I collapsed in tears. He was right; my world was collapsing! How could I even think such a thing as to say the Mass;

I was clearly deranged.

Basically, I couldn't deal with the fatigue. I also think the medications impacted, because at one time I experienced some sort of tremor episode in church, and was shaking so much a girl standing next to me had to turn the pages of my prayer book for me. Rev. David was presiding, and was so concerned he came up to me afterwards and enquired,

"Are you okay?"

I wasn't. But I didn't want to let him see.

Again and again, I experienced these horrible primordial urges rising up from below the level of waking consciousness. I was totally aware and awake, but it was as if I was watching from afar. I couldn't stop these enormously powerful sensations; emotions, moods and feelings: immense energy gusts *like whirlwinds* tugging at my own psyche. I would lie down

and feel,

my feelings and emotions being pulled by strings ... turned off and on and up and down ... emotions dancing to this tune.

That bloody awful pop melody that seemed so nice once! Long ago, when I was in the everyday world, before the tune dragged me to this outer world on the edge of awareness, this nightmare zone, where I was becoming the unwilling plaything of something infernal buried deep in my psyche; even touching the universal psyche. As if it was eating away at my freedom, trying to consume me.

At other times, still beyond my control, as I would try to rest: some force or forces had a hold on me,

spiritual, emotional, psychic. And I really didn't want to go there,

I wanted to be me; to have control back.

What the hell was happening?

A sort of psycho-physical manipulation I couldn't tune out of?

A breakdown?

A breakthrough?

This would happen once, maybe twice, in a week. Always when I was at home and trying to rest. So there was no rest.

That word, "*warlock!*" would recur with menacing intensity.

So slowly the strange spiritual episode (again, I am denoting this as 'Christian-Prophetic', because there are no suitable concepts I can find in Judeo-Christian spiritual literature which give the essential experiential sense) took hold;

a world of instinctive desire and compulsion.

I seemed to enter the world of animals, and could tune into their primordial feelings. Again, it often began with the music,

the warlock singing his territory.

It wasn't all bad. I recall – on two occasions at least – I woke up *to hear the birds singing in English, "Glory and praise to God!" As if, at the same time as I was tuning into an intense negativity, I was also experiencing the way creation itself praises God. Each time it went on for about twenty minutes before dying down;*

the horrific, repetitive music was not there.

In fact, I couldn't listen to a lot of music after these experiences, I'd have to leave restaurants, cinemas; even churches. But this was different –

this was …

"the time of singing has come,

and the voice of the turtle-dove

is heard in our land." (The Song of Solomon; esv)

The language of the birds. Glorious, incandescent.

Something I will never forget. The birds,

Creation itself,
Praising God.
God was there with me in all of this!
Whirling me round like sand, like dust, in dark infinity;
His child.

Yet darkness falls: Night!

Again, the glass was shattering.

Once, as I was kneeling in church praying;

I began hearing voices praying for us. Inside and outside the church.

(I believed it was happening.)

The Church Militant praying.

I rose from my seat, and rushed outside the church to confront a group gathered around a priest in the porch. My words had the tenor of a manifesto, as I commanded them,

"Could you please stop praying for me!"

I couldn't see anyone else, so in my confusion I assumed these people had to be "them" – it was that real! The priest took it all in his stride, thank God, and got rid of me by politely shooing me away, and ignoring me at the same time, (I suppose there are a lot of crazies out there). Michael had come to the church looking for me, and discovered me as I was verbally challenging these people who, from what I understood, were gathered for a wedding rehearsal. I was both embarrassed and humiliated, but Michael was furious. I don't think he understood what was going on;

I needed help.

Back home – in desperation – I searched out Canon John's number. I had lost contact with him, his health being poor. But, as I was so distressed, I determined to telephone John in England. Daisy answered the telephone, and told me the Canon was too ill to speak. I felt dreadful. I remember trying to explain to Daisy something of what I was experiencing; she must have thought I was stark-staring mad.

I put the telephone down after we finished speaking and thought, "How could I have imposed on Daisy and Canon John? What's wrong with me?"

I loved them, they had gone out of their way to help me. And John was gravely ill.

Oh dear God, I was there again; grovelling! A wreck, a despicable thing; torn apart with no confidence left,

rock bottom.

Turn your eyes from me; They overwhelm me.

The Song of Songs

Some short while following,

I picked up my Bible, and found a strange force pushing me away from it. I struggled, but it was no good. I was intensely distressed, I couldn't look at my Bible! I fought to open the pages, I wouldn't put it down. *It was as if the incredible holiness of the book shone into the interior darkness I was experiencing.*

I would later read an account of the experiences of a woman known as Mary of Egypt. This fourth century saint's vita describes an incident in which she attempted to enter the Church of the Holy Sepulchre in Jerusalem, but was barred from doing so by an unseen force. Following this, Mary repented and led the life of an ascetic in the desert, displaying remarkable prophetic powers. Strangely enough, I have picked up that Bible, which has notes I wrote alongside the text during my period of intensive study of Judaism, and have sensed;

an incredibly holy feeling.

Another night, I woke up *and experienced a brilliant light being shone into the depths of my being; it was terrifying. I could see the light everywhere, and it seemed to be probing my entire soul. I was just darkness, compared to the light. It went on for quite a while and then just stopped.*

I was awake, and

God was shining in my soul.

So

God was unbearable, dazzling brilliance.

While I was desolate, profound darkness.

I recall thinking about the dead sleeping in light. Yet I realized, "I can't exist with this light. No-one can exist with this light."

Nowhere to hide from the light.

On the surface life continued as normal, while in reality my world was falling apart; fragmenting. I remember Michael stopping the car to fill up with fuel at a petrol station. I was hazed with fatigue; psychic, emotional and physical. Later, Michael told me this was a moment when he looked at me and thought along the lines, "This is my beautiful wife. And she looks like an old woman, haggard. All the beauty gone, gone for ever".

Michael couldn't conceal the expression of anguish on his face. What had I become?

Sometime about this time I had another vivid and intense vision. This vision went on for quite a while as I was asleep. And then washed over into waking,

it had something to do with Fatima, something to do with war.

And it was focused on the Middle East, on the area around Afghanistan and Pakistan.

I saw, even as I was awake,

vast fields of incredibly beautiful poppies waving in the wind. Red poppies. And the seeds of the poppies were blowing,

blowing on the wind,

spreading out across the world. Some terrible evil spreading from that incredible beauty:

Opium.

It was so vivid and disturbing I told Michael about it. He can't remember now. But I reminded him because I heard a programme on the radio recently, relating to the opium trade, and how it had spread world-wide and become incredibly dangerous.

Another horrible vision I had *was of a baby being wired up to a computer. As if some attempt was being made to harness human intelligence to computers in this perverted way.*

A baby! An innocent baby! Wired up! My God!

At another time,

I heard a voice telling me to pray for the Jewish people;

the words repeated over and over again.

I wrote (and here I refer to notes written at the time),

"The voice said the Jewish people didn't know what to do. That they wanted peace, but were sick to death of seeing their people blown to pieces in buses. The voice said they wanted peace, the voice said;

Pray for the people of Israel."

And the music of the soulscape changed to become,

O come, O come, Emmanuel;

the music of the end-time.

Not so much then, as now. As I write. As these words pour out, as I look back. From where we are now.

At another point, it was as if I reached into a dimension where *a bell was tolling out the coming of the end times,*

the sound of a clock beating in the background;

tic-toc, tic-toc.

And the words,

"The books are being opened and the courts are being called ... everything you have done will be weighed!"

The Day of Doom.

Of course, any attempt to 'get on with my life' was about to fail. I had slipped over into what our society defines as madness. My psyche was shattering over and over. One day in a church, near breaking point, a lady standing next to me realized I was in considerable distress. And there was this strange waking experience, standing at Mass, a sense – very, very vague, but there;

as if the veil of heaven had been drawn back. I felt the whole court of Heaven was watching me. It was almost as if my fate was being decided.

But it was very vague, and yet it was terrifying; is terrifying!!! Even to write this now.

A lady, whose name might be Ravenna (I guess it is her name on the book) handed me a little book *The Divine Mercy Message and Devotion*. The book was pressed into my hand,

by *a keeper of the flame.*

I had come across The Divine Mercy Devotions before; now it was one of those important moments in time. This woman of the Church was reaching down and giving me a hand up, because *I was in danger of falling off the mountain.* The book contains the Revelations of a Polish nun and visionary who died in 1938 whose name is Sister Faustina. Sister Faustina's revelations reiterate Christ's words calling for Mercy. Again, I felt this simple act of charity averted disaster in some way (although many aspects of Sister Faustina's visions do not resonate for me). But this Catholic Christian woman was, in fact, performing the ministry of angels by reminding me of God's promise of forgiveness to all who truly repent.

The total breakdown happened suddenly. Michael went away on business for a few days, I really can't remember it all. When the taxi came to pick Mike up and take him to the airport, I ran out of the house after him, barefoot, to say farewell. He looked acutely pained, touched by my affection and vulnerability, as I reached for him to kiss his cheek. He would have told me to,

"Take care."

This he almost always does. My mind was crazed, although I probably just appeared distressed at his departure. Then the taxi drove off, and Michael was gone. Forlorn, I went back inside the house and shut the door. Once inside, *I felt I was being commanded to cut my hair off as a penance.*

So I started cutting it off. Crying and wailing, my hand slipping on the scissors, as I thought of how it may have led others into sin;

crazed!

I started hacking chunks out. But a remnant of sanity (and vanity) stalled me, and I put the scissors down. A good clump of hair lay on the table before me. What was I doing? *Did God really demand this?* I looked round

windows in my soul opening.

It was a dark house, but a good rental for Oz. A nice place. But in a bit of a gully. Not far from the road. The house had an expanse of lawn before it. I had lost our Samuel there. So, for me, it was a house tainted, a place of mourning, a place of tears and regret. Sparsely furnished, because we never had an awful lot of money. Plain and functional, with an open-plan living area.

I wailed my way up the stairs, praying and crawling, and begging forgiveness of God – and asking for mercy – in a heightened state of extreme anxiety, an altered state of consciousness,

I remember looking in a mirror, and thinking I was the witch or whore or something out of the Apocalypse.

That horrifying beauty ... of me ... of *It?* Or *Her?* Or whoever the hell it was?

Loveliness tainted by madness, and some sort of heavy, cloying evil.

The

Apocalypse ...

The whore of the Apocalypse.

As if, more accurately, there was some force trying to turn me into Her. Or maybe some version of Her. It was unbelievably terrifying;

my psyche tore apart in sheer terror and panic. I was everywhere

a time slip ... As if a tear had breached reality

and I fell through.

This fragmentation, the shattered glass of consciousness ...

This group of Satanists, witches and this warlock from the college, were after me: literally 'tuning in' to me,

hunting me down like an animal;

I was an animal being hunted.

I *had* to get out of the house ...

But I felt I didn't know who to trust, or where to turn. I was so crazed I couldn't think but

I had to get out of the house.

Reality was tearing

Michael was on a plane. *Nowhere seemed secure. No-one seemed safe anymore.*

I ran outside taking just a bag, then walked, and then sometimes ran. No-one was around on the street in the beautiful Australian morning. The garden I'd left appeared so ordinary, just that expanse of grass and a tree ... *but the land was opening up.*

The landscape of the soul, the landscape of my soul. *Of all our souls* in a sense.

The sequence of events blurs now ... the terror again ... that sense of fear. The sequence here not quite as it was. So words fail, and fall meaningless, in a landscape of a fissionary event, become pathetic in any attempt to elucidate such experience in written form. This is a description of an atomic bomb exploding; imploding the entire fabric of the construction of reality … a massive surge of psychic energy, breaking open the illusory forced constructions we have placed upon our minds and souls,

the deconstruction of our reality; of phenomenal reality as we experience it.

This I term the 'Omega point'. So this explosion

like glass

shattering through time,

re-forming, re-aligning.

(Even the sense of a spell breaking: as if this artificial construction of reality was some sort of psychic web of illusion)

"Now we see but a poor reflection as in a mirror; then we shall see face to face," wrote the Apostle Paul.

The image of who, and where, we are revealed. In this *Hiroshima of the soul.*

So the atomic bomb finds its metaphysical resonance in the seismic impact of God on the psyche. This is like death.

"And many will be purified." (The Book of Revelation, again.) Perhaps. Where we really are. In the landscape of time, real time;

sacred time.

I walked, strode, to the college. The campus was busy with students hurrying to lectures…people like a blizzard, while *I was in the eye of the storm.* I walked past one man, my stride rapid, strands of hair flying.

I was in time. Our time … then … out of time

a time slip.

The man's eyes interrogated with just a glance, a look. A moment of genuine concern etched across his features. Recognizing insanity in my eyes. A wild woman. Determined to confront one of the lecturers in the department, and so tell them,

"I know what you're up to! I know what's going on!"

I got only so far, almost there. Quite near a reading room. Then stopped. A pin-point of rationality broke through, or maybe *something more supernatural guiding me.* I turned back, and found the bus-stop. Got on a bus, and realized I'd come out without any money. Or perhaps I'd thrown my purse away. I don't remember. I do recall saying to the bus driver,

"I've left my home to serve Jesus. I have no money."

I knew, in a hesitant fashion, he would let me on. He did. For his part, the driver seemed used to this sort of thing. (I guess he was another nice Aussie.) The bus bumped along, zigzagging streets. For a while I seemed to be the only one on board. I got off in a suburb close to the city. I'd made up my mind to go to a church and offer myself to God, maybe as a nun. Or religious of some sort. But I knew I was crazy! So that was hopeless, I couldn't go there. The churches didn't take mad people.

So I went on, wandering round the suburbs ... all day

a long, slow day.

Pacing fast. Bowing to the ground every fourth or seventh step, begging forgiveness of God. Pleading for mercy for myself, for anyone and everybody. People in cars stopped at lights must have looked. (I saw them and thought that.) But I didn't care, I was beyond all that. Anyway, there was a lot of traffic at points. And here was just another mad woman, but this one deranged, in torment for her sins.

Walking. Walking. In desperation and anxiety and fatigue and loathing and unearthly terror

through the afternoon. Into the night

Night.

Darker and darker. Walking into the maelstrom of consciousness broken open, *walking the winds of eternity*

It was then that it became really, unbelievably, terrifying

the tear in the fabric of reality broke. Like a woman in labor giving birth

life spurting forth;

from Gehenna. From out of the Apocalypse

a time slip

Reality was a landscape where I was like a deer, an animal being hunted. At one point, I was hearing what I took to be the Virgin Mary screaming at me,

"You killed my Son!"

over and over again.

Oh my God! The Mother of God herself was condemning me; the Mother of God! The Virgin! What hope was there? I was near a shopping centre in one reality, while in another reality I was hearing the Virgin screaming at me in anguish and anger. I couldn't believe it! And the terrifying horror of sin once again hit home;

you don't even fantasize, you turn away, you get out of the situation; you don't go near evil.

This was not the God of the philosophers and theologians, this was not even the beautiful and weeping Theotokos. I was hearing anguish; terrible suffering at the heart of God, no dispassionate God this. This was a God who suffers agonizingly when his children stray. God who died in terrible circumstances, and who went down to hell, into that most horrendous and eternal of all places. We all murdered God, not just the Romans and the Jews. All of us; Christians, Muslims, Buddhists, atheists. No one has hands free of the blood of Christ;

this was God *of the Passion.*

The Virgin, in sheer and total and utter torment and agony – and even rage – at the foot of the Cross as her innocent Son, God

Incarnate, paid the horrific price for our sins: screaming out now, and across eternity for it to stop!

God alive. God dead.

Dead! Hanging there! For me, for you; for all of creation. This is what I had done, what we all have done.

I'd probably done nothing in the eyes of the world, in the eyes of some, if not most, priests even; so precipitously weak has our concept of sin become. And yet I'd slipped, fallen, all because I didn't listen to the Holy Spirit warning me to get out of that terrible place.

God is not to be mocked, you avoid all possibility of sin. You don't murder, or lie, or steal, or commit fornication or adultery, or wizardry or abuse yourself or anyone else or the world in any way. I repeat, you do not even fantasize. We are not in this world to destroy or harm; we are here to heal, to worship, to be with our God.

But I could, and could not, work out what on earth was happening; I was totally beside myself. With all my years of research, I'd never heard or read of anyone who'd ever experienced anything like this,

the Virgin screaming in agony and rage.

And I, so terrified and so horrified there were not even tears in my eyes. My beloved Virgin who had always interceded for me,

(were there also tears in the eyes of my God?).

So I just kept walking

walking the winds of eternity. The maelstrom. I had to. I was

nowhere and somewhere. Between Eden and Armageddon, with the distant sense of wars and rumors of wars, the battlefields of the First World War, strewn bodies, and a time of

the Angels of Mons.

Night.

Existential Darkness;

no light.

The screams ceased. I kept on walking. Into a suburb of houses with lights on, people eating and drinking: twentieth century, our time;

but eternity unraveled, God's time ... Real time.

Walking. Now

I kept hearing the word,

"Imprinted."

As if I had been 'imprinted'. I felt there was some sort of tagging system being used, a pheromone or something on my clothing, which I won't go into because it really disturbs me. Quite possibly this is, was, madness ...

I could hear them, *like some sort of howling lupine-like animals. These followers of Satan hunting me;*

there was a terrible sense of fear out across the landscape, a landscape beyond normal consciousness. Reality had opened up, and I was tuning in to all these dimensions of existence. I was an animal with the hounds after it. I believed this was some sort of modern crucifixion. And that it was 'out there', happening to other Christians,

others;

other people across time, and in our time,

people being psychically, spiritually, crucified.

Realities and dimensions of existence intertwined. Past and present and future in this terrible landscape of the soul,

reality had torn open and I was walking in Biblical time

some point in Revelation

the no-man's land of the wilderness of the lost

The existential experience of Paul's runners,

the runners of Paul the Apostle; those figures I saw in the Far East … running the race through the landscapes of the soul … running the race that "is set before us".

I had become one of Paul's runners

and I could trust no-one here.

Which timescape was I in? Which house of reality or illusion or imagination or *cyber world*?

Something awful had happened to Michael? I could hear, far off, a sort of crazy laughter

(I can't go there again.)

Reality and illusion and other realities

Past. Present. Future.

I had slipped through the timescape of the phenomenal world;

I was walking worlds,

I was a woman walking through the walls of the Houses of Time

In the early hours of the morning, in a street by a major hospital, *I felt I needed to divest myself of everything I owned, and bury myself alive to escape the Satanists.*

So I took off everything.

Including my rings and watch and my father's cross: my beloved cross. And then threw them away. The clothes, I recall, landed in a pile, then another pile. Until they were all gone.

Now I could be safe. This was the exit;

they could not pick up my scent if I was buried beneath the earth.

I buried myself as much as possible.

(Later, and even as I was doing it then, for some reason I seemed to see this as some *sort of death and rebirth experience,*

some sort of primitive ceremony?)

It was as if I had become a character in my own visions; a*s if realities had coalesced:*

I was moving through time and space and consciousness

I was moving through time and space and consciousness …

Burying myself like this – to escape from something terrible – had been a recurring theme in my dreams for decades; now I was doing it. The ground was cold, the earth clumpy, as I dug with my hands and feet; pushing at the earth, covering my body with dirt and leaves. Even my face I covered, tasting the soil between my lips, prodding it into my ears. And then it became quieter, quieter. I lay there. Passive in the limpid night, eyes blacked out to the moon and stars. In a sort of passive tranquility. It was not cold, it was cool. A clear, Australian, darkness.

I was in The Night

Beyond an endless dreaming.

Safe. Buried alive

In the haunted night.

Time passed.

It was some while before I decided to get up. The sense of near and present fear, of danger, had lifted somewhat. Enough for me to think it was okay; I was going to be alright. The scent had been lost. The sound of the baying of those

lupine-hybrid creatures

had passed by. I could now take the risk, and emerge from my *makeshift grave*. I shook off the dirt from my skin, even spitting it out from my mouth as I stood up, attempting to dislodge soil from my hair. But the soil had turned to mud, and not much would come out. Unsure of what to do, I wandered round a bit in the street and began to feel chilled. A young man must have emerged from a house, because I suddenly noticed his presence. At a guess, he was in his late twenties or early thirties (I really didn't want to look). The man seemed amused, smiling at me with slight menace as if he were watching a prey

I had nothing on ... naked and lost in this *place between places.*

But the fracture, the tear in reality, was closing up

I was rational enough to realize I was in danger, and had to do something. The young man started to move towards me. I cried out to him to

"Call the police!"

He didn't react, except to seem disturbingly amused. I asked again; still, no reaction. I picked up a short stick, and exorcised him and began to call out – over and over – my name and address. Calling, shouting out, for someone to,

"Please, please call the police!"

A resident must have heard and acted quickly, because it wasn't long before the police arrived to confront this strange Mexican standoff. I recall that the officers wore what looked like guns, (this didn't faze me; I was too relieved for that). One young cop stared pityingly at me, as if not wanting to be part of this. It was all over his face, and transmitted by his demeanor, as if he were thinking, "Oh my God! This poor woman ..." He seemed a really nice fellow who didn't want to be there.

I exorcised the police with my stick anyway; I thought, "Just in case."

A woman officer approached warily, and began to talk me down, down, down and out of my heightened anxiety. I acquiesced, glad to get away from the man who remained watching, (I even think he was still smiling). The police led me to a car and took me to hospital. I was nervy, edgy. A bit difficult to deal with. In the police car, a woman officer tried to give me a sheet to cover my nakedness. I kept trying to shrug it off,

I was convinced the sheet had chemicals on it, poisons;

chemicals, poisons, evil seeping through at all levels ... we are poisoning the landscape, the world. I was being poisoned ...

At the hospital, the police left me in safety with a nurse. Then, a woman medico questioned me about what had happened. I remember saying some strange things. *It was rather as if I had been on a metaphysical low and was floating, drifting back up to our reality.* I recall being somewhat stupefied, vaguely bemused by it all, light-headed, making odd, rather absurd remarks relating to the way I felt and what had happened. And being idiotic and confused and not truthful. This made me problematic to deal with. I was given a straight choice by a hard-faced woman medico: either I take something to help me sleep, or I'd be forcibly medicated. The latter notion didn't seem an option at all, so I shut up and acquiesced. I felt totally intimidated, but it was for my own good. A nurse helped me shower. I recall my acute thinness, the almost childlike quality of my tall body, the straggly hair clumped with mud. The sensation of just an occasional involuntary, physical, *spiritual* shaking, as if my body and interior spirit were reintegrating.

And the water too cool and unpleasant. Sending me shivery in the extreme. All that horrible mud was so very difficult to remove from my hair that I had to drag out strands, and still it wouldn't come out. The wretched stuff would be there for all of several days; maybe it was even a week. My lovely hair was now a mess, with a clump missing on one side. And there was the embarrassment of my physical exposure with this nurse, this woman whom I did not know, helping me. After showering, I was provided with a hospital gown and medication so strong it knocked me for six. I have just a vague recollection of an uncomfortable bed and pillow and not enough sheets in the coldness, and a ward with two other people (I think they were male). The two seemed to be in some sort of coma, and were rigged up to monitoring devices on the opposite side of the room. I forget the rest and fell into a deep, deep, sleep from which I don't recall waking.

I am sick of love ...

Song of Solomon; kjv

(**in a time when Men have gone mad, and when the *love of God is sickness*;**
echoing the prophecy of St. Anthony of the Desert.)

In Perth, Michael received a telephone call from the police in the middle of the night. It woke him in his hotel room. He was informed I'd been found wandering the streets. He flew back immediately.

To what?

I remember, only vaguely, the first time Mike saw me after I was admitted to hospital. I was so doped I can't remember the circumstances. I do recall the expression his face held as being one of utter bewilderment. Michael didn't seem to know what to say, or even what to do; he was falling apart. His wife was a certified mad woman, what is termed a 'regulated patient' in Australia. That is, even Mike guaranteeing he would look after me couldn't get me out of the enclosed ward I was held in: I was forcibly incarcerated. My husband couldn't speak to me about some things, to this day he still can't. He was just too terrified by what had happened, and, worse, of what might have happened. Out there. On the streets. As someone remarked later, if this had happened in the UK, I'd be dead! Thank God for the relative safety of Australia, and for the professionalism of the police that night. Australia gets to me sometimes, of course. But it's not a bad place to be for an awful lot of reasons;

God bless Australia forever!

Mike was questioned concerning my background, and the events leading up to the illness. I was so thin, the suggestion was made I might be anorexic. David, who was on retreat when my breakdown happened, came immediately: what a priest. I had a stream of visitors from the church, they were wonderful. The kindness of friends.

Apart from that, hospitalization was an eye-opener. At night, and as I got better, I would sometimes wander the dimly-lit corridors with a Bible, praying. And would gently enquire of the night staff on the reception desk,

"Would you like to pray with me?"

Bleary-eyed, the staff would be fighting to stay awake with pens dangling from limp hands. But they didn't make a fuss. Their dedication, kindness and patience was astonishing. And they would amiably respond, "No", they really would rather not pray. And so I would meander happily away. Many of the nurses were like angels. I remember one, dressing with loving care, a minor abrasion I'd got along the way. I also had a personal nurse assigned to my case who was simply brilliant and wonderful to talk to. Mike was allowed in at visiting times, and brought me pizzas from one of the ritziest pizza cafes in town. These we would eat together, alone in a vacant consulting room. I was determined to put on weight and demolished the pizzas, sometimes not leaving Mike much at all, (which was mean of me because I don't think he'd had dinner himself).

Mike rebuked me – after I'd come out of hospital – for this wanton gluttony.

All in all, the humdrum routine of institutionalization was blissfully calming, although initially I did harbor pathetic notions of making a break for freedom. There is something about having your freedom taken away that is unsettling. But even the food was excellent; cereal and fruit juices for breakfast, and a good vegetarian selection for lunch and dinner. The daily round of lots of sleep and good food was broken only one night when the police brought in some bloke who was in a terrible state. Panic swept the ward like a gale, because the guy had freaked out, and I saw four or five male ward nurses wrestling with him to get him into a secure room; it took all of them. Some of the female nurses became distinctly unnerved, and one marched round and round the ward with a note-pad, as if she wasn't quite sure what to do. The room the man was taken to had a big glass window, and I could see the staff, I think they were trying to inject the guy with something to pacify him.

Towards the end, I would go to Mass in the Hospital Annex almost every day. Heinrich, the psychiatrist assigned to my case, appeared rather puzzled about certain details. And amused, even surprised on occasion, coming upon me in the lift between floors after I had washed my hair (apparently it's unusual for mentally disturbed people to be attentive to their appearance, whereas I can't stand being dirty or unkempt). Anyway, I must have been incarcerated for about two weeks. I got to quite like it in a way. For a start, it was very nice not to have to wash up and do housework.

More recently, I hinted when talking with Heinrich, at the idea of spiritual experience and psychotic episodes, and began to talk about how individuals who enter deeply into mystical experience can experience a psychotic episode; an acknowledged position by some writers on the subject. Heinrich seemed quite open to discussion. Which is nice. No identifiable illness,

just this sickness called Christ.

I divested myself of everything, and got everything back. Except one of my most treasured possessions, my father's cross. It was one of the only things I had from him. And it had been with me through my years with Canon John. It's still something of a great sorrow to me. I took it to mean I had in someway failed,

I had gained my possessions, but lost my cross.

I don't fully understand this 'psychotic' experience. Sometimes I feel it was, again, a death experience. But more now, looking back, it was as if I was, just possibly in one sense, 'tuning in' to some sort of pagan ceremony. And, if so, doesn't it recall the Apostle Paul reminding us,

"I believe neither life, nor death, nor angels nor principalities nor demons can separate us from the love of God in Christ Jesus."

How incredible is the love of God for those who trust in His mercy!

It took me many years to come to grips with what I went through and, again, an extended period of healing. The trauma rendered me emotionally fragile, and sometimes depressed; occasionally I did wacky things or behaved in an erratic and nervous manner. Now I pray I am a little more sensitive to the intimations of the Spirit when I feel it; I need to be. We all do.

But I would still like my father's cross back.

Christ walks the lightning.

Like lightning breaking the darkness of the Night.

The vision from Israel; a vision of the imagination and of the senses: *of Christ walking the lightning. Existence as we know it disappearing in a flash of enormous energy,*

Night Lightning.

And also, for me, that deep sense I felt; *of walking upon tectonic plates of consciousness. Worlds, and realities, coinciding in the holiest place on earth;*

Israel, which the prophet Ezekiel describes as the "centre of the world".

That existential loss of cohesion; as if the very fabric of reality as we perceive it is tearing. Shearing, from the apocalyptic explosion of the energy of evil, the evil we have done. The sense, everywhere now, of beings from other dimensions finding their way into the human psycho-physical world; beings from the Apocalypse and from the earliest times of the Bible. For the Bible itself is reality: it is the breath of God. It is in this supernal space that we live, and move, and have our being. The breath of God is love itself; it is life and light and truth and freedom. It is the essence, the pure energy of existence, and it comes from God and is God and is our true home. But what we see is only our misconception brought on by spellbinding, and the distortive force of evil.

So, we have beings only hinted at in parts of the Bible breaking through the mindspace: they are the real enemies of mankind. Rulers, Powers, Principalities and people in this world ... coming under their dominion ... becoming their slaves;

so we are deceived.

And the implosion of the Universe of energy collapsing back upon itself: imploding under the weight of negativity. Returning to nothingness. The negative energy of evil, like a black hole in time and space. People themselves becoming black holes; vortexes within vortexes. That was the experiential sense of hell, of gehenna. A place that is no-place, a place that exists with no existence. If evil is negative energy, sin is, psychically, spiritually speaking, anti-matter: spiritual anti-matter. And it has a force, a negative pull. And without the Blood of Christ we cannot resist. That is the fundamental problem: pride. We are going it alone when no-one can fight evil alone –

to turn from Christ is to be eaten alive, emotionally, psychologically and spiritually.

It is to become a husk, a shadow;

A Ghost-Walker.

Darkness Visible.

This is the devouring, all consuming, power of the demonic. That is why you never touch the occult, whose power comes from this horrendous negativity that pollutes the psyche and the soul.

When we turn from God reality shatters. And the pull is intensifying with the death of every innocent, with every violation of the Law of the Most High God, with every violation of Biblical truth. We have brought on the Apocalypse;

and the only way out now is prayer.

For Christ will walk the Serpent Power. And crush it beneath his feet.

And that is Judgment Day. And that day every man, woman and child who has ever lived will be called to give an account.

When the fire of love will meet the fire of evil and wipe it forever from reality.

So that glimpse of nothingness? 'touching the void'

that strange mystics sometimes talk about,

what is it really? Where is this really all taking you?

It is taking you to hell: the ultimate Black Hole. The place I saw. Of non-being that has being;

and those who do not repent will never see the light of God again.

And the vision I was spared, the never ending fire, will be the fate of those who do not wake up.

This is reality

This is the Apocalypse

Christmas in Oz.

When I was in deep spiritual trouble, a very kind lady called Margaret Bater used to ask the priests in the Catholic church where she regularly read aloud (for God more than for us I'm sure) to say a Mass for me. When she recently went to Heaven, I felt it was like a reprise of my earlier experiences in England. One of the last things she said to me was,

"I'm going to be with the Lord."

I wasn't too happy, I didn't want her to die.

But now, looking back and thinking of incidents like the death of Margaret, I realize I can say it really was all worth it; that mountain climb, I mean. (The mountain I'm still climbing, by the way.) Because, I can honestly say, that when I stand in church at the Lord's Table; time stops. And somehow we are all together; one in Christ. And that is what Christmas is all about; the promise. That one day all will be made 'good'. I don't know how or when, but I do know. To love, in this world is to suffer. But in the next world it is to be alive forever. Love is the key. And there is nothing so beautiful as trust. And trust is faith. So we learn to trust. Not in Man but in Christ Jesus.

So it's time to go now. I, back to my life of prayer and writing. Didn't I tell you? I write poetry now. Michael quite likes some of it. At the moment things don't look too good, not in the Church and not in the world. But if you want to change the world, why not begin by asking the One who made the world? We have a Church to rebuild. Terrible things have happened, and it's pretty lonely at present. There aren't many people at the Lord's Table every day any more, and we could do with some more people praying in prayer groups, and more Bible study groups and such. There is room for everyone. We're a family. There are Orthodox Christians and Catholic Christians, and Anglican Christians, and Evangelicals, and so on; many marvelous people. Christianity is not really about denominations and subtle differences at all, but about relationship; a relationship with a real living person, Christ Jesus.

Christ loves you, he died for you, he went to hell for you. No-one else, no matter how much they love you, would do that. Take the chance; ask for Christ to reveal Himself to you. Keep asking. I'm writing this as a testimony that those who come to Christ will be saved, for they have passed from death to life. Christ has paid the price. He loves you more than you can imagine, and through him God is opening his hand and offering you forgiveness and eternal life. Take the chance, you have nothing to lose. And know always that I and many, many others will be praying for you;

Because

the Houses of Time are opening.

So, as I leave one of the main churches I worship at, I frequently pause. And place my hands on the open Bible. To remember who and where we really are;

As dust whirls in the sandstorms of time

Place your hands on the Book of the Apocalypse
Dissolve into Greek and Hebrew script
As those golden letters blow through time
And the winnowing staff dissemblers call 'history'
Falls vacant, as the Temple veil itself is ripped

A man born God; and the breath of Christ
Through a torn veil blows Spirit-truth at pagan war-lords
Sworn to but another lie.

The blood of Christ opens a window in your soul
as the Satanic warrior hordes,
Hooves of blackness, death and sickness fail.
For evil shrivels in terror as the face of the Living God
Annihilates fear ... And pain ... And vanity.
Our loved ones only seem to lie
Under the darkness of pain, and earth's humble sod.

We drift in the landscapes of eternity
Across those veiled, starlit words of the Book of Life
Whirling we dream (as in the Song of Songs) and stir.

We live here, and there

And find our place
Within the Alpha and Omega ... Beyond the tear

in the veil.

To where we really are. Now. All of us.
Dawn over the Lake of Galilee and Mount of Olives
Prophets, martyrs and the saints of time
I reach in Spirit, to wipe away the sorrow in your hair:
One in the Lord, because of love turned wine.

I have known love and I have known fear. And there is a place beyond fear

And it is called love.

"I slept but my heart was awake.
Listen! My lover is knocking:
Open to me, my sister, my darling,
my dove, my flawless one.
My head is drenched with dew,
my hair with the dampness of the night."

... *The Song of Songs*

Christ is knocking

For me,
For the Church,
For us all.

Completed Easter. Year of Our Lord March 2010. Catholic and Orthodox Easters coincide. The Passover of the Jews also occurred during this period (March 30th – April 6th). The core text was given to the Catholic and Anglican Churches as Hannah sensed was dictated by the Holy Spirit. Clarifications and revisions were made after that point with intense prayer.

April 1st is kept in the Church of England as the feast day of Mary of Egypt, the Patron saint of Penitents. Mary Magdalene is also a Patron saint of Penitents.

The last section of the book is an extract taken from a recent poem, "Melchizedek's Prayer". It is written in the form of an Icon poem of healing.

God bless you

Keep me, keep us, in your prayers.

Amen.

With love,

in Christe. A penitent; by the Mercy of God:

Hannah

2013 The Dust Poet

Epilogue: Hannah's Song ...

St. John warns in Revelation that no-one is to change one word of the Bible, of the prophecy.

But can we repent? Can the entire human race repent in sackcloth and ashes and reach out to God and beg forgiveness?

So that billions do not go down to the fires of hell?

We cannot stop the Apocalypse as sacred time. But if we repent in sackcloth and ashes and call on the Mercy of God ...

Is it just possible for God to hear our prayer?

Can we pray for the impossible?

Endnotes

Biblical Interpretation

The Bible is interpreted as an emanation of the Most High God, as the very breath of God mediated by inspired prophecy.

As the Canticle of Canticles or Song of Songs is interpreted in this life story, we also discover an exploration of the relationship between Man and God. As an inspirational prophetic poem, the Song of Songs can be read and interpreted as multi-faceted; one facet being the relationship between God and Eretz Israel and the Jewish people, and yet another between Christ and the Church. It can also be read as a love song between a man and a woman, breathing a sense of the intensely mystical nature of marriage and the marriage bond and the sanctity of marriage. At this level, it in no way denies the body because the body is a temple of the Holy Spirit.

All these levels of interpretation interweave, and yet can be separated. Each reading of the Song of Songs reveals new facets of the unending Divine Mystery which lies at the heart of authentic spirituality and Man's search for God.

At the heart of that search is the Mystery. The mystery of God and the mystery of Being; the Mystery that the subject of this book glimpses and glimpses yet again.

This being so, the broad theological approach is most consonant with Orthodoxy, in that theology itself is seen as the experiential way of union with God. So theology is prayer. When the Christian prays and witnesses to faith, this is prophecy. When a Christian prays, meditates and witnesses to faith in Jesus Christ as Messiah, this is theology.

Terminology

This book was originally far longer, but I have now decided to publish the latter section of the manuscript as a sequel in the coming months. I would just like to stress that my central character does not claim to be prophetic, in the sense that she has not clearly heard the voice of God calling her to prophesy future events in the name of the Church. However, she does see herself being called by God to proclaim the truth of the Risen Lord, and the Bible as the literal Breath of God. There is a difference between prophecy in the Old Testament, and prophecy in the New Testament period (today). The Canon of Scripture is closed; the Word of God is complete, unerring and unchangeable. So 'Prophetic-Christians' might be seen as individuals who are waking from the slumber of the night. They are shrugging off the sheet or covering prophets in the Old Testament talked about, that prevents mankind from realizing who – and what – we really are. Hannah realizes there is a sense in her visions of the New Testament idea of prophecy as the prediction of future events; or, more precisely 'discernment of the times we are in'. She feels that we are at a point in Revelation where the forces of hell are now being unleashed. Not just against the followers of Christ, but against all mankind; because if mankind wakes and turns to God then our real enemies will be vanquished. And we will become the incredible creations we are meant to be.

The sequel to this book will discuss not just the dreadful phenomenon of the 'false priest', but also the terrifying 'false mystic'. These are the individuals hinted at in this manuscript who possess the ability to shape reality as we see it. To project negative energy and imagery. They are the literal 'walking demons'; the sorcerers of the Book of Revelation, who are at the bidding of worldly principalities of power, using subterfuge to drag the human race into a horrendous new age. As Hannah describes this; a future where individuals will be totally dehumanized, a future she has glimpsed and is dreadful to contemplate. This is where the 'walking demons' are taking us;

"You don't know how evil we are".

All one can do is pray for such people. That they too will repent.

Etymology/stylistic note

Butterfly laughter: Here I am imaging for the reader laughter that is not just infectious, but brings to mind a sense of place and atmosphere. Such a joyous moment of transcendence – a peak spiritual experience – evokes a sense of dancing light and evanescence. Thus, the imagery of the butterfly with its beauty, dancing color, and symbolic association with the transformation of reality; resurrection. The term 'butterfly laughter' appears in a forthcoming collection of poems, *The Poetry of Hannah's Song*, where it occurs in the poem "Singapore Rain".

The slight break up of punctuation at the end of *Hannah's Song* is deliberate, and intended to reflect the sense of psychic fragmentation.

Author's disclaimer

This book takes the form of a biography. It is, therefore, not a theological treatise. It is written with the caveat that the conclusions reached are for discernment; I am a woman and have no authority at all to teach men. But, given the nature of what has been written, I have to at least raise a voice and call on the Mercy of God. (Here I am especially referring to the very last sections of this book.) To remain silent would not be true to my calling as a Christian.

At all times in writing Hannah's story, I have tried to be as accurate and truthful in reflecting this person's life as possible. In my human frailty it is the best I could do. All that is good about this work comes from God. The flaws are mine alone.

Notes

Addendum to the story:

Note 1. The holy water bottle Sister Molly left Hannah is made of green plastic, and the letters IHS are inscribed on it. The initials denote the name of Jesus in Greek, or possibly 'Jesus Savior of the World'. The letters were clearly visible in the vision.

Note 2. The words 'Love is the key' are written in the text without punctuation, and so exactly as they appeared in the vision.

Note 3. Hannah's visionary image of an angel flying over houses and painting doorposts with blood is related to Passover, the Jewish festival commemorating the sparing of the Jewish first-born, when the first-born of Egypt were slain by the angel of death. She, of course, didn't make the connection when the vision first occurred.

Note 4. April Fools' Day in France is sometimes kept by the wearing of the symbol of a fish on a person's back. The Ichythus, or fish symbol, was used by early Christians to identify themselves as followers of Christ.

Note 5. Many people may doubt the existence of devils, but scientists are affirming their existence. Hence, a leading neuropsychiatrist in the US refers to "... entities whose bodies are composed entirely of emotional, mental and etheric substance ... They are of many natures and some are malicious, cruel and cunning ..." (Green, Elmer "On the Meaning of the Transpersonal" in *Journal of Transpersonal Psychology*, vol. 3, no1 1971.)

Note 6. For information on telepathy and dream states, I would refer the reader to research carried out by the Maimonides sleep research institute in New York. Recent experiments have shown the possibility of telepathy influencing the dream state.

Note 7. A guide as to how to psychically target an individual both within the dream state, and in the waking state, was recently published in a popular Australian magazine.

Note 8. With regard to the incredible vision of light Hannah received, it has been suggested – with regard to these sorts of experiences – that the very impact of God on the psyche is so powerful it can shatter the mind. A seminal writer in this area, and a good place to start, is the classic book, *The Idea of The Holy*, written by Rudolf Otto and published in 1917.

Note 9. To reiterate: visions and voices must be treated with extreme caution in the area of the spiritual life, because it is sometimes very difficult to determine where they are coming from (malevolent, angry, voices such as those demanding Hannah cut her hair off and the voice of the Virgin screaming – for instance – are indicative of Satanic attack. Indeed, Hannah feels that some instances might well have included human involvement: telepathy). Satanic forces can duplicate almost all spiritual experiences. Look for the signs of the fruit of the Holy Spirit in an individual's life. Always, always, check experiences against the Bible. Where no spiritual director, or friend, or confessor, is available keep close to the Bible and ask the guidance of the Holy Spirit. And be very careful about repetitive prayer. Rather, meditate on the Bible and seek the will of the Holy Spirit in all things.

Note 10. With regard to exorcism: using things like incantations and herbs to dispel evil spirits or the Evil One, is calling on the forces of nature to rid a person – or a place – of the demonic. This is nature worship, in that it ascribes powers to created forces and not the Creator. It is shamanic witchcraft. There is, for the Christian (and in the ultimate sense) no such thing as 'white magic'. All magic is demonic.

Note 11. With regard to the writings of John of the Cross, the author is indebted to his incredible legacy, but has deep reservations about the erotic imagery sometimes suggested by his poetry. Similarly, I have reservations about some aspects of both William Blake's spirituality and that of Stanley Spencer. (My remarks have to be taken in the context of what has come down to us through the process of history, because these undoubted geniuses have left a legacy of great and inspirational work.)

Note 12. Even since beginning to write, things in the Church have deteriorated dramatically. So Biblical literacy is very important. Pray to the Holy Spirit to guide you in your reading. (I thank God myself for some American Evangelicals.)

Sources

Biblical quotes, unless otherwise stated, are from the *New International Version of the Bible*, copyright 1985; The Zondarvan Corporation. Other translations used are: the King James Version (kjv), the New Jerusalem Bible 1985 (njb) Douay-Rheims Bible (d-rv), English Standard Version of the Bible (esv). And the New Revised Standard Version with Deuterocanonical Books (nrsv).

Scripture quotations taken from the HOLY BIBLE NEW INTERNATONAL VERSION. Copyright 1973, 1978, 1984 by International Bible Society. Used by permission.

Sections from the New Revised Standard Version with Deuterocanonical Books (nrsv) – copyright 1989 are given by permission of the Division of Christian Education of the National Council of Churches of Christ in the USA. Used without written permission when five hundred verses or less are used. All rights reserved.

Scripture quotations are from The Holy Bible, English Standard Version*(ESV*), copyright 2001 by Crossway. Used by permission. All rights reserved.

Excerpt from *The New Jerusalem Bible*, copyright 1985 by Darton, Longman & Todd Ltd. And Doubleday, a division of Random House, Inc. Reprinted by Permission.

Extracts from the Authorized Version of the Bible (The King James Bible), the rights in which are vested in the Crown, are reproduced by permission of the Crown's Patentee, Cambridge University Press.

Other Sources

The translation of the Breastplate used is that by Mrs. C. F. Alexander, and can be found in The English Hymnal, Oxford University Press. First published 1906.

The quotation from St. Augustine's "Confessions", is taken from the translation published by Hendrickson Christian Classics; St. Augustine *The Confessions* St. Augustine. (USA 2004) Hendrickson Publishers. Peabody, Massachusetts.

William Blake's words to the hymn *Jerusalem*; can be found in *The English Hymnal* published by Oxford University Press, Walton Street, Oxford OX2 6DP. The edition was first published in 1906 and the forty-second impression was published in 1977.

The traditional hymn *Faith of our Fathers* is Text 88.88.88; Frederick W. Faber, 1814-1816. The line of the song actually reads "We will be true to thee till death." Faber Music, London.

W. B. Yeats poem "The Song of Wandering Aengus" can be found in the collection *The Wind Among The Reeds,* first published in 1899. I have been instructed that this poem is in the public domain worldwide except for Spain. Spanish rights to use an extract of *The Song of Wandering Aengus* in Spain in print and e-book form have been obtained by permission of A P Watt at United Agents on behalf of Grainne Yeats.

Green, Elmer "On the Meaning of Transpersonal" in *Journal of Transpersonal Psychology,* vol. 3, no 1 (1971)

Kinnock, Lord Neil. Extract quoted taken from his speech given at Bridgend 7 June, 1983.

Permissions have been sought, and obtained, for all of the above.

(The original manuscript has been altered slightly because, as a self-published book, I could not find out how to obtain permission in certain instances, and had to omit some quotations. Perhaps one day there will be a "Dust Poet's Cut" to remedy this situation!)

Acknowledgments

My thanks go to my husband for his love and patience, and to our families and others for the gift of faith. Also many thanks to my editors Barbara, Jenny and Virginia (although I did re-write things, so many of the faults are mine). To Barry, for his advice and proof reading. To Kerry and Dina for useful criticism in regards to character development and other aspects of the manuscript's development, and to Carolyn for reading through a draft and for her amazing cover design. I cannot omit thanking Robin for encouragement, and Ian Howe S.J. for seeing something of promise in a very rough first draft. Also, I would like to send my thanks to Bishop David Chislett who read the near-finalized project giving very welcome praise and a letter of critique.

This book especially honors the memory of Tessy, Kathleen and Gran. I offer God thanksgiving for the inspiration and legacy of John of the Cross and Teresa of Ávila.

So much gratitude for my mentors of former years! Most particularly, Prof. C. du P. le Roux, Prof. Kubus Kruger and Dr. Shirley Thorpe. These three academics and theologians gave encouragement and aided me in the form of the memory of their wisdom and deep spirituality. They were too, too, kind to me at the time I was privileged to know them. But it was the very memory of this kindness that gave me confidence through the dark times of writing. Many thanks also to those who prayed with me from time to time for the guidance of the Holy Spirit when writing.

I must also include the help given from listening to many sermons, especially in the Anglican Church. Also to Sr. Joan Cusack (notably for a comforting word of knowledge) and to Eva L. for her prayers for me. And for the spiritual, charismatic, support of Mary Stone; a friendship in the Lord that has withstood the years. To Jacqueline Latter and Christa Kernick, for their love and enduring camaraderie. And to Pat Thompson, our neighbor, for being the lovely person she is.

It would also be wrong not to mention those who helped Hannah in a special way; a secretary at a Jesuit church who showed great compassion, and whoever telephoned the police that Dark Night. Not forgetting for a minute the medicos – particularly her personal psychiatric nurse and psychiatrist at the hospital – and the police themselves. Indeed, Hannah wants to thank anyone who smiled in truth on her as she made her way through life.

My publisher, Paul Higgs, deserves words of thanks for his patience. So, too Joy Childs for always being quick to answer my questions. And I would also like to express my gratitude to Helen Christie for her input in the final stages of book production.

And always, for those priests and pastors, teachers, lay persons and others who keep the flame. And to our beloved pups, Muffin and Bubba. There are too many others for me to include: just God bless you all.

A note from Hannah

These last few pages are intended primarily for the discernment of people living a deeply spiritual Christian life. In line with the New Testament command to test the Spirit (1 Thess 5:19 – 22: esp. v. 21: "Test everything. Hold on to the good. Avoid every kind of evil.") These visions are to be prayed about and tested –

"Test the spirit! Test the spirit! Test the spirit!"

Hannah has discerned (possible) plots of negative forces that do not come to pass because of prayer. Her predicament is that she is in a vacuum at the moment, with many Christians in her area falling away into apostasy and heresy under the impact of the spirit of the age.

But first to sum up much too briefly: you cannot totally cut off areas of reality and take no responsibility. Human beings are – in a sense – part angel and are born to do no evil. And evil is anything that contradicts the law of the Most High: that is, the Biblical law. When an individual moves away from this law they open out to the potential to sin. When they do not repent the psychic/spiritual strain increases until it becomes intolerable, and the person/personality literally implodes. This is symbolized (in one sense) as the Biblical 'pit'. Hence, the individual literally drowns in the fictitious 'unconscious': which is the waters of death. This happens because the psychic/spiritual tension of continued suppression/repression of this fictitious or constructed realm becomes unbearable. Sin, repression of your own evil, has a force; it is an energy. It saps the psyche. Good, which means living in accordance with the law of God also has a force: it repels evil. No-one can fight evil alone; that is pride, and it is the mistake of everyone out of touch with Christ. We all have to choose: either good and life or evil and death. That is freedom. If you choose to be evil then you open up to the demonic, and if you do not repent you will be literally torn apart, devoured alive; although you may still function as a human being on this level of reality. But you are no longer free:

you have entered the House of Bondage.

Similarly, for the Christian there is no such thing as a 'shamanic episode'. The psychotic experience here can be seen as the opening up of an individual to a previously closed down reality; existence as it is. No-one is totally out of contact with God and the Spirit of God or they would cease to exist. God is everywhere. The shaman or diviner or person of the occult, however, chooses to be demonically possessed; that is where they get their limited access to knowledge and divination. They place themselves outside the mercy and grace of God, unless there is repentance. The Prophetic-Christian has to remain at all times in contact with God. They are called to do no evil. They are called to intercede for mankind, and function in their different roles as proclaimers of truth: as witnesses.

–

A final Antichrist is on the horizon. Even possibly here. As I am writing things are changing; he is moving in a power circle. This person appears to be a priestly figure; waiting in the wings. Beware of a new seemingly Christian 'fundamentalism/ fanaticism'. No-one should ever kill in the name of God – and particularly – no priestly figure should ever order this. This person is of the occult. Beware miracles and shows of miraculous powers; look for the source of the 'energy' (spirit). Beware anyone who puts themselves in the place of Christ and seeks to establish a New World Order.

The occult in the church: moving into power positions; especially the followers of Lucifer. Their symbolism is worldwide and *in many places they are in control*. They will foster and support the Antichrist and his way of evil and the unforgivable sin: that *Lucifer rose from the dead, not Christ. So the Antichrist in this sense almost as Lucifer himself* in the place of Christ. *This seems to all be linked to the horrendous Abomination of Desolation: instead of the Imago Dei people will bear the symbol of Satan* (the rest of this I cannot write). *But this is happening, and will happen in full force when the Abomination is set up. There will be nowhere to run. I would just say that there is a little time remaining to return to the Bible. It is as if after a period of mercy the full power of judgment will be unleashed.*

So the Church seems to be withdrawing, *but in the sense that the Holy Spirit is withdrawing.* Hannah *has never felt anything like it before.* Hannah asks for prayer in that she now feels, following what has been said in her biography, the way forward for Christians who live in areas where there is a fallen church – and a polluted priesthood – is for families to start carrying out the Agape meal in their own homes, if possible at times with other Christians. This requires spiritual purity, and especially if persons have been part of these apostatizing churches, they will need to repent before doing this.

People may need to memorize the Bible. The Holy Spirit will always guide the remnant.

A great whore figure: an incredibly powerful witch. The whole of the human psyche is being polluted/ has been polluted, by what can only be described as a 'Wine of Whoredom':

a negative energy twisting, serpent like. An ether seeping out where reality has ruptured. Sometimes it is like a thick, viscous fluid. And yet other times strands of energy. Thought energy in a very damaging form.

In New Age circles there is talk about people feeling surges of energy. *This is not a result of solar flares, sun spots etc* (as New Age sources may suggest) *this is the 'unconscious' erupting.* The increase in sleep problems is another symptom of this phenomenon.

Reality is tearing apart: sheering under the weight of human evil. A child is raped, the earth vomits. What happens on one level of reality impacts across existence. Anything to do with evil or the occult fractures reality and provides an opening through which evil can seep in. Damaging energies to assault mind, body and spirit.

We are in the time of (an expansion of) the Cathedral of the Witch.

UFO's and other 'extra-terrestrial' phenomena: phenomenon of spiritual attack of frightening power to penetrate and disturb consciousness, the soul and the psyche. We have 'torn' reality and rather than looking to outer space for the source of these phenomena, we should be looking to our own inner space: the vortexes of our own minds and spirits. The origin of these phenomena is the occult itself; that is how powerful we have allowed the Satanists to become.

We have opened up the landscape of hell itself. The increase in electromagnetic energy is impacting our minds, bodies and psyches and tying us in to the ultimate Tower of Babel: worldwide paganism and telepathy as a method of communication. The end result will be a total loss of human freedom; everyone will be controlled. No secrets where the webs will not reach. Mankind will be encased in the spider's web.

There are places where time and space and the whole fabric of reality are losing cohesion. The illusion cannot be maintained totally by the spellbinders. That is why human bondage is the answer: a New World Order and human enslavement.

The Beast. A fundamental source of negative energy. This seems (to Hannah) more 'machine entity' than animal – (although it has had the appearance of an animal at times). There is the sense that if we do not repent many of the saints will fall under direct attack; (energy! Negative energy). The saints are being targeted.

Many of modern sciences 'miracles' are not of God. That is why they have disastrous side-effects and results: we have deified science and this has brought disaster.

Hannah's beloved Australia; This Great South Land of the Holy Spirit. *The warriors of the --- now feel you are surrounded, capitulating, immoral, decadent. Rescue from them will come by sea from the people of the serpent if we do not repent. This will be the beginning of bondage for every man, woman and child and even the animals and land itself; horror untold in the history of humanity. The floods: psychic and in reality. Once again, what happens or is happening on one level of reality impacts on other levels of reality. Australia is now under massive psychic (spiritual) attack. And many are falling. To fall, and not repent, is to become Satanized. The telepathy demon has arrived, by sea. (666 – the time of the Beast – is starting here).* I pray that everyone, from whatever nationality or religion in Australia turns to God, and that we will be the ones to repent and ally ourselves with the heavenly hosts to hold back (at least here) the greatest terror that has ever threatened humanity.

For the United Kingdom, the situation is much worse: the train with its cargo spoken of in vision in this text has now crossed the UK and arrived to a location that seems to be West of England or even possibly Wales. This is the serpent power. Christians now have to stand firm under increasing pressure to compromise on Biblical values and resist what amounts to passive persecution. *Repentance must begin with the Church, because the Satanization of the United Kingdom – the people who never would be slaves – is underway. The people of England should wear sackcloth and plead for the Mercy of God.*

The future is cyborg. Out of the cryogenic chambers will come the new ruler of humanity and others. This is no resurrection; these are demons. Their appearance at present is reptilian. Drone-humanity will supply their spare parts. Eternal fire will be the fate of those who submit to this rule of horrendous terror with the Antichrist as High Priest and a 'resurrected' ruler. This is why humans have been systematically de-humanized: cut off from God. We have seeded our progeny; the human genome; our sperm and eggs. We have given away our humanity. We are now expendable. These people have gone so completely mad they believe they will be the new 'Immortals'; the super-race. Their leader will possibly be a 'resurrected' past human leader; a demonic individual with demonic power. There is only one 'little' problem at present; and that is God. That is why the crosses have to go, authentic prayer has to cease, and the Church corrupted entirely. Which is now happening. They want humanity to have no recourse to God; no sign, no symbol, no sacrament – no hope and no escape. Humanity will be ruled by demons.

We should pray earnestly for Russia, China and Islamic nations.

Israel. Yom Kippur. You are a target. (This vision of the prophetic is abbreviated and was written "Like wind blowing through my fingers".) Hannah is very cautious about such spiritual insights, and is sensitive to the predicament of the Jewish people. So she was unsure whether to include this. Pray for Israel and *Benjamin Netanyahu*.

Sackcloth for the Church. Real sackcloth; not fancy dress that looks good, but the sackcloth of the heart; sackcloth for all of us. Across the board celibacy is not Biblical. It is contrary to the Word; the Bible. Women's priesthood, in the way it is being introduced in Anglicanism and other Christian denominations, is contrary to the Word; the Bible. The crisis of the Church is because it has made rules not founded, not anchored, in the Word; Jesus Christ: the cornerstone.

To clarify what has happened on a spiritual level:

to move away from the Word, which the Church in many places has done, opens a door for the Evil One to penetrate and cause chaos – you place individuals in a position that opens them up to Satanic attack they may well be unable to withstand. You place human rules above the Divine Will. This, in itself, is idolatrous. Spiritual pollution seeps through. At the concrete level of the priesthood, this has been seen in disharmony and the disgusting cases of sexual and physical abuse. Yes, the Church on earth can make mistakes; it is composed of human beings. So Paul rebukes Peter in the early church. But evil becomes entrenched when the mistake is perpetrated. When this happens the entire Church suffers and becomes spiritually polluted by false doctrine. The laity also suffer from this spiritual pollution. So, we become spiritually unclean and impede the Spirit; our collective and individual vision is skewed. The result is disharmony, division, rivalry and false accusations with different factions of the church proclaiming they have the 'unerring truth'. The touchstone of truth, of the Word where Christ is the cornerstone, can be seen when the Spirit in the Church flowers and empowers the Body to function as a harmonious whole.

In the terms of spiritual discernment; when things seem unclear you look at what is happening. At results,

"You will know them by their fruits."

In this time of unequaled evil, it is imperative the Church repents and performs the work of Christ in proclaiming the incredible blessing for all mankind of the Good News and the Resurrection. This is our job. Not just that of the Bishops of Rome, Constantinople, Canterbury and the Evangelical and Lutheran leaders. Repentance must start with the Church, and the opening of the Communion tables to baptized and confirmed people professing the apostolic faith as a sign that we are the Body of Christ. By doing this we can effectively witness, with power, to people headed to a situation of unparalleled horror.

Christ depends on us. Each and every one of us. And the fate of mankind is now in the balance. The Church is unity with diversity. That is why I feel the Holy Ghost impelled me to give the initial draft of this manuscript to the Church at the particular time I did. That is, the time when the Orthodox and Catholic Easters combined and when Passover occurred. I have had many visionary experiences. But the sense of the Spirit of God empowering me to hand that very rough draft to certain priestly figures will never leave me.

The role of the prophetic voice is not to be hidden away, but to speak openly, and then to step aside in the spirit of Divine Grace and allow the elders of all the churches to decide: to pray to the Holy Spirit for discernment.

In relation to these insights as a commentary and to reiterate:

to turn away from Biblical teaching, to break the Law of God, renders you evil if you do not repent. Our problem is that when huge swathes of population turn away from God and become spiritually polluted, or bad, they are then liable to go collectively, insanely evil. This collective insanity can, of course, be state sanctioned as in Germany before the Second World War, in Russia under Lenin and Stalin, and in diverse other places.

In this sense Christianity has not failed; Man has failed Christianity.

We have sown the wind. We are reaping the whirlwind.

www.ingramcontent.com/pod-product-compliance
Lightning Source LLC
Chambersburg PA
CBHW031324230426
43670CB00006B/229